BEYOND THREAT

BEYOND THREAT

Finding your centre in the midst of

uncertainty and change

Nelisha Wickremasinghe

Published by:
Triarchy Press
Axminster, England

First edition: 2018
Second edition: 2019
Third edition: 2021
Fourth edition: 2022

info@triarchypress.net
www.triarchypress.net

ISBNs:

Paperback: 978-1-911193-34-0
ePub: 978-1-911193-32-6
pdf: 978-1-911193-33-3

Printed by TJ Books, Padstow, Cornwall

For Saul and Jude

Reviews of the book

There is increasing recognition that how we perceive and deal with threat has a big impact on many of our relationships including work and organisational ones. This well written and fascinating book brings together many different ideas from neuroscience through to psychotherapy to explore ways we can deal with threat, learn to generate compassion for self and others and be more effective and supportive in our work and everyday social relationships. A benefit to all. **Prof Paul Gilbert OBE, author of *Compassionate Mind* and *Mindful Compassion***

At work and home, we believe we are reasonable, 21st-century adults. But this highly readable and relevant book has opened my eyes and deepened my understanding of a parallel reality. Our nervous system and vital parts of our brain tell us it's a jungle out there and we are under threat. If we can recognize, understand and manage these embodied 'messages', the implications for ourselves, our families and friends as well as the organizations we work in - are simply enormous. **Jim Cookson, Director Client Solutions Ashridge/Hult International Business School**

Regulating our motivational system by paying more attention to and nurturing our safe brain is, I believe, at the cutting edge of leadership learning and practice. I have run leadership development programmes based on Dr Wickremasinghe's work for over four years, deeply immersing our leaders and managers in these practices. Participants have been inspired and energised to lead more courageously and act as catalysts for change within organisations. It is very timely to see this work appearing in print. **Tom Jones, VP, Rolls-Royce**

Take your time while reading this book. It brings discoveries about human nature that need to sink in. More importantly, it gives you hope, courage and curiosity to embark on a journey of compassionate self-discovery. The Trimotive Brain is like a three-headed fantastic beast whose heads need to agree on the direction and then the beast can fly!" **Mike Houghton, Programme Director, Amec Foster Wheeler**

In these complex times so-called 'wicked' problems are the norm. In order to come up with creative and innovative solutions leaders must ensure their people speak openly, challenge each other, take risks and experiment. This requires them to be free of fear. This timely and insightful book offers a compelling case for promoting psychological safety in organisations so people can do good work and flourish.

Mike Brent, author of *The Leader's Guide to Influence*

I believe trust is at the heart of great leadership and that understanding what is really driving our behaviour is fundamental to creating the environment where excellent teamwork and transformation can take place. Over the last five years I have worked with Dr Wickremasinghe, developing our high potential future leaders to embrace the challenge of leading global teams within a complex business. I am delighted that her insights will now reach a wider audience through this book.

Christoph Debus, Chief Airlines Officer, Thomas Cook Group

Dr Wickremasinghe's translation of the neuroscience of motivation through the Trimotive Brain concept has resonated with Fujitsu's global leaders and helped develop a deeper understanding of our behaviours and relationships at work. In the leadership development programmes we run, high-achieving participants quickly recognise their own *threat-drive brain* loops and appreciate the importance of managing their inner critic and developing self-compassion. I am convinced this kind of learning and understanding is fundamental in helping organisations to unlock the potential of their people.

Ian Parkes, VP, Global Talent & Leadership Development, Fujitsu

Leaders are focused on today's results and tomorrow's plans. Seldom do we consider the importance of reflecting on past experience and how it informs current responses. *Beyond Threat* is an incredible distillation of Dr Wickremasinghe's many years' research and practice and shows how the power of reflection and noticing allows us to understand and overcome the threat loops which inhibit our ability to lead. Her detailed use of real world examples allows leaders to draw practical insights from many disciplines so we can gain a deeper understanding of why we do what we do and how to become more conscious and effective leaders.

Chad Dreas, Managing Director, Media Analytics, Nielsen

Contents

List of Figures and Tables

Some of these images can be seen in colour at www.bit.ly/Trimotive01

...the acceptance of oneself is the essence of the moral problem and the epitome of a whole outlook on life. That I feed the hungry, that I forgive an insult, that I love my enemy... these are undoubtedly great virtues. ...But what if I should discover that the least among them all, the poorest of all the beggars, the most impudent of all the offenders, the very enemy himself -- that these are within me, and that I myself stand in need of the alms of my own kindness -- that I myself am the enemy who must be loved -- what then?

C.G. Jung, *Modern Man in Search of a Soul*

Preface

Looking for answers

In the summer of my first year at university I enrolled, for reasons mysterious to me now, in an Artificial Intelligence class where we were supposed to teach machines to solve our problems. Our first task was based on the (in)famous ELIZA therapist program that processed a patient's symptoms using standardised language scripts and offered, in return, a 'diagnosis' or intervention. This was in the years before we became glued to screens or talked to our computers and before we became used to relating to each other in the abrupt text that mediates many of our relationships now. So back then I was dismayed. I did not understand or want to be part of a profession that 'fixed' human problems as if they were machines with technical faults.

In my program the problems were never fixed. When my patient typed *"I feel depressed"* I was not inspired to create a list of multiple choice questions to diagnose the cause or determine the remedy. So I made my Eliza end all her consultations with, *"I suggest you talk to someone about that"*. I didn't do very well in the assignment, although I did meet Colin, a long-haired computer scientist, who showed me how electronic mail worked and we whiled away the summer staring at bulky monitors and pinging each other messages. We didn't know or imagine, as we chatted through our machines, just how much our lives were about to change as a result.

My second memorable experience that year was a lunchtime viewing of *One Flew Over the Cuckoo's Nest*. In the film, Jack Nicholson plays a criminal seeking escape from a hard labour camp through transfer to a mental institution. Although he thinks life on the ward will be a soft option he is soon subject to the humiliating

9

and, at times, inhumane social and medical regimes of the asylum. The most difficult part was watching the medical treatment of distressed patients which included the administration of electric shocks, large doses of mind-numbing drugs and, in the final scenes, a lobotomy.

These experiences did not put me off my hoped-for career; if anything, they propelled me further along the path. I wanted to be a psychologist to understand how to be understood. More than that: to find out whether it was possible to be known and accepted for who I am. That yearning was so strong in me that I imagined it must exist in other people too. The less we are understood and accepted, I observed, the more likely it is that we will have problems. My father used to say to me, *"when you grow up and have lots of problems come and tell me"*. He wrote this in the bottom of my birthday cards until I was six years old. It worried me that he believed problems were inevitable, and later it grieved me that he was not available to fulfil his advisory role.

These days it's not so fashionable to talk about problems. Not since positive psychologists told us about the benefits of joy, gratitude, serenity, hope, love and awe. Yet problems keep appearing and, when they do, they are, at least for me, very distracting. It's hard to be serene when anxiety unsettles my stomach or when anger and depression paint a grey wash over even the sweetest smile.

Problems thread their way through my family history, sometimes visible like broken veins, but mostly buried deep under the skin of our lives. There's a hushed story about a Great Aunt who drowned herself in the warm waters of the Indian ocean. She was found washed up on the shore with her sari floating behind her, glinting like a golden fishing net. Then there was Uncle Chandra, Harvard scholar, talented doctor and photographer, who drank himself in to a poisonous oblivion, perhaps to escape the racism and hatred of 1960s' America. And what happened to Uncle Fritz, who ate grass in a prisoner of war camp? Many years later he showed me his cellar in Stuttgart piled high with Ritter chocolate. He never wanted to go hungry again. Closer to home, nearer to the surface, my father meets the Ginger Lady who teaches him to rant and helps him soothe his passion and pain in her warm auburn glow.

Machines and drugs can standardise, obliterate or anaesthetise our problems but they don't give us understanding, forgiveness, compassion and acceptance. And, in the stories I hear, this is what most people want.

I went to university looking for answers to problems both general (what motivated Hamlet's procrastination?) and specific (why is my father so unhappy?) and I found them, I thought, in the work of people like Ronnie (R.D.) Laing, the outspoken Scottish psychiatrist, who argued for a *relational* approach to human suffering. Laing maintained that even extreme mental distress was an attempt to cope with and heal the wounds inflicted by society and in particular, the family. What was needed, he said, were more people (and not necessarily 'professionals') who were prepared to listen *deeply* in order to truly understand one another.

As a young psychologist, Laing's thinking appealed to me, whilst drugging, incarcerating and electrocuting people did not.

Experimenting

My first job was as a 'dependency counsellor' in Arlington House, London. This huge Victorian hostel for the homeless opened in 1905. By the early nineties it had become a 'wet' house allowing homeless people to live there despite their addiction to alcohol and other drugs. My brief was to apply a 'harm minimisation' approach to the more severely addicted to enable them to maintain their lifestyle of choice in relative dignity. I was not expected to persuade them to stop drinking, get work or change – unless they wanted to.

Here was a form of Laing's method in motion. My colleagues and I in the 'dependency team' spent hours talking to the residents and forming empathic relationships. However, the residents mostly just wanted to be left alone to drink themselves to death. Once a week I was assigned the early morning 'death round' which involved touring this vast building to check whether anyone had died in the night. If no one responded to my loud knock I had to open their door with a master key and investigate. It was a dispiriting job and I didn't last long.

Afterwards I joined the health service, where change, health improvement and recovery from addiction *were* on the agenda. I managed clinics and an in-patient unit for addicts with a multidisciplinary team of doctors, nurses and social workers. I had become part of the medical profession that my earlier self had so mistrusted, and it wasn't so bad. We worked with addicts using detoxification drugs and a wide range of therapies to try and provide holistic and relational care. Yet the harsh reality was that relapse rates amongst the acutely addicted were, and probably still are, appallingly high. Most of my clients only maintained their sobriety or drug-free status for short periods before returning to their old habits. This recurring, vicious cycle of addiction frustrated me, not least because at the time my father and others close to me were also caught in that loop. During those years I was passionately driven to solve the problem of addiction, not realising that the 'answer' was not to be found in one method or another. Of course, I did not succeed in achieving my unrealistic goals and after ten years of failing to significantly interrupt or even understand the reform-relapse cycle, I resigned from my work in mental health services.

I wanted to put the dark days of addiction behind me and so I started an organic food business and restaurant. Yet, along with the weddings, birthdays, anniversaries and christenings, I also witnessed and shared bottles of wine with those who were bereaved, divorcing, facing financial ruin, struggling with old age and family rifts. No-one and nowhere, it seemed, was immune from life's quotidian challenges and disappointments, and once more I found myself trying to 'solve' human problems and understand the messages of ordinary madness.

When I sold the restaurant I found work as a business psychologist and leadership development consultant. I imagined I would be working with the successful, relatively problem-free members of society who had money, status, optimism and exciting jobs. Yet here too problems appeared like damp patches in a freshly painted wall, indicative of deeper, hidden complications arising out of a compulsion to compete, achieve and accumulate.

Coaching and developing people in business and the corporate world is no less challenging than working with the mentally ill or drug addicted. When *any* of us becomes caught in the vicious loop of an unhelpful habit we encounter problems. It doesn't matter whether that habit is alcohol, work, competitiveness, Facebook, our smart phone or long-distance running. In this book I will share some stories of ordinary people I have worked with who were caught in such loops and who were suffering as much as the people who came into my mental health clinics.

Hard-earned lessons

Working in the clinics, the restaurant and in organisations has taught me two important lessons. First, that a singular approach to complex human problems is misguided and ineffective. As a young psychologist, I was attached to a narrow set of beliefs about how change 'worked' and it took me a long time to evolve that understanding. Medical intervention, mindfulness, psychoanalysis, family systems therapy, yoga, low sugar diets, cognitive behavioural coaching, attending the gym, running a marathon and, more recently, neuropsychology, *all* offer helpful ways of expanding our human capability. As psychiatrist and author Dan Siegel so aptly puts it, *the mind is embodied and relational.* To me this means that *both* nature and nurture matter, that we are the sum of both biology *and* experience and that our bodies, minds and relationships all count when it comes to appraising and adapting our life. Our problems deserve a creative approach that draws on and synthesises many different insights.

Second, there is no perfect solution to human suffering. Suffering is part of the human condition and cannot be avoided. By understanding suffering as an experience that arises from certain *habits* of feeling, thought and behaviour we may be able to cultivate a different approach to that experience which potentially leads to growth, resilience and a richer, more enjoyable way of life. The way to 'get out' of a problem – or our suffering – may, in the end, be much simpler than we imagine, although simple does not mean easy. *"The way out is through the door"*, said Confucius. *"Why is it that no one will use this exit?"*

The power of habit

We don't use the Confucian door because it is hard to leave the familiar and known place we are in. We all have beliefs and preferences about how life is or should be that are expressed in the habits and routines that define our life. Once acquired it is not easy to lift out of or expand these habits of feeling, thought and behaviour. Habits, after all, have *become* habits because they once served us well. But when our habits no longer help us and when sometimes they do us harm, why is it so hard to let them go? Why do we persist in feeling, thinking and doing things that cause us problems? This is the ordinary 'madness' of which I speak and there is method and message in it.

All around us we can see the evidence of our problem habits. We might ask: why do they argue about the same things over and over again? Why does he drink until he passes out? Why does she spend money she doesn't have? Why do we work for an employer who bullies and denigrates us? Why do I keep trying to please a partner who is unfaithful? Why am I so anxious about my son's daily walk to school? Why can't I stop checking my phone?

Questions about habit are at the heart of this book. Such questions have puzzled and frustrated me for a long time and, after thirty years of professional and personal inquiry, I no longer expect to uncover their mystery for the roots of habit are buried deep in our unconscious and most of us will not travel far into that labyrinthine underworld. However, I have come closer to the experience of living with clarity, purpose and peace which represents for me a *break* with habit and a movement towards Confucius's open door.

Such moments arise when my feelings and thoughts are 'centred', when I am not overwhelmed by particular emotions or trapped in thought-loops that undermine, deceive or mislead me.

Through the door, at the centre of my experience, anything feels possible, yet there is no sense of urgency or compulsion. The feeling is one of quiet acceptance and focused energy.

This book is about how to find and return to your own centre which, I believe, is the outcome of personal and social *observation, inquiry, reflection and experiment*. These are the same activities involved in the scientific method, yet the goal is very different. Here, we are not so much concerned with measuring, proving and predicting as we are with discovering deeply subjective and compassionate truths that enable us to live with dignity, peace and integrity. Some of these truths are buried and obscured in our unconscious experiences and it takes time, effort and courage to reach them. Yet, when we find our centre we strengthen the core stability of our body and mind, enabling us to face and respond to difficult and challenging life events and discoveries with resilience and equanimity.

Even though we will fall from our centre every day, and some of us will fall often, the measure of our health is how quickly we can *return*. When we get angry, fearful or high on excitement, are we able to bring ourselves back to a state of internal equilibrium when we need or want to? We may never be able to completely rid ourselves of unhelpful habits or fully understand the unconscious forces that motivate them yet we can learn to live more freely within our human constraints and uncertainties.

Introduction

It is not our fault that we get trapped in bad habits or 'loops' of unhelpful and sometimes destructive behaviour. Or that we are easily irritated, sometimes less than truthful, suspicious of others and inexplicably anxious and afraid. It is not our fault because most of what we feel, think and do is motivated by unconscious memories of how to survive the environment into which we were born. These memories, without our knowing, continue to exert a huge influence in our adult lives.

At work, these hidden motives play out in unexpected and often unwelcome ways. We can be ruthlessly competitive, frequently disengaged or dangerously compliant. We can say and do things that we regret, make mistakes, upset people and feel miserable and defensive. Not all the time, of course, but sometimes. And as we get older, if our problem habits go unaddressed, the 'sometimes' becomes 'often'.

Along with their extraordinary tales of resilience, brilliant accomplishment and profound company loyalty, my organisational clients also talk about, exhaustion, dissension, lack of appreciation, fear and doubt – and they wonder what to do about this. Such experiences affect us all but in organisations we are rarely encouraged to talk about them openly. Instead we are told to be positive, innovate, grow, inspire and win. Yet we cannot do these things if our bodies and minds are in threat.

So, I have written a book which *does* talk about these experiences directly. I have written it for people leading, working in and changing organisations and, for this reason, I have adapted the language, theories and practices of mainly neurobiological and psychological disciplines so that they can be applied in this organisational context.

I hope, especially through the case studies of three people working in ordinary organisations, to persuade you that with understanding, awareness, insight and practice, we can live and work more freely and bravely. I strongly believe that doing so will enhance organisations in ways that may be beyond their current imagining.

In the first part of this book – *How has it come to be this way?* – I weave together insights from neuroscience and developmental psychology to explore the way in which our biological heritage (nature) and our early individual experiences (nurture) combine to make us who we are. We start by considering how we are motivated by three neurological systems – threat, drive and safe – which together form what I call the *Trimotive Brain* which is a metaphor (not an actual brain) that I find useful when trying to understand human motivation. When these systems are working well together we are 'centred' and we can respond to our experience with focus, calm and accuracy. When our *Trimotive Brain* is 'dis-integrated' we experience problems. Usually this is because the 'threat' part of this system is overactive and/or the 'safe' part is underactive. We learn how and why this happens by considering how childhood experience influences the development and functioning of our *Trimotive Brain* and how our formative relationships shape our adult orientations to life. When experience teaches us that people and events are mostly hostile, unpredictable, dangerous and uncaring then our *threat brain* emotions start to dominate and we get trapped in rigid behavioural patterns of *moving against* people/events (fighting/controlling), *moving towards* (freezing/ submitting) and *moving away* (fleeing/disengaging). These patterns are explored in Part Three through the three coaching stories.

Our biological inheritance and our childhood experiences are preserved in and by our memory and so we end Part One by taking a look at what memory is and how it works. This sets the scene for an exploration of unconscious processes in which implicit memory plays a large part. Here we discover that most of our feelings and thoughts happen outside our conscious awareness and we consider the implications of this for our decisions and actions.

In Part Two – *What else is possible?* – we dig down towards the roots of our habits by exploring the unconscious processes in our body and mind that sustain them. We learn that to become aware of these processes we need to develop self-compassion – or 'warm awareness' – in order to tolerate and accept some of the unpleasant or unwanted truths that fuel our problem habits. We explore what self-compassion is and how the experience of mindfulness, kindness and acceptance of our shared humanity helps us to increase *safe brain* emotions that regulate threat and bring equilibrium to our *Trimotive Brain*.

Once we have cultivated basic self-compassion we are ready to enter our unconscious and discover the hidden or unnoticed intelligence that resides there and we end Part Two considering three simple practices that help us become aware of our unconscious processes. The new material that emerges from this exploration provides ample inspiration for re-authoring our lives. In the new stories we tell about ourselves it is possible to let go of old habits and develop different, more satisfying responses to our experience.

Finally, in Part Three – *Panning for Gold* – we examine the coaching stories of three clients working in different corporate environments but each trapped in the problem habits arising from their overactive *threat brain*. We return to the patterns of *moving against, away* and *towards* to understand these habits and to learn how to soothe our threatened brain. In sharing these stories I also hope to make a case for the value of *depth coaching* which includes an exploration of the unconscious forces influencing behaviour and sustaining the habits we wish to change. Depth coaching seeks to support profound and lasting change and to nurture healthy 'drive' motivations by ensuring that goals and objectives are informed not by *threat brain* motives but by the conscious, compassionate and wise motives emerging from *safe brain*.

The *Trimotive Brain* metaphor and the cultivation of warm awareness through self-compassion have helped me to make sense of and travel beyond experiences that for a long time have held me captive, confounded and immobilised. These ideas and practices represent my way of comprehending and working with the inherent complexities and challenges of ordinary life and I have discovered in their research and application the possibility of living beyond threat that is both conscious of our mortal vulnerability and no longer overwhelmed or enthralled by it.

PART ONE:

HOW HAS IT COME TO BE THIS WAY?

Chapter One: Our Emotional Brain

The emergence of brain

The feeling, thinking and doing person that each of us is today is the product and sum of billions of years of evolution. Four billion years ago, life on Earth appeared as single cells such as bacteria. Fast forward three and a half billion years and life forms we are more familiar with started to appear, beginning with arthropods, fish and reptiles. These early life forms contain nervous systems that are no longer single cells but *networks* of neurons that carry messages between parts of the body. As it evolved, this nervous system supported basic functions like moving, eating, breathing and reproducing. As it evolved further, it came to form the oldest and still very active part of our brain, which I refer to in this book as *threat brain*.

Understanding how and why our brain has evolved over millions of years helps us to appreciate why we feel, think and act in the way we do. When our feelings, thoughts and actions are sometimes ineffective or even destructive, evolutionary science offers insights that help us see how this is not our *fault* – even though it is our problem. Instead of blaming ourselves, we can begin to see our frailty as a shared human experience. Although we have evolved into astonishingly conscious, creative, social beings, these new capabilities are grafted onto our old *threat brain* and this causes us problems. Our earliest ancestors, living in harsh environments amongst numerous predators, needed to be highly vigilant, cautious and ready to attack or run. Their sensitivity to danger and urge to survive is still in us even though the contexts in which we live have changed considerably.

Just as we would not blame someone for being born with one leg shorter than the other or for having motor neuron disease, we need not blame ourselves for the irrational, damaging or debilitating feelings and thoughts that sometimes direct our action. Understanding ourselves as an organism in the flow of evolutionary life helps us become more aware of our previously unconscious drives and motivations and enables us to cultivate self-compassion and tolerance towards our mistakes and failings. This 'warm awareness' will also help us manage the problems that our *threat brain* can cause in our relationships with others.

Neuroscience – the study of the brain

Neuroscience is the study of the brain. In recent years, the work of neuroscientists has spread into many disciplines including physiology, psychology, computer science, engineering, physics and education. Sophisticated scanning technology showing how the brain works may be responsible for this surge in interest – perhaps because people are fascinated by, and liable to believe, propositions backed by brain scan imagery more than other psychological findings.[1]

When I use images depicting the brain's evolution and how it responds to certain kinds of stimulation I notice how quickly my students and clients become curious and motivated to explore their feelings, thoughts and behaviours. Understanding ourselves in terms of the moment-by-moment brain states that we experience seems to offer more immediate possibilities for change than talking about our childhood or our personality profile.

However, as much as I too am fascinated by these emerging insights, I don't suggest we jump onto the neuroscience bandwagon just yet. Who we are and what we will or can become is a complex and dynamic subject best illuminated and understood using insights from many different disciplines. Before galloping off into a future filled with scans, screens and magical mind control, I invite you to pause and consider the extraordinary *connections* and synchronicities between contemporary science and the historical, non-technological, intuitive insights of, for example, writers, artists, psychologists, sociologists, anthropologists and philosophers who were equally absorbed and challenged by how we have come to be

---

[1] (Munro & Munro, 2014)

this way and where we are going. So, throughout this book I will refer to work which may no longer be in fashion but which has significantly influenced today's popular theories.

Our *Trimotive Brain*

Without motivations we would not be alive. Living creatures need to experience the energy and desire to seek food, stay safe and if possible, reproduce. In organisms with nervous systems the brain mediates motivation through three neurological systems which I call the *threat brain*, the *drive brain* and the *safe brain*. In reality they are all part of one interconnected system, which I refer to as the *Trimotive Brain,* but it helps to understand their various functions if we separate them. Remember the *Trimotive Brain* is a *metaphor* to describe our complex motivation system and is not intended to suggest an anatomical fact. It is an adaptation and representation of ideas first outlined by Professor Paul Gilbert in *The Compassionate Mind,* where he describes three emotion regulation systems that give rise to different feelings, desires and urges related to threat/self-protection; incentive/resource-seeking and soothing/contentment.[2]

These motivation systems are responsible for directing our feelings, thoughts and actions and if we want to change the way we feel, think and act we need to understand and manage these systems. We will discover, however, that this is easier said than done because most of their functions are carried out without our conscious control or knowledge.

Our motivations are activated by emotions produced by the sympathetic and parasympathetic nervous systems. Emotions are neurochemical reactions in our body that are triggered by experiences we have and occur without our conscious control. (Those experiences, as we shall see, may be happening now, may have occurred in the past or we may be imagining or anticipating them.)

---

[2] The *Trimotive Brain* metaphor, as well as adapting Paul Gilbert's 'affect regulation system model' (Gilbert, 2010), draws on work on emotional regulation systems described in Depue & Morrone-Strupinsky (2005) and research on the 'emotional brain' carried out and described by Joseph LeDoux (1998).

Emotions are not the same as feelings. A feeling is our *representation* of what is happening in our body. Distinguishing emotion from feeling is important because it is our conscious 'naming' of our body responses that determines how we act. Let's say, for example, that someone I do not know walks into the room and I experience a fluttering sensation which is the result of chemical and neural changes in my body. This fluttering sensation is an emotion. Usually I consult my prior experience (which I have stored in my memory) to help me name and understand the sensation. I may decide it is anxiety, attraction, excitement, or nerves and label it as one of these. These are feelings. It is this naming of what is happening in my body that orientates my subsequent actions.

Throughout this book, I emphasise that as we become more conscious of what is happening in our bodies and minds we are more able to exercise choice in our naming (feelings), interpretations (thoughts) and responses (actions). Behaviour starts in the body. In particular, we learn that our memory is not always a reliable source for interpreting 'here and now' experience.

The purpose of human emotion then is to motivate action in order to achieve the basic goals of survival, accumulation and affiliation. *Threat brain*, our oldest motivation system, enables us to recognise and respond to danger. *Drive brain* motivates us to seek out pleasurable and rewarding experiences. *Safe brain* motivates us to rest, recover and form relationships with others. Ideally, we need all three motivational systems working together in a balanced way and regulating each other. Unfortunately, many of us get caught in unhelpful habits which are sustained because our motivational systems are 'dis-integrated' and out of balance. Usually the cause of dis-integration is an over-active *threat brain*. Many of our personal and social problems can be attributed to this over-activity: high blood pressure, anxiety, loneliness, addiction and shame are a few of the consequences we can trace back to the innate and learned responses of our *threat brain*. To overcome these problems we need to recognise when we are in a state of 'dis-integration' and we need to learn what to do in order to restore equilibrium.

When our *threat brain*, *drive brain* and *safe brain* motivating systems are working well and regulating each other we experience motivational integrity. Our feelings, thoughts and actions become more coherent, calm and considered. We feel centred and at peace with ourselves. The neurologist Andrew Curran describes this as "*a state of being where your entire brain is harmonic with itself*".[3] This is when we are most likely to experience and act from our full potential.

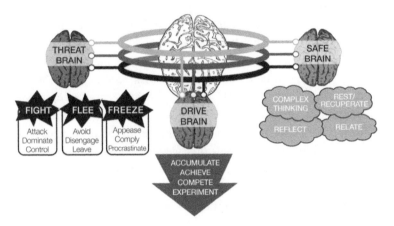

Figure 1: *The three motivation systems of our Trimotive Brain. Our threat brain system is the earliest; our safe and drive brain systems followed and have continued to evolve.*

It is only when a situation demands extreme and intense focus or response that over-activity in parts of the *Trimotive Brain* may be useful:

- If I am climbing Mount Everest or about to give a crucial presentation to my board of directors I may want my *drive brain* to be working hard – to give me a good dose of dopamine to keep me alert, enthused and energised.

- If I have just given birth or I'm managing the fallout from a mass organisational redundancy programme, I need my *safe*

---

[3] (Curran, 2008)

brain to do a little overtime. I'll need some oxytocin to reduce my stress and to support excellent relational skills that can help soothe a troubled team or a new-born child.

- If I am stepping into a busy road and notice a bus a few feet away, then I want my *threat brain* to kick in quickly. Cortisol and adrenalin will get me moving fast.

These are all moments when I may be 'off centre' in a useful way. I can focus my attention and energy on a situation that is specific, transient and legitimately demanding of a particular neurobiological and behavioural response set.

If, however, I find myself 'off centre' most of the time I will start to experience difficulties. Workaholism, compassion fatigue ('caring too much') and anxiety disorders are recognisable examples of what happens when our *drive brain, safe brain* and *threat brain* motivations are stuck in unhelpful and probably deeply rooted habits. This is when our feelings, thoughts and actions become inflexible, repetitive, less effective and sometimes harmful. So let's look in more detail at how these motivation systems work and how our biological heritage, which has given us this brain, shapes the way we are.

Threat Brain – fight, flee, freeze

The brain's oldest and primary purpose is to ensure the survival of the species. In order to do this it must sense, process and store information that enables us to detect and respond to threat, to find a mate and to protect our offspring. Of these three motivations the most significant is avoidance of threat and danger. The organism has to remain *alive* as its first priority. Our sensitivity to threat and our reflex response to react are at the core of our brain function and our being.

Robert Sapolsky is a stress biologist. In his book, *Why Zebras Don't Get Ulcers*, he explains that our stress response is designed to respond to life-threatening, physical challenges. In other words, being killed, wounded or starved. Stress for an animal is a *short-term* crisis which either passes or doesn't. In other words, you live through it or you die. The physiological reactions triggered by short-term physical emergencies are highly effective. The combination of cortisol (a steroid hormone), adrenaline and noradrenaline increases blood pressure, blood sugar level, breathing rate and muscle contraction. This gives you a boost of energy and prepares your body to act fast. These chemicals also narrow your attention (to focus on the threat), constrict your memory (to store only threat-related information), impair digestion, lower sex drive and suppress the immune system (to save energy and keep you alert and awake). In summary, the threat response stops any bodily function, feeling, thought or behaviour that might 'waste' energy and detract from either fighting or escaping danger. *When in threat, your emotional, cognitive and behavioural range is significantly reduced.*

It is good to be hyperalert and to respond with speed and strength when we are in life-threatening physical danger. However, our brain can also turn on this physical reaction simply by imagining, worrying or ruminating about potential risks and dangers. The zebra in Sapolsky's book does not get stress-related illness because, once the danger of being eaten by a lion has passed, he resumes his relatively peaceful grazing life. We, on the other hand, have a tendency to think about and anticipate danger even when it has passed or does not exist. Sapolsky draws on a significant body of evidence to show that stress-related illness arises when we regularly activate and sustain our threat system which was originally designed to respond only to acute and immediate physiological emergencies. The net result, Sapolsky says, is that *the stress response can become more damaging that the stressor itself.*

Many of my clients say they frequently experience states of mild to moderate threat at work and in their personal lives. These experiences of threat (micro management, poor performance scores, customer complaints, divorce and debt are just a few examples) feature highly and are complex and not easily dealt with by either fighting or running away. For example, in this volatile economic climate many people have at one time or another feared losing their job or being demoted. This experience does not constitute a direct threat to survival yet for some people it produces the same physical responses such as raised blood pressure and the increase of stress hormones. This is because our brain can *anticipate* problems and *imagine* the threatening consequences of being out of work. It can also make associations and connections between 'being out of work' and personal inadequacy or even shame. Our ability to think in this way is relatively recent; however, this evolved response is not necessarily helpful to us.

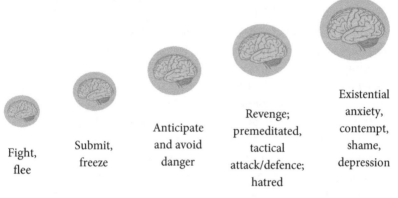

| Fight, flee | Submit, freeze | Anticipate and avoid danger | Revenge; premeditated, tactical attack/defence; hatred | Existential anxiety, contempt, shame, depression |

Figure 2: The basic threat brain emotions stimulate anger, disgust and fear. As we have evolved, these basic emotions have become more complex in their expression/action.

Job insecurity, when handled through our *threat brain*, may motivate us to compete aggressively, treat others ruthlessly or become so consumed by anxiety and depression that the quality of our work and relationships suffers. These *threat brain* reactions are unlikely to secure us the job we fear losing and so our problems compound and our fears are fulfilled. Karen Horney, whose work we will look at in the next chapter, gives us more insight into the complexity of the human threat response. Often we do not realise that our habits – especially those that cause us problems – are sustained by the real or imagined experience of threat.

Luckily, as our brain evolved we developed higher brain centres that gave us more response options. The next part of the brain to develop was the limbic or emotional brain which is concerned with complex behaviours like social interaction and nurturing. This part of the brain first supported the emergence of *safe brain* and *drive brain* motivations. Later, with the arrival of our uniquely human, prefrontal cortex these motivations became capable of even more sophisticated expression.

It is something of a 'chicken and egg' debate as to whether the development of new higher brain centres such as the limbic brain encouraged social (drive) and nurturing (safe) behaviours or whether these behaviours came first and in doing so stimulated the development of the limbic brain. If, however, we agree, that the more nerve cells you have the more potential you have for new and complex behaviour, then it would be reasonable to argue that the brain cells came first. Furthermore, research suggests that throughout our evolution we have carried 'spare cells' which are ready for use. For our brain to grow we need to feed those cells with *experience*. Mammals engaged in new and different behaviours which seemed to improve their survival and probably stimulated these spare neurons to fire and create new specialisations in the brain. The proposition that behaviour, occurring sometimes by chance but repeated over time, alters structures in our brain supports many theories of learning and growth. Later we will see how it is possible to use this capacity to 'learn by repetition' to let go of some of our problem habits when we practise acting 'as if' we did not have them.

Safe brain and *drive brain* motivations, emerging about 150 million years ago, found a lasting place in our evolution because caring for our young and living in larger social groups significantly improved our chances of staying alive and controlling essential resources. About four million years ago, at around the time our ancestors in Africa began to stand upright, we see the brain develop again. This time it is the emergence of the *neocortex*, bringing with it the capabilities of language, imagination, abstract thinking, problem-solving and introspection. In humans, this cortex has grown in size and complexity. The newest and uniquely human part – the prefrontal cortex – offers us even greater potential to learn, reflect and collaborate and to develop accurate, creative and effective responses when faced with life challenges. However, to access all these advanced human capabilities we first need to regulate our threat reactions because they can interfere with – and sometimes close down altogether – the functioning of our higher centres. It is *safe brain* that helps us do this.

Safe Brain – rest, repair, soothe, bond, reflect

Our *safe brain* motivations were successful. In other words, caring helped our offspring survive for longer and increased their chances of reaching maturity and, in turn, reproducing.

In this way, caring was genetically favoured. This is in contrast to, and a developmental leap from, reptilian (*threat brain*) strategy, which does not prioritise caring for others. Consider, for example that a turtle – a member of the reptile family – lays hundreds of eggs but once hatched the young are left to fend for themselves and only a small percentage survive. In 2016, the BBC Planet Earth documentary highlighted the plight of baby turtles in Barbados. In this programme, we see distressing footage of hatchlings emerging from their solitary shells and becoming quickly disorientated by the city lights. Instinct should propel them towards the luminescence of the moon and the relative safety of the shoreline but on this Barbados beach they mistake neon for moonlight and so turn away from the sea and head towards the busy road. With no parent to guide them, most of the hatchlings meet their end under the wheels of the oncoming vehicles or fall through the grills of the urban drainage system. These turtles are at the mercy of their basic brain which is not equipped to deal with an increasingly complex environment. Without the help of conservation projects they would be extinct.

Caring is not exclusive to mammals, of course. Basic caring capabilities and behaviours can be observed in a wide range of species. The Kildeer bird, for example, displays an unusual type of parental care behaviour – it nests on the ground and when predators try to take its eggs or chicks it lures them away by pretending to have a broken wing. These behaviours are effective but fairly basic – feed offspring and defend the nest. By the time we get to humans, the caring relationship and social mentality has evolved into a much more complex set of emotions and capabilities. Compassion towards others, the experience of love, and care of and mourning for the dead all represent evolutionarily recent capabilities.

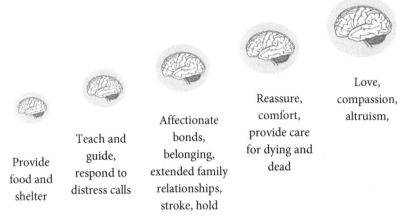

Love, compassion, altruism,

Reassure, comfort, provide care for dying and dead

Affectionate bonds, belonging, extended family relationships, stroke, hold

Teach and guide, respond to distress calls

Provide food and shelter

Figure 3: The basic safe brain emotions stimulate calm, relaxation and safety. As we have evolved, these basic emotions become more complex in their expression/action.

Safe brain motivations are triggered by the activity of the *parasympathetic nervous system* (PNS) which releases feel-good hormones such as oxytocin and endorphins which activate our body's opiate receptors and help us to feel calm and relaxed. The PNS conserves energy in our body, is responsible for ongoing, mellow, steady-state activity and is associated with a feeling of contentment. A calm, stress-free environment and the experience of kindness and love can activate our PNS. We can also induce its activation through meditation, deep breathing, gentle exercise and restful sleep. When our *safe brain* is active we are better able to bond with others, care for ourselves, rest and reflect. In addition, a calm brain provides optimal conditions for the growth and function of our *prefrontal cortex* which enables us to focus attention, think creatively and solve complex problems.

33

Safe brain and the prefrontal cortex

The prefrontal cortex is the newest part of the brain and unique to humans. It gives us consciousness, which is the ability to look inward and think about our thoughts. We can scroll back through our memory, anticipate or plan the future, use language and symbols to communicate, express ourselves appropriately and understand moral and social rules. When our brain is 'safe' – when it is in a relaxed and calm state – we are able to access and use our prefrontal cortex to feel, think and behave in non-reactive, complex and usually more effective or 'intelligent' ways. It has long been known that sleep and rest are essential for intellectual growth and emotional balance. These are *safe brain* states which significantly influence the way our brain develops over time and performs in the moment.

The prefrontal cortex does not work if it is damaged or if our brain is in threat. People who have suffered injuries to this part of the brain experience changes in their moods and behaviours. Typically, these involve feeling lethargic, uninspired, distracted, disorganised, forgetful, inattentive and bad-tempered.

One of the earliest and best-known examples is Phineas Gage, a US railroad construction worker. At the time of his accident in 1848 Gage was a supervisor on major projects and seen as an efficient, capable, "shrewd and smart business man". Colleagues described him as energetic, enthusiastic, mild mannered and meticulous. One day, whilst stuffing blasting powder, fuse and sand into holes with an iron rod, Gage became distracted by a co-worker. He turned to speak to his colleague and in that split second the tamping iron sparked against the rock, causing the powder to explode and the thirteen-pound rod to ricochet into and through his head. Gage survived the accident and remained fully conscious in the aftermath of the injury.

John Martyn Harlow, the doctor responsible for Gage's emergency care and long-term recovery, noted after the accident:

> *The equilibrium or balance, so to speak, between his intellectual faculties and animal propensities, seems to have been destroyed. He is fitful, irreverent, indulging at times in the grossest profanity (which was not previously his custom), manifesting but little deference for his fellows,*

*impatient of restraint or advice when it conflicts with his
desires, at times pertinaciously obstinate, yet capricious
and vacillating, devising many plans of future operations,
which are no sooner arranged than they are abandoned in
turn for others appearing more feasible. A child in his intellectual capacity and manifestations, he has the animal
passions of a strong man. Previous to his injury, although
untrained in the schools, he possessed a well-balanced
mind, and was looked upon by those who knew him as a
shrewd, smart business man, very energetic and persistent
in executing all his plans of operation. In this regard his
mind was radically changed, so decidedly that his friends
and acquaintances said he was "no longer Gage".[4]*

Gage lived for twelve years after the accident and for a while was a
stage coach driver in Chile. However, he suffered recurring health
problems, including epileptic seizures, which made it hard for him to
hold down a job. In 1860 he had a severe seizure from which he did
not recover. Six years after Gage's death Dr Harlow contacted the
family and asked that his skull be exhumed. The skull and the iron
rod remain on display at the Warren Anatomical Museum in Boston.

Damage to the prefrontal cortex impairs our ability to process
moral and social codes and is related to delinquent, anti-social
behaviour and dispassionate, impersonal reasoning. People lose
their capacity to listen well, empathise with others and act
compassionately. These same effects occur when people feel
threatened. Even if it is not damaged, our prefrontal cortex will not
function well under stress.

The prefrontal cortex does not fully develop until we are in our
mid-twenties, which is why young children and adolescents are less
likely to manage their emotions, be socially adept or engage in
complex reasoning. In Bruce Perry's[5] images on page 45 we see how
the brain of a severely neglected child has atrophied in this cortex
area. Dick Swabb[6] suggests that when children are deprived of love

---

[4] (Harlow, 1869)

[5] (Perry, 2002)

[6] (Swabb, 2014)

and care their oxytocin levels are lowered and may be permanently depleted. If oxytocin encourages *safe brain* states that reduce stress and facilitate growth, its absence could explain atrophication and why adults who have had extremely abusive, isolated or lonely childhoods struggle to activate their *safe brain* responses and find it hard to experience the full feeling and thinking capabilities that are made possible by the frontal cortex. They may have laid down such a deep and pervasive network of negative memories that their *threat brain* remains permanently on and cannot be soothed. Repeated stress and the absence of *safe brain* respite alters the structure and function of the prefrontal cortex and can permanently affect our ability to concentrate, organise, remember and control our emotions. Without *safe brain* to soothe us, we can get locked in a *threat brain* loop that is very difficult to interrupt.

Although *safe brain* states are highly desirable, I am not suggesting that we try to achieve or sustain these states as a permanent or even dominant mode of experiencing. Too much *safe brain* can prevent us from sensing danger or responding to it quickly and it can also make us complacent and unwilling to try new things. For example, a couple I once knew were very much in love and delighted in each other's company so much that they decided to give up their jobs and start an idyllic new life together in the countryside. They lived in relative isolation and peace producing their own food and maintaining a small income through online sales of their produce. They said they felt more healthy and fit, they never argued and hardly ever experienced stress. They anticipated a future of blissful partnership and actively avoided situations or people who might have disturbed their calm life style. Unfortunately, after some years, one of them was killed in a car accident leaving the other alone and responsible for everything. Feelings of fear, anxiety and loneliness overwhelmed the widowed spouse who had become unused to experiencing or responding to these emotions. It took a long time and considerable support to reintroduce her to a life which is unpredictable, inevitably painful and demanding. Too much *safe brain* had *reduced* her resilience and adaptability.

People *do* choose to retreat from life and to cultivate a peaceful existence away from the pressures of modern living. Journalist Sara Maitland,[7] for example, describes how she spent ten years looking for a place to live which would offer the solitude and quiet she desired. During her search she wrote about the many experiences of silence and seclusion *including* the difficult emotions that arose when she was alone. She did not try to create an idyll or deny the unpleasant.

When you nurture *safe brain* capabilities through contemplative practices such as meditation, writing or walking in nature a whole host of feelings is likely to arise including anxiety and sadness. Learning to accept these feelings is one way to cultivate motivational integrity. Trying to banish them in order to create an illusion of perfect happiness is misguided and inevitably short-lived.

Drive Brain – explore, achieve, accumulate, consume

Our third motivational system, *drive brain*, encourages us to compete, accumulate resources, achieve, play and learn. These basic motivations emerged early in our evolution and like those of *threat brain* and *safe brain* have become more complex. Early *drive brain* helped us to learn (animals use play to teach and learn) and motivated us to join, and manage our social status in, groups. Modern *drive brain* can inspire us to climb Everest or addict us to Facebook.

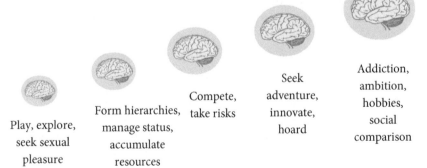

Play, explore, seek sexual pleasure

Form hierarchies, manage status, accumulate resources

Compete, take risks

Seek adventure, innovate, hoard

Addiction, ambition, hobbies, social comparison

Figure 4: The basic drive brain emotions stimulate excitement, curiosity and desire. As we have evolved these basic emotions become more complex in their expression/action.

[7] (Maitland, 2008)

The *drive brain* motivation system is potentially a great asset. It is responsible for fuelling the energetic, progressive, inventive, risk-taking aspects of our personality and at its best enables us to participate fully in life and to experience the rich varieties and challenges of the world in a healthy way.

The *drive brain* is a reward-based system and uses the potency of the neurotransmitter dopamine to make us curious, excited and brave. Drugs such as cocaine and speed mimic the effect of dopamine yet it is naturally stimulated when we win, fall in love, get promoted or enjoy extreme sports. However, these natural dopamine 'highs' are as potentially addictive as the synthetic ones. The feelings of excitement that dopamine produces and the 'hyped-up' sense of pleasure it brings can lead us to want more and more. We become over-attached to computer games, 12-hour working days, alcohol, Facebook, shopping and checking our phones because when we stop these activities we experience unpleasant withdrawal symptoms such as boredom, restlessness, inability to concentrate and anxiety. We can get rid of these uncomfortable feelings by continuing the dopamine-stimulating activity and, in doing so, the addictive cycle is strengthened and sustained.

Our *drive brain* is frequently over stimulated because we live in a society that encourages us to want more, have more and be more. Brené Brown[8] calls this a "scarcity culture" where:

> *everyone is hyperaware of lack. Everything from safety and love to money and resources feels restricted or lacking. We spend inordinate amounts of time calculating how much we have, want and don't have and how much everyone else has, needs and wants.*

Social comparison *can* be useful in helping us gauge how to fit in and belong to groups, however it becomes debilitating and addictive when, as in Brené Brown's version, we compare ourselves to unattainable, media-driven images of perfection. We push ourselves to achieve, accumulate and compete but never feel that we measure up. This is not our fault – it is the basis upon which many

---

[8] (Brown, 2012)

goods are marketed and sold to us. Under these conditions our *drive brain* becomes motivated by fear and other *threat brain* emotions aroused by the possibility of hostile judgement, rejection and abandonment. These fears are deeply embedded in our *threat brain* templates. To be excluded from our group can constitute a life-threatening danger. When our *drive brain* is motivated by threat we are likely to get stuck in toxic 'loops' of addictive activity that represent our most problematic habits.

Threat brain and *drive brain* looping – a toxic combination

When our motivation to compete, achieve and prosper is supported by *safe brain* logic, focus and calm, then our *drive brain* works well and what we do feels purposeful and rewarding. Healthy drive promotes value-aligned achievement, prudent risk-taking and the enjoyment of and energy for new challenges. However, when our *drive brain* is fuelled by *threat* emotions our motivation to achieve and compete becomes ruthless, exhausting, addictive and compulsive. Toxic drive is a common experience amongst high achievers who feel constantly stressed, overworked and controlled by external expectations. An example of this is when we are compelled to work long hours not because of a positive joy in our work but because we are fearful of losing our job or being judged incompetent.

Our *drive brain* is stimulated by the Sympathetic Nervous System (SNS) which is the same system that controls our *threat brain*. When our *drive brain* is highly active the hormone adrenalin is overstimulated. Adrenalin makes us hyper-responsive and ready to act but, like cortisol in the *threat brain*, in heavy, regular doses it can affect our blood pressure and immune system and increase stress-related symptoms. This is why simultaneous over-activity in our *threat brain* and *drive brain* is a toxic combination. Our SNS revs up and floods our bodies with concentrated stress hormones.

Toxic drive is an increasingly common experience in highly competitive societies which reward winning performance. It is not at all unusual for people to be living in a permanent state of anxiety and fear – one that is driven by misplaced ambition and sustained by deeply rooted feelings of inadequacy or unworthiness. Many of us are driven to keep going because we fear being exposed as vulnerable or incompetent and because of this being rejected by our family or work group. The problem is that we are usually not *consciously* aware of these fears and motivations and so cannot choose to act any differently.

Figure 5: Safe brain triggers Healthy Drive,
while threat brain triggers Toxic Drive

In Part Two we will explore the extent and significance of *unconscious* motivation and how it affects our ability to be aware of or change our habits. We will also consider how warm awareness creates optimal conditions for an exploration of the unconscious, allowing us to discover the truth of our history and within it the origins of our beliefs and assumptions and favourite habits.

Motivational Integrity

We have seen how, in different ways and to different degrees (depending on our intention and purpose in the moment) we need our *threat, drive* and *safe brain* to be working and regulating each other. *Integration* of our *Trimotive Brain* enables us to live at our best. Too much threat and we will become defensive and stressed. Too much drive and we become hyperactive, anxious and unfocused. Too much safe and we become complacent, unrealistic and unprepared.

We become 'dis-integrated' when there is over- or under-activity in parts of our motivational system. Dan Siegel writes:

> ...*integration is the key mechanism beneath both the absence of illness and the presence of well-being. Integration – the linkage of differentiated elements of a system – illuminates a direct pathway towards health. It's the way we avoid dull, boring rigidity on the one hand, or explosive chaos on the other.*[9]

Siegel argues that how we *focus our attention* is key to promoting integrative changes in the brain and there is certainly growing evidence to support the argument that the brain, unless it is organically damaged or atrophied, is able to change itself through repeated and *targeted* stimulation of neurons or brain cells. If we can train our attention to focus fully on the thing we want to learn – be it a new skill or the unlearning of an old habit – we can help our neurons to strategically fuse together to form new templates or networks.

Plastic brain theories[10] suggest we can 'flex' neural circuits in our brains just like we can flex muscles in our body. By flexing these circuits and encouraging our neurons to fire, we strengthen and expand synaptic linkages between neurons which create learning and new habit formation. If we are often anxious, stressed or focused on our problems we will be flexing our neurons to develop strong and extensive networks that support our *threat brain* motivations. Conversely, if we are able to focus attention on nourishing, kind, appreciative feelings, thoughts and opportunities, we will start to flex the neural connections required to support our *safe brain*.

Research shows that a self-compassionate inner voice can trigger our parasympathetic nervous system which, as we have seen, enables our *safe brain* capabilities to function well and to regulate the threat and drive systems. This means we can think more clearly and deeply, relate to others more effectively and feel more rested and healthy. Self-criticism does the opposite. It triggers our sympathetic nervous system which floods our body with threat and

---

[9] (Siegel, 2010)
[10] (Begley, 2009)

drive hormones and significantly narrows our emotional and behavioural range. Additionally, research carried out at Aston University by Olivia Longe and colleagues[11] shows, using fMRI scan images, how self-criticism and self-reassurance appear to activate different areas related to *threat brain* and *safe brain* responses.

In this chapter we have learned that we have come to be this way because we are part of an evolutionary flow of life. We have developed brains and bodies that enable and constrain us in particularly human ways. However, we are not *just* evolved brains and bodies and 'selfish genes' feeling and acting in predictable ways. The way we feel, think and act is also the result of a complex and nuanced interaction between our evolved biological needs and potentials and our relational and physical environment. In Chapter Two we continue our exploration of how has it come to be this way by looking at the significance of childhood experience in forming our habits and character.

---

[11] (Longe, et al., 2010). See these images at www.bit.ly/Trimotive01

Chapter Two: The Significance of Childhood Experience

Relationships matter

Professionals working in the field of adult development are increasingly influenced by advances in neuropsychology which emphasise the brain's potential for change and its lifelong ability to adapt and grow. Neuropsychologists researching 'plastic brain' theory argue that by training our mind to regulate threat responses and to be positive, appreciative and focused we can overwrite negative templates and re-wire our neurons to form new networks that offer more relevant, current and useful information. This is good news, for not long ago psychologists believed that our character and capability is fixed by the time we are 30.[12] As a result of these developments, coaching and psychotherapy are increasingly focused on 'here and now' experience, attention 'in the moment' and how physiological balance or 'integration' supports a mindful approach to threat-based, destructive emotions and habits. We don't have to be enthralled or held prisoner by our past.

However, no matter how alluring and compelling this argument and no matter how much we want to believe in the ability of humans to adapt and flourish, many people who seek help, and even more who do not, *never* manage to lift up and out of their preferred and sometimes problematic habits. Re-wiring may be possible but it is a machine metaphor that oversimplifies the organic, dynamic and complex reality of human life. Humans are not robots, even though we may feel like them sometimes. We are mysterious, chameleon-like, creative, symbolic, compassionate,

---

12 (James, 1890)

conflicted, imaginative and dependent on our primary carers for a considerable time. This dependency, upon which our survival depends, forces us to pay attention to and learn about others quickly. What we learn is mediated through a complex system of *symbols*, including language and *context*, including social norms and expectations. Even though we may de-prioritise them, the belief systems, meanings and associations that we learn in our first years of life stay with us for ever.

Over the last 70 years a number of studies have looked at children neglected in early childhood. The majority of these studies focused on children living in care or similar institutions. Bruce Perry's[13] harrowing research involving Romanian orphans shows how the developing brain may be irreversibly damaged when subject to sensory, physical, emotional and social deprivation. Neglect included lack of food, conversation, touch and play. In some cases it also involved physical and verbal violence and abuse. The children and babies in these infamous orphanages were found confined in, and sometimes tied to, their cots. Some could not speak at all whilst others screamed continuously, often rocking and biting themselves to get some sort of stimulation.

Perry and his colleagues discovered striking differences in the head sizes of these orphans against an expected growth norm. In the brain scan below, an image from a healthy 3-year-old is contrasted with one from a severely neglected child of the same age. The brain size is significantly smaller and the dark areas indicate damage or atrophy in certain areas of the brain which support cognitive, social and emotional functions. This is a dramatic image and stark evidence to show how significant our formative experiences are. This kind of research finds corroboration in many other studies including L. Alan Sroufe's thirty-year longitudinal study of risk and adaptation from birth to adulthood.[14] Sroufe concluded that 90% of the children who experienced maltreatment went on to develop a mental illness by the age of 18.

---

[13] (Perry, 2002)
[14] (Sroufe, et al., 2009)

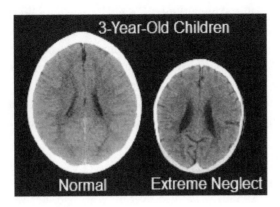

Figure 6: *The impact of neglect on the human brain (Perry, 2002).*

Thankfully, most of us are not severely neglected and are unlikely to have brain damage or atrophy. Nevertheless we still get stuck in harmful habits which affect our emotions, thoughts and behaviours. That's because childhood – even without severe neglect – leaves its imprint on our brains and bodies. It is not so much that early experience is *more* important than later experience but simply that early experience occurs at a time when a person is highly receptive to certain kinds of information. Early experience is so significant because it gives us first press information about *how to survive,* a core component of which is *how to relate to others.* This potent information is stored deep in our unconscious memory. It retains its intensity and influence because it got us through childhood alive. Some researchers have referred to this store of early learning as our *prototype* which influences us throughout life in complex and nonlinear ways.

That childhood matters is not news. Over 100 years ago, and without the help of brain scans, Freud drew attention to the significance of childhood and proposed that the early primary relationship was the blueprint for all subsequent relationships. Freud worked mostly with adult patients and their remembered narratives. In this sense, he worked 'backwards' from the adult story to the childhood experience. Others who followed began to work directly with children. The carefully documented observations of pioneering clinical practitioners Karen Horney, John Bowlby, Mary Ainsworth and Alice Miller lent weight to some of Freud's speculations and added new insights into the *quality* of childhood relationships and the impact of cultural conditioning. These findings still have a strong influence on how we understand the physical, mental and behavioural consequences of our upbringing and provide further support for the need to regulate our *Trimotive Brain*.

Basic anxiety – a brain in threat

Karen Horney was an acute observer and interpreter of human behaviour. Although she died over 50 years ago, her work is still echoed in many of the psychological theories in use today. In the 1920s, early in her career, she lectured at the Institute of Psychoanalysis in Berlin. A contemporary of Freud, her interests were broader and encompassed feminism, Buddhism and existential philosophies. Horney was the first psychoanalyst to strongly link adult psychological problems with disturbances in the *quality* of early relationships. She was one of the first to argue that people were not just driven by a pleasure principle,[15] as Freud had originally stated, but by a need for *basic safety* in the world. Horney evolved Freud's psychosexual theories into *psychosocial* concepts and emphasised the importance of kindness, consistency, autonomy and trust.

According to Horney, we feel safe when we experience consistent warmth, love and affirmation from our carers. We feel unsafe or anxious when we are maltreated. Maltreatment can range from constant criticism, isolation, neglect and emotional blackmail to more extreme forms of abuse, including sexual and physical violence. Horney observed that nurturing, loving relationships in early childhood create inner security which enables healthy growth and maturation. Horney calls this *self-realisation* and explains that it involves a person developing:

> *...the unique alive forces of his real self; the clarity and depth of his own feelings, thoughts, wishes, interests; the*

---

[15] The instinctual seeking of pleasure and avoidance of pain to satisfy psychological and biological needs.

ability to tap his own resources, the strength of his will power; the special capacities of gifts he may have; the faculty to express himself and to relate to others with his spontaneous feelings.[16]

Horney's concepts of basic safety and basic anxiety anticipated insights from neuroscience which support *Trimotive Brain* theory. Self-realisation in Horney's terms corresponds to the idea of *integration*, which begins when we regulate our motivation systems. In Horney's description we see the activity of *safe brain* influencing *drive brain* and regulating *threat brain*. In her detailed clinical studies we see that self-realisation also entails a fundamental move away from self-contempt (the inner critic) towards self-compassion.

Horney argued that children frequently experience *unfavourable* childhood conditions. She writes:

...such unfavourable conditions are too manifold to list. But, when summarised, they all boil down to the fact that the people in the environment are too wrapped up in their own neuroses to be able to love the child, or even to conceive of him as the particular individual he is; their attitudes towards him are determined by their own neurotic needs and responses.[17]

Parents and carers can be dominating, over-protective, erratic, intimidating, irritable, over-exacting, over-indulgent, show favouritism to other siblings, sexist, hypocritical, sarcastic and indifferent. The list, as Horney rightly notes, could go on. This kind of environment triggers anxiety in the child, which Horney describes as a feeling of *not belonging* and a sense that others are hostile.

Once more we see in Horney's observations strong connections with contemporary neuroscience. Basic anxiety, as she describes it, is an expression of our brain in threat. It is terrifying to feel that we

---

[16] (Horney, 1950)
[17] ibid

may be hurt or rejected by our caregivers. This is a significant risk to our survival. So we quickly learn ways to respond to, and overcome, the danger. Horney called these our *survival solutions* and over thirty years she refined these solutions into three behavioural patterns which closely resemble the fight, flee and freeze responses of the threatened brain. Behaviour which emerges from a brain in threat is narrow in range and scope. Horney used the word "cramped". Her description of the survival solutions and the patterns of behaviour that emerge from them illustrates very clearly how our basic reptilian threat response has, over time, become much more complex. Our threat responses are no longer simply to run, fight or freeze. A human being senses and reacts to threat in a multitude of ways.

Our *threat brain* in action – three survival solutions

Although our *threat brain* is our oldest motivation system we have come a long way from the basic emotions and responses of our reptilian ancestors. Horney's survival 'solutions' help us to understand the way our *human* brain processes threat and creates strategies to deal with these life challenges. Horney observed and categorised our strategies into three core patterns of behaving. The three patterns are *moving against people/events,* which involves mastering and overcoming threat; *moving away from people/events,* which involves cultivating independence and self-sufficiency and *moving toward people/events,* which involves a dependency on others to protect us from threats.

We will gain greater understanding of these patterns and see how they appear in our day-to-day routines when, in Part Three, we consider the coaching stories of Maggie, Carl and Ronnie. Before that though, it is useful to understand how these solutions arise and, if overused, become our general orientation not just to threat but to life in general.

When, as children, we experience a risk to survival – and remember this may be as subtle as noticing that our mother is distracted – we will quickly work out which behaviours are most likely to secure us again. We instinctively ask, how can I make mother attend to me when she is distracted? Shall I shout and cry (*move against*)? Shall I smile and gurgle (*move towards*)? Or will she become more interested in me if I stay quiet and amuse myself for a while (*move away*)? These strategies are not consciously calculated because at this age we do not have words or complex cognitive capabilities. They emerge as a series of 'trial and error' responses, motivated by our innate urge to survive.

We quickly learn that when difficulties or threats arise – and they will even in the most secure circumstances – sometimes we will have to stand up for ourselves, sometimes we will need to give affection and sometimes we will need to back off. In a safe environment and within healthy relationships these moves are not mutually exclusive – they are used flexibly and only when appropriate.

The solutions become problems – or harmful habits – when we are *constantly* experiencing threat and anxiety. Then the solutions become overused and rigid because we become hyperalert to threat and see it everywhere, even when it does not exist. Furthermore, our *safe brain*, as we have seen, may under-function due to lack of nurturing and soothing. Without the regulating function of *safe brain* our *threat brain* can go into overdrive.

Healthy *moving against* when overused and misapplied becomes a tendency to dominate, control and rebel and corresponds to our brain in fight mode. Healthy *moving away* becomes avoidance, resignation and cynicism and corresponds to our brain in flight mode. Healthy *moving towards* becomes clinging, people pleasing, and self-subordination and corresponds to our brain in freeze mode (we freeze when we diminish or disappear aspects of our self in order to please others). Eventually, because they are employed so frequently, these solutions become our orientation toward life.

Our survival solutions, which may become our orientation to life, are born out of challenging childhood experiences. We *all* experience challenge but for some of us these challenges are very difficult and sometimes even dangerous. The way we apply our solutions – in other words the way we respond to threat – is dependent on the nature and severity of the original challenges we experienced.

Healthy, flexible solutions usually develop when our environments are favourable whilst unhealthy, rigid solutions develop when they are not.[18] Most of us can, however, learn to recognise and adapt this early learning so that our adult response to threat becomes more accurate and effective. We will discover how in Parts Two and Three.

Separation anxiety – *safe brain* and attachment

Karen Horney observed how we develop certain orientations to life depending on whether our childhood environments and relationships were favourable or not. In particular, her research supports our discussion about how the *threat brain,* manifesting in our survival solutions, controls and constrains behaviour.

John Bowlby's research drew attention to the importance of *attachment* in early childhood and his work provides evidence to strengthen the case for the existence and cultivation of *safe brain* capabilities. Bowlby's seminal studies expanded our understanding of the importance of nurturing relationships in ensuring survival and ongoing health.

John Bowlby trained in Psychiatry at the Maudsley Hospital in London and in 1936 he also qualified as a Psychoanalyst. Following service in the Royal Army Medical Corps he joined the Tavistock Clinic and from 1950 he was Mental Health Consultant to the World Health Organisation where he was asked to advise on the mental health of homeless children. It was during this period of research that Bowlby saw for himself the lasting effects on young children who had been separated from their mothers. He wanted to understand *why* maternal deprivation might influence such developmental problems.

Throughout the 1950s and early '60s he and his colleague, James Robertson, carried out studies to explore the impact of loss and

---

[18] Sometimes we develop rigid and problem habits even when our childhood experiences were favourable and the reverse is also true. Not everyone who had a troubled past becomes hostage to their threat brain. However, the exceptions are few and often come about because of later experiences of significant trauma or deep and enduring compassion/love that override the original experience templates.

suffering experienced by young children separated from their primary caregivers. In 1952 they made a documentary film, *A Two-Year-Old Goes to Hospital*, which was instrumental in changing restrictive parental visiting policies.

Bowlby proposed that the way we form and sustain relationships as adults is dependent on the quality of our first attachment relationship. An attachment represents a *significant bond* between the young child and her primary carer. This relationship is crucial to our survival and as babies we are instinctively aware of how important it is to maintain proximity and closeness with this person.

When Bowlby was researching attachment theory, psychoanalytic perspectives were popular and a child's separation distress was understood as a product of unconscious fantasies. Bowlby challenged this and argued that children were responding to real-life events which threatened their survival. Bowlby also opposed popular behavioural theory which claimed that infants attach themselves to and are contented by whoever *feeds* them.

Bowlby, following Horney, saw that healthy attachment involved more than having one's physical needs met. A baby also needs someone who helps them feel secure. Thus attachment required a *psychological connection* between the infant and carer which develops as the infant learns to trust that the carer will be "*nearby, accessible and attentive*". Like Horney, Bowlby observed that a child will "experiment" until she finds the pattern of behaviour most likely to secure proximity and care.

Bowlby collated the results of many studies which recorded the anger, grief and insecurity that young children express when parted from their mothers. He concluded that:

> *The young child's hunger for his mother's love and presence is as great as his hunger for food.*[19]

Bowlby proposed that for some children these responses of "*protest, despair and detachment*" remain active into adulthood and interfere with the ability to form close and trusting relationships. It is

---

[19] (Bowlby, 1997, p. xiii)

probable that what he witnessed – as did his colleague Mary Ainsworth – were threat response patterns not dissimilar to Horney's *moving towards* (insecurity and clinging), *moving against* (anger, hostility) and *moving away* (detachment, grief).

Bowlby concluded that intimacy with a *particular* and *consistent* carer made a significant difference to a child's development. Separation from this carer, usually the mother, was extremely detrimental and could produce irreversible consequences. Whilst his claim may seem obvious to us now, at the time it was not universally accepted that maternal love or presence was a necessity or that the formation of an ongoing and lasting relationship with the child was foundational to the child's healthy development.

In later studies Bowlby observed that not all children respond to separation from their mother in the same way. He refined his theory to acknowledge that separation by itself did not create lasting insecurity. This inspired Mary Ainsworth to develop the famous 'strange situation' technique to explore the nature of these differences.

In the strange situation studies, one-year-old children are observed in a laboratory setting being separated from and reunited with their mothers. In the studies, around 60% behave in the way suggested by Bowlby's 'normative' theory. They become upset when the parent leaves the room but when the parent returns they are easily reunited and comforted. Ainsworth called this *secure* attachment where separation anxiety is experienced at a normal level.

Other children (about 20%) appear uneasy even when their mother is with them. When their mother leaves, these children become *extremely* distressed. However, upon the mother's return the child is hard to soothe and can also behave in angry, punishing ways towards her. Ainsworth called this attachment pattern *ambivalent*.

The third pattern of attachment, again observed in about 20% of children, is called *avoidant*. Avoidant children don't appear distressed when the mother leaves or particularly pleased when she returns. In fact, when the mother returns they actively avoid contact with her, often seeking out toys and other distractions in the room instead. Ainsworth's studies went on to explore how these individual differences in the laboratory corresponded to parent-child interactions at home. Children who appear secure in a strange situation tend to have parents who are responsive to their needs. Children who are anxious (either ambivalent or avoidant) often have insensitive, rejecting or inconsistent parenting. These findings have been replicated in many studies since.

Bowlby's work and the research it subsequently inspired provides a vast body of evidence to show the role of *safe brain* motivations and capability in soothing threat (or in his language, insecurity). Reciprocal, nurturing attachments in our childhood confer significant benefits on us as adults and when they are lacking we suffer by getting locked into *threat brain* responses to relationship.

Adult attachment – the pattern repeats

In 1984, Carol George, Nancy Kaplan and Mary Main developed the Adult Attachment Interview (AAI) which enabled clinicians to assess attachment behaviours in adolescents and adults. In this interview, respondents reflect on their childhood relationships and evaluate the possible impacts of these experiences on their current personality and behaviour. The questionnaire, when used in a skilled way, helps people to reflect and make sense of early experience.

AAI Research shows that if we are securely attached as children we will generally grow into securely attached *autonomous* adults. In other words, we are able to form, nurture, value and enjoy reciprocal adult relationships. If, however, we showed ambivalent attachment style as a child we are likely to express a *preoccupied* style as an adult. Although we want to be close to people we feel we cannot depend on them. We try to manage this by controlling and dominating relationships and we become aggressive and hostile when others disagree with us or act independently. We feel undervalued and so we are constantly on the lookout for approval and affirmation. As a result, we may come across as attention-seeking, self-centred and demanding. Preoccupied adult attachment styles correspond to *threat brain's* 'fight' response or *moving against*.

If, however, we were avoidant as a child we are likely to develop a *dismissing* or a *fearful* avoidant style as an adult. *Dismissive-avoidant* adults are comfortable living independently and do not seek or desire close emotional relationships. If we have a dismissing style, we *fear* intimacy and 'emotionality'. We believe feelings are better suppressed and we can seem cold and aloof. We probably regard the need for human closeness as a weakness yet the appearance of high self-esteem and self-sufficiency is a compensation to hide the belief that we are not truly worthy of love and attention. Dismissive adult attachment styles correspond to *threat brain's* 'flee' response or *moving away*.

Fearful avoidant adults also lack self-confidence and carry negative views about themselves. Unlike dismissives, we openly crave love and closeness even though we believe we are not worthy of it. Like other insecure people we are mistrustful of partners and friends and anticipate abandonment, rejection and betrayal. However, we try to manage this fear by pleasing and placating others. The problem is when people respond and move closer we become anxious again because intimacy feels dangerous. Fearful adult attachment styles correspond to *threat brain's* 'freeze' response or *moving towards*.

Attachment research provides significant evidence to show how childhood relationships inform our adult patterns and studies suggest that around 40% of adults are likely to be 'insecurely attached'. I would suggest the figure is higher as increasing numbers of very young children are regularly separated from their parents as childcare outside the home grows and family break-ups and 'mergers' continue to challenge and interfere with healthy attachment relationships.

Feeling insecure in our adult relationships is, I believe, a very common and shared experience and is part of the fabric and colour of our everyday encounters. The most talked about issues of personal significance in my coaching practice are memories of family breakdown and divorce and the inability or lack of opportunity to relate to one parent or the other. These have become ordinary life experiences. Thus, whilst labels and categories can be useful in helping us notice patterns we should be careful in their application and resist polarising these patterns into 'normal' and 'abnormal'. This is because when we feel or are told we are abnormal our *threat brain* will activate. In Maggie's story we will see that whilst her diagnosis of 'narcissistic personality disorder' offered some clarity around her problem habits it also made her feel ashamed and inadequate – which set off her *threat brain* loops.

Although *moving against, towards* and *away* are also, to some extent 'labels', I have found them more spacious than the labels we tend to find in psychiatric diagnostic manuals. Perhaps this is because they attempt to describe an *orientation to living* rather than a narrow cluster of behaviours that constitute a 'disorder'. They are also less about pathology – which connotes illness and disease – and more about habits we have learned and, perhaps, got stuck in.

These relationship habits can cause us distress and frustration though and they should be taken seriously. However, when we begin to see that they are the result of events beyond our control and are, to some extent, inevitable, we feel less ashamed and isolated. It is not our fault or at all surprising that we have learned to avoid relationships, for example, when all our former experience and memories of close relationships are filled with disappointment and pain.

Reframing our 'problems' as out-of-date solutions is the first step in soothing our threatened brain and entering into a deeper exploration of what else is possible. In Part Three, we will see how Maggie, Carl and Ronnie began to understand how their habits had once helped them and how, with a new and warm awareness, they could overwrite their childhood patterns and learn to relate to others in more reciprocal and fulfilling ways.

Making the connections

Brain science	Developmental psychology		
A Brain in threat	Horney's Survival Solutions	Bowlby and Ainsworth's infant attachment styles	George, Kaplan and Main's adult attachment styles
Fight	Move against	Ambivalent	Preoccupied
Flee	Move away	Avoidant	Dismissive
Freeze	Move towards	Avoidant	Fearful
A Safe brain			
Bond•relate•reflect Complex thinking	Self-realisation	Secure	Autonomous

Table 1: Brain science and developmental psychology

You can see the connections between how evolutionary brain science and developmental psychology describe the experience of threat in the table above and how, when our brain is in threat, our emotional and behavioural range narrows.

However, a person who is able to regulate their *threat brain* response will not be held within the narrow confines of these patterns and can develop their potential as well as experience security and autonomy as an adult. A secure and autonomous adult is able to think freely, openly and coherently about their attachment experiences. They can reflect on negative or difficult past experiences with compassion and forgiveness. The ability to understand and reflect in this way is facilitated by the activity of our *safe brain* as it both regulates our *threat brain* and supports the functioning of our prefrontal cortex, which enables complex and integrated thinking.

Even if we were deprived of loving relationships in childhood, research shows that most of us can re-stimulate *safe brain* later in life by cultivating new relationships that are reciprocal, trusting and enduring. For those of us who are struggling to do this, self-compassion becomes a core and primary practice. *The ability to love and take care of our self comes before we can love or take care of another.* Although the severely neglected orphans in Bruce Perry's study (page 45) may have brains that are permanently damaged and unable to achieve full integration, most of us *do* have the means – even if we do not have the will or dedication – to create new experiences and meaning in our life.

Before we look at how to create new experiences and meaning, let us turn to the work of Alice Miller. Miller helps us understand why, in spite of outward success and achievement, we are sometimes left with a feeling of emptiness or inadequacy. Her work foreshadows and supports recent research into the workings of our third motivational system, *drive brain*. We have already seen how this system can energise and motivate us to accomplish astonishing things. But if our drive motivations are fuelled by threat we will develop unhealthy, addictive habits and our achievements will feel hollow and fragile.

Unintentional harm – *drive brain* and the false self

Alice Miller, writing and researching in the late 1970s, suggested that *ordinary, non-traumatic and conventional parenting* can also interfere with a child's ability to experience and express his true feelings and needs. Miller drew attention to the everyday, unintentional and often unconscious ways in which our parents make demands of, and set expectations for, us which suffocate our own desires and ambitions. This happens easily, even in the most caring and loving environments, because, as children, we are acutely sensitive and responsive to how we can secure love, attention and eventually approval from our parents. If our parents have unmet needs of their own (and many do) they are likely to try and meet those needs through our vulnerable and easily manipulated selves.

Miller stressed that most parents do not *intentionally* seek to harm or stifle their children yet the child's extraordinary adaptability and intuition when it comes to pleasing the parent enables their willing subordination to the parents' wishes. This leads, said Miller, to the formation of a 'false' personality where we feel, think and behave as *others* expect or want us to. Our 'true' self becomes stunted and repressed.

In *The Drama of Being a Child,* Miller shares her experiences of being alongside adults as they re-discover their 'true' selves through a painful but necessary acceptance of how they have been 'loved':

> *It is one of the turning points… when the narcissistically disturbed patient comes to the emotional insight that all the love he has captured with so much effort and self-denial was not meant for him as he really was, that the admiration for his beauty and his achievements was aimed at this beauty and these achievements and not at the child himself.*[20]

Miller was particularly interested in the experience of the 'gifted child' who excels, performs and achieves in line with his parents' goals. The gifted child usually goes on to become a high-achieving adult whose *drive brain* motivations are strong. However, because our achievements have been motivated by fear of losing our parents' love, our adult behaviours become 'narcissistically disturbed'. Miller identified 'grandiosity' and depression as two of the most common consequences of narcissistic disturbance. A grandiose person is one who is admired everywhere and who *craves* this admiration. We set impossibly high targets and standards for ourselves and believe we must excel in everything we do. We might recognise these as 'perfectionist' habits common in those of us who find it hard to tolerate failure, rejection or personal limitation. Yet, writes Miller:

> *Grandiosity is the defence against depression and depression is the defence against the deep pain over the loss of self.*[21]

I have coached numerous people in organisations who appear to lead rewarding, happy and bountiful lives. Yet their personal and often hidden story is quite different. Many of these executives and leaders are insecure individuals carrying a burden of pain they are often not conscious of until it manifests as illness, an angry outburst or depressive disengagement.

The term *corporate psychopath* has become common but is misused. Most people are not psychopathic – which is a rare and

---

[20] (Miller, 1987, p. 30)
[21] (ibid, p. 56)

severe personality disorder. The more common problem is an inability to manage subconscious feelings of threat and to regulate *drive brain*. Usually this does not lead to dangerous and extreme behaviour. Sadly it *does* contribute to a whole host of *socially acceptable* destructive habits such as excessive drinking or eating, the inability to sustain relationships, workaholism, the overuse of digital technologies and the insatiable desire to accumulate material goods.

Nowhere is this more apparent than in the endless stream of media stories recounting the antics of the rich and famous. We are familiar with people in the film industry, music business and sport who amaze us not just because of their talent and achievements but also because of their propensity for deep unhappiness and self-harm. For the curious, Wikipedia provides a list of some of these well-known people and their problems,[22] yet there are plenty more who do not achieve notoriety or fame but who share the childhood experience of needing to excel in order to gain love. Oliver James in his book, *Not in Your Genes*, refers to this group as the 'miserable talented' and urges that these and millions of less successful sufferers get the help they need to explore the roots of what I call their toxic-drive-based behaviours.

In 2011 Amy Chua, a Yale law professor, wrote a book on her philosophy of child-rearing called *Battle Hymn of the Tiger Mother* and it became a global bestseller. 'Tiger mothering' refers to a strict, rigid and aggressive approach to parenting that aims to achieve educational excellence in children. It involves longs hours of study, very little play time and sometimes harsh and coercive methods to achieve focus and commitment. When the book came out Chua's children were frequently pitied and labelled 'abused'. In 2016, *The Telegraph* newspaper carried an interview with Chua's now grown-up daughters.[23] Sophia and Lulu both went to Harvard and Sophia went on to postgraduate study at Yale. They had become the Ivy League educational success story their parents intended.

In this interview both daughters claim to have happy memories of their childhood and say they would parent their own children in a

---

[22] www.bit.ly/Trimotive03
[23] www.bit.ly/Trimotive04

similar way. Sophia goes on to say, *"everyone talks about my mother threatening to throw my toys on the fire, but the funny thing is that was not a major memory. I remember my childhood as happy."*[24]

Thirty years before the Chua sisters' fame, Alice Miller noted a strong tendency in highly successful adults with 'narcissistic disturbances' to be completely unaware of their own personal needs and yearnings. Miller saw that these adults:

> ...*are never overtaken by unexpected emotions and will only admit those feelings that are accepted and approved by their inner censor – which is their parent's heir. Depression and a sense of inner emptiness is the price they must pay for this control.*[25]

Sophia and Lulu Chua may be able to maintain their appreciative and partial memories of childhood for years. This might serve them well as they work hard to establish their status and independence in the world. It is often not until mid-life that successful people with a troubled past begin to experience a confusing unease which is a sign that other memories, needs and yearnings are seeking expression. Many people dismiss or joke about this unease as a 'mid-life crisis'. However, in Part Two we will see how important it is to turn towards such feelings and follow them if we wish to discover and integrate the split off fragments of our divided self.

Whilst there is growing evidence to show the link between high achievement and ill health, not all talented, successful and famous people suffer from emotional or social problems. Those who achieve in healthy ways have regulated their threat-based motivations so their *drive brain* can function normally and does not go into 'overdrive', causing addictive, relentless, exhausting and ultimately unfulfilling habits. Yet this is easier said than done. If you find it hard to let go of unhelpful childhood habits, be comforted: you are not alone. We all have a *memory* and that memory, when working, is tenacious. It holds on to habit, is slow to learn from new experiences and unconsciously influences (some would say determines) our actions. Sometimes our memories make it very hard for us to be in our *safe brain*.

---

[24] ibid
[25] (Miller, 1987, p. 37)

Chapter Three: Memory – The Orchestrator of Self and Identity

Our biological heritage and childhood experience provide the ingredients for creating our unique self. Yet it is how we *make sense* of this heritage and personal experience that produces who we are and what we do. Sense-making differentiates us. It is, for example how one person is able to cope with stress at work and another ends up burning out. Or why a relationship breakdown will trigger a depressive cycle in some, yet motivate others to travel abroad, make new friends or learn a new skill.

Research shows that when we believe stress is bad for us we are much more likely to suffer from it than if we believe it is a useful experience that is going to help us deal more effectively with a particular challenge.[26] Thus the way we *think about* our experience matters. However, it is not always easy to direct our thoughts in ways that are beneficial to us. This is because strong emotions associated with significant memories can 'take over' the way we feel and make sense. To understand how this happens it is helpful to understand how our memory works. Then, in Part Two, we will explore in detail how memories influence unconscious processes that direct the way we feel, think and act.

Making memories – experience, neurons and templates

At birth, our brain is full of single, disconnected neurons or cells. Billions of them. These isolated cells need experience to activate them and to find other cells to bond with and form *templates*. Everything we 'know' is stored as part of these templates. What we

---

[26] (Jamieson, et al., 2012)

have learned is not a 'thing', it is a collection of neurons grouping and firing together when we have an experience. An experience, such as feeling hungry and being fed by mother, becomes 'encoded' and stored the more often it is repeated and the more my neurons build up connections with other neurons as a result of this repetition. Over time (as I am repeatedly fed and comforted) I might build up a template that stores information about how to get fed, that food equates to comfort and that females are important caregivers.

If an experience is *emotionally charged* and we have focused our full attention on it, then our neurons will fire more strongly. This might be when we are excited, fearful or experiencing joy. Core neural templates carry information that is deeply memorable, meaningful and important to us and, as a result, they are more accessible and available. Traumatic experiences that constitute a threat to our survival carry the strongest emotional charge and are immediately prioritised, encoded and stored. This is not because we are negative, 'glass half empty' people, it is because there is a clear evolutionary *advantage* in encoding danger, problems and threats and learning how to survive and anticipate them.

The structures in our brain that support these memory functions are the corpus striatum, amygdala and hippocampus. We have learned a lot about how these structures work by observing how they grow and what happens when they are damaged through injury or strokes. Understanding these structures illuminates distinctions between our conscious and our unconscious mind and will later help us to appreciate the difficulty in both noticing and changing our habits.

The corpus striatum and amygdala – unconscious, implicit memory

The *corpus striatum* is one of our earliest brain structures and is involved in storing *implicit memory* – memories related to our basic functions including breathing, blood circulation, moving and digestion. When we are born it is the corpus striatum that holds and manages our memory.

Within it there are specialist centres for storing cognitive, psychological, sensory and motor memory where we hold the patterns that dictate the habitual nature of our lives.[27] In humans, the corpus striatum has evolved and is capable of storing all sorts of memories relating to our essential 'habits' which are no longer exclusively concerned with basic bodily functions and needs. As our brain has grown in size, complexity and capability so too has its ability to discern, tag and store a broader range of experiences which contain physical, psychological and social information about how to survive – which is still the brain's primary mandate.

Decisions about what to store as 'essential' memory are made by our *amygdala*. The amygdala acts as an emotional radar, detecting and processing experiences that are 'value laden' – in other words, ones that are meaningful to us. Whilst the amygdala is receptive to all emotions it will always prioritise those which relate to threat. It will ensure that *survival information* relating to danger, pain, attack and abandonment is seared into our implicit memory system. This is why some of our most deeply buried memories are negatively charged. Experiences which have little emotional intensity have a higher likelihood of being tagged 'unimportant' and will in time be 'lost' or hard to retrieve.

Memories stored in the corpus striatum *unconsciously* influence our feelings, thoughts and behaviours. In other words, we don't have to think about them in order for them to 'work'. This enables us to breathe and move 'automatically' and also to react with speed to danger. These memories influence us in other ways. They enable us to understand the meaning of the cultural cues, symbols and signs that we have been socialised in and they give us involuntary 'gut feelings', aversions, attractions, surges of unexpected emotions and a sense of déjà vu.

One way to think about our unconscious is as a memory bank containing vast numbers of 'deposits' that we have forgotten about or, having been left by our ancestors, not even known were there. Our unconscious sends us information about these deposits – especially

---

[27] Caudate nucleus (cognitive storage), nucleus acumbens (emotional storage), putamen (sensory and motor storage) – described by Curran (2008)

through our imagination, dreams and our somatic symptoms such as digestive pains and headaches. This powerful energy or force makes us feel, think and behave in ways we often do not understand or want to take seriously. Most people ignore their unconscious until they get in trouble with it, which is usually when they experience physical, psychological or social discomfort and distress. Psychosomatic symptoms such as stress-related headaches and stomach ulcers are easier to treat and often relieved when we become aware of the unconscious thoughts and feelings that give rise to them.

It was, of course, through these kinds of psychosomatic cases that Sigmund Freud, Carl Jung and others observed, detailed and illuminated – *without the help of modern science and technology* – the vast and complex workings of our unconscious. Contemporary brain scientists owe a lot to these pioneers of the unseen mental landscapes that exert such a strong influence on what we feel, think and do. Neuroscientist Brian Eagleman,[28] affirming Freud's work, notices that we still don't have much awareness about the "roots of our own choices". He's right. However, over time we have gained greater understanding of the unconscious, making it more possible to notice its processes and use its intelligence to review and adapt our choices. We will see how in Part Two.

The hippocampus – conscious, explicit memory

By the time we are in our second year of life our *hippocampus* has matured enough to provide a second memory function. The hippocampus acts as a search engine. It is responsible for retrieving information from different templates and connecting them up, like a jigsaw puzzle, to produce coherent *conscious* memories.

Explicit (or declarative) memory is at work when we are *aware* that we are remembering something. Spoon, cup, kettle, sugar, milk, hot water, tea bag. My hippocampus collects and connects with extraordinary speed. I remember what these objects are and how to make tea. When my hippocampus is damaged these objects remain unconnected and I become confused about what to do with

---

[28] (Eagleman, 2015)

them. My corpus striatum won't come to the rescue because making tea is unlikely (for most of us) to be an important survival memory protected and stored within its deep unconscious recesses.

The well-documented case of Henry Molaison shows just how important our hippocampus is in memory formation and retrieval. In August 1953, at the age of 27, Henry had his hippocampus removed in a well-meaning operation to cure him of severe epilepsy. Whilst the operation did relieve his seizures, it left Henry unable to store or retrieve new experiences. Although he could remember facts about his life before the operation he was unable to make *connections* and *associations* to give those facts meaning. He was also unable to imagine the future.

For 55 years after the operation and until his death in 2008, Henry participated in hundreds of research studies carried out at the Massachusetts Institute of Technology (MIT). Suzanne Corkin, lead researcher at MIT, worked with and assessed Henry for 46 years. She described Henry as a happy, friendly person who was rarely sad or depressed.[29] She recalled his stamina and interest in memory test tasks that others would find repetitive and boring. For Henry, everything was always new and interesting. Without his hippocampus, he was able to be fully engaged in the moment without the distractions of past or future. However, whilst living in the present may have contributed to his cheerful disposition it also made it difficult for Henry to contextualise or make sense of his experience. Corkin remembers Henry telling her that he was always 'arguing with himself' and she reflected:

> *His unrelenting amnesia kept him riding on the horns of a dilemma, which must have been unsettling. He could never be sure if he had acted improperly or like a gentleman, whether he had met a particular individual before, how old he was, what month and year we were in, and whether his memory for current events was accurate.*[30]

---

[29] (Corkin, 2014)
[30] www.bit.ly/Trimotive05

Thanks to Henry Molaison and other research participants, we know how damage to, or absence of, the hippocampus impacts memory. Research also shows that the healthy hippocampus shuts down if it is flooded with alcohol or stress chemicals such as cortisol or noradrenaline. As before, not only does this mean that my ability to retrieve and connect information is impaired but also that my capacity to store *new* information is reduced. I remember fewer *details* when I am drunk or scared and I make fewer connections and fail to grasp or construct complex meaning. For these reasons it is not a good idea to engage in learning, serious conversations or activities that require skill and focus when you are drunk or in threat.

When my hippocampus is not functioning, I can still store certain kinds of new memories in my corpus striatum or unconscious memory. This is because my amygdala – my emotional radar – is constantly alert and will ensure that emotionally intense experiences are not lost. By increasing its activation it will 'burn' these memories into my corpus striatum. Thus, whilst they are not easily available to my *conscious* mind, they are still exerting their influence through unconscious processes. This is why I can still feel worried and fearful the morning after a reckless office party, even though I cannot remember the details of it.

Growing me – learning, understanding and wisdom

As babies and young infants we are *impressionable*. Our single neurons are ready and waiting to connect. We are set up to learn and all we need is experience. Without varied and nurturing experiences or what researchers call 'rich environments' our brains grow more slowly. In extreme cases – remember Perry's pictures of childhood neglect on page 45 – our brains can become stunted. The more we experience things the more we learn and the more we learn the greater the number of neural networks in our brain. *Knowledge*, in brain terms, means having a large conceptual framework made up of many strong templates. Being able to use that conceptual framework with skill and accuracy constitutes *wisdom* or *understanding*.

I may have a lot of knowledge from reading books, having children, travelling the globe, participating in pub quizzes and tapping into Google twenty times a day. My head may be full of templates containing all sorts of information about my world. However, unless I make links *between* those facts through a process of reflection and interpretation, the facts remain isolated, their *meaning* is limited or trivial and my understanding is shallow.

It is the increasing complexity of our sense-making through connecting and associating templates that defines growth and development. To achieve this we need our motivation and memory systems to be working well. *Safe brain* states support full functioning of both the hippocampus and our prefrontal cortex which work together to enable higher-level thinking. Wisdom is the result of *connecting* our learning (templates) in order to respond optimally to the complexity of life in accurate and meaningful ways. In making the connections we are able to translate the *content* of our brain into coherent and effective feelings, thoughts and actions.

Connecting templates of information is part of the work of integration. As adults we are still prone to over-using certain templates and not making connections between others. A 'dis-integrated' memory is one in which connections have been lost (through trauma, injury or illness) or have not been made at all (lack of experience, education and reflection). The result is a person held captive by a few 'energised' templates that dictate how he experiences and responds to life. Some, if not most, of these templates are likely to have formed from intensely charged early experiences and will thus contain rigid, anxious and limited options for feeling, thinking and behaving. For example, here are some facts about my current work situation: *I have a new manager. I notice he looks a little like my father who died some years ago. Sometimes he behaves like my father. He has set tough targets for me and wants results quickly. I'm aware he likes to go drinking with colleagues after work.*

I have a strong template containing information about my troubled relationship with my father and I retrieve that template every time I see my manager. As a result, I notice more and more similarities between them. This triggers unpleasant feelings in me, similar to those I felt as a child in the company of my father. These feelings are so strong that at times I find myself getting into arguments with my manager, just like I did with my father. I get especially annoyed when my manager asks me to 'work harder' to achieve targets. My father was a taskmaster and a drinker too.

The relationship I have with my manager is difficult for me because I am drawing on only one template to understand and respond to this current experience and much of my sense-making about the experience remains at an unconscious level – in other words I react 'automatically' to my manager sometimes without knowing exactly why. In reacting unconsciously I am not engaging my hippocampus and making explicit connections *between* templates that help me to see and respond to the situation in a more informed, complex way. I have other templates that contain information about the current economic climate which could help me understand the target-setting process differently. Or my template about how to cultivate friendships, which could help me to notice that the 'drinking after work' takes place only on a Friday for an hour and most of the team go along. I may also have a template about power and authority which contains some information about my pattern of rejecting male authority figures.

By consciously connecting information stored in other templates I am more likely to release myself from negative – and often unconscious – emotional memories about my father in order to feel, think and act with greater insight and choice in the relationship with my manager.

The neuroscientist Susan Greenfield writes:

> *The insight and the knowledge that characterises a gifted mind is more than the regurgitation of facts. …real intelligence requires a synthesis between facts, context and meaning that encompasses far more than efficient responding.*[31]

"Real intelligence" is not just cognitive. In other words, it is not just about how we collect, process and use facts to judge, evaluate, reason

---

[31] (Greenfield, 2014, p. 251)

and problem solve. Emotional, social, physical and spiritual intelligences[32] also help us navigate our complex world with resilience and efficacy. The synthesis of facts, contexts and meaning that Greenfield talks about (*"seeing one thing in terms of another and thereby understanding each component as part of a whole"*) is the method at the heart of coaching and other forms of adult development. It is involved in the work of *integration* – making whole.

In Part Three we will see how synthesising information helped Maggie, Carl and Ronnie to 're-sense' their experience and construct new and more useful versions of their life story.

Being me – am I the sum of what I remember?

As our brains grow, the number of individual neurons reduces due to a process called *neural pruning*. Neural pruning starts from birth and reaches a peak in adolescence. The purpose of pruning is to make our brains more efficient. We keep the neurons we use and have connected to form strong templates and we lose the ones we don't use and haven't connected. Neural pruning is like a spring clean for the brain and by early adulthood our brain has become optimised for the particular environment we find ourselves in. Core templates – or groups of active neurons – have formed. They hold information about our particular beliefs, patterns of behaving and skills. Our adult personality, the one that enables us to adapt to and live in our unique life and environment, has emerged. The experiences we have stored in our neural templates constitute what we know about our self, our relationships and our world. This leads some people to define who we are in terms of what we remember. However it is not that simple.

First, as I have said, we are not *consciously aware* of all our memories. Those stored in our corpus striatum (implicit memory)

---

[32] Emotional intelligence refers to being aware of our own and other people's feelings; social intelligence refers to our awareness of and skill in relating to others; physical intelligence involves the awareness of our bodily experience including breathing, heart, muscle and digestive function. It also involves managing our energy well. Spiritual intelligence refers to our values, sense of purpose and our compassion for causes and life beyond the self.

unconsciously influence our body and mind. According to researchers George Lakoff and Mark Johnson,[33] only 5% of what we know reaches consciousness. This claim is supported by numerous studies[34] showing the degree to which people fail to accurately predict or explain their feelings, behaviour and motives when these are being controlled by unconscious processes.

In one such experiment, passers-by were asked to select the best quality nylon tights from a table displaying what were, in fact, *identical* pairs of tights. After people made their choice they were asked to explain how they arrived at their decision. Participants described at some length their preference for differences in sheerness, elasticity and knit. Given that the tights were all the same, these accounts could not have been accurate; nevertheless, people felt strongly about their choices and invented reasons for their judgements.

Added to our unconscious assumptions and beliefs we also have feelings and thoughts that we hide because they are unpleasant to us. Freud called this repression. These ignored, denied, projected and disassociated parts of us comprise our unconscious 'shadow' self and play a major role in our life even though we are mostly unaware of how and when we are being guided by these hidden forces. Most of the problems we encounter as individuals and in groups arise because we think and act without full consciousness of our real motives. The psychoanalyst Ken Eisold says:

> *Consciousness is a thin shell that screens out most of what we could know and much of what might actually help us to know in conducting our lives.*[35]

The second reason we cannot define who we are based on what we remember is because when a memory *is* consciously re-called, the act of recall is one of *dynamic* re-construction. In other words, the memory is influenced and *changed* by our present state of mind as well as elements of memory from other experiences. Research into

---

[33] (Lakoff & Johnson, 1999)
[34] (Wilson, 2002)
[35] (Eisold, 2009)

false memory[36] shows how easy it is to manipulate people to make them 'recollect' events that did not actually happen. Such techniques have been controversially used in advertising campaigns as well as prison torture. It is also a potential problem in psychotherapy when the words used to frame questions and to elicit a patient's history can heavily influence the response given. Everything you remember, therefore, is a *new* thought containing some memories, some omissions and some 'in the moment' additions.

If we cannot define who we are based on what we remember, how can we understand selfhood? The psychologist Timothy Wilson suggests that our personality or 'who we are' resides in two places: in our unconscious mind and in our conscious construal of self. According to Wilson, the unconscious self is rooted in childhood experience, is partly genetic and not easily changed. The conscious self on the other hand is the story we tell about ourselves based on the limited and changing information we have access to. Wilson, who has carried out many experiments to test his hypothesis, concludes that not only do these two selves exist but also that the constructed conscious self bears little correspondence to the unconscious self. We are, as Ronnie Laing[37] pointed out, *divided selves*.

The split between our conscious and unconscious self has occupied scientists, artists and philosophers for a very long time. That we have these two sources of knowing is probably the most significant and defining characteristic of being human and whilst it confers great survival advantages it also causes us a lot of problems. By understanding and becoming aware of some our unconscious processes we can exercise greater intention and choice in our responses. If we remain totally unaware of these influences, not only do we miss important and useful information, we also end up being controlled in troublesome and confusing ways. We get hijacked by strong emotions we do not understand, make decisions based on gut feelings that are only partially accurate, or experience 'knee jerk' reactions to people and situations.

---

[36] (Shaw, 2016)
[37] (Laing, 1959)

However, it is not useful to become aware of everything. Conscious and unconscious processes have evolved alongside one another for a reason, even though, as we have already discovered, evolved design is not always good design.

So far

We have considered how the emotions of *threat brain, drive brain* and *safe brain* motivate us to perceive and respond to our experiences and how *regulating* these emotions optimises our response potential. An integrated or centred brain has access to a greater range of evolved human capabilities and is more observant, accurate and calm.

We have also learned how childhood experience plays a significant role in shaping our response repertoire and how our adult 'personality' represents habits and preferences we have learned as our brain and body interacts with, and adapts to, the environment and relationships into which it is born. Many of these habits have become deeply internalised and operate automatically outside our awareness and this is why our character often feels fixed and difficult to change.

Our biological inheritance and our childhood experiences are preserved within our memories. Memory plays a significant role in how we make sense of our lives. It is our memory that encodes, stores and retrieves information received from both inherited and lived experiences. Memory gives us access to our past, informs the present and anticipates the future. If we are not careful it can also *dictate* the future. Ultimately it is how we manage and use our memories, particularly those that operate unconsciously, that determines how we feel, what we think about and the decisions we make.

In Part Two we learn more about the unconscious and how self-compassion creates the conditions in which we may gain access to more of its intelligence and intent. Our evolution depends on increasing consciousness. We can do this by opening our self to new experiences – both internal and external. Our unconscious, if we learn to pay attention to it, offers many such experiences that can provide information to help us revise out-of-date self-conceptions and strategies.

PART TWO:

WHAT ELSE IS POSSIBLE?

Chapter Four: Bundles of Habit

The paradox of plasticity

For many years I have worked at the boundary of management development and psychotherapeutic practice assisting organisations, groups and individuals to change. Usually, the 'going in' question, which can be applied systemically or personally, is whether prevailing behaviours and processes (business as usual) will enable the organisation to meet and eventually exceed its current and future goals and if not, what needs to change?

Organisations, which are living systems comprising humans 'organising' together, develop 'habits', just like individuals, of feeling, thought and action. We refer to these as culture. Culture is in essence, a 'collective habit'. When addressing the question 'what needs to change?' it is useful to begin with an inquiry and conversation about the habits that both hinder and help the organisation meet its objectives. Habits that hinder offer a starting place for development and are the leverage point for introducing 'culture change'. They are often discovered in the individual and small group behaviours that make up organisational life.

I know a man who made significant changes in his life during our coaching. He rescued his failing marriage, rebuilt a close relationship with his estranged son and became an admired and high achieving leader. However, when I met him again, by chance, a few years later he told me he had slipped back into his old ways. The previous week, he told me, he had ruthlessly fired a person, under humiliating circumstances, for daring to challenge his commercial strategy. My client was troubled by his behaviour. He had, he said, 'become bad' again and he wondered whether his true colours were more dark than light.

My 'bad' client had in early childhood lived in a community where young boys gathered in gangs on street corners and menaced those who were not part of their crowd. Initially he had resisted joining them but it became clear that survival in his neighbourhood depended on it. This once quiet child who spent his time reading, rescuing spiders and marvelling at the moon became a rough, intimidating and, at times, violent teenager.

He had been able to genuinely engage and develop in coaching probably because his most formative experiences had nurtured and cultivated his *safe brain* capability. His family had been loving and supportive and he could associate close relationships with warm emotions. In Part One we called this 'secure' attachment and it probably helped him, at this point in his life, to reflect, adapt, reconnect with his wife and son and to nurture his team.

However, this man had other significant memories. For most of his adolescence he had lived in threat and as a result formed and sustained new, aggressive habits. When I met him – two years after our coaching sessions had ended – he was under significant pressure to turn around a failing part of the organisation. He took on this leadership role as a 'favour' for his Chief Executive, who in his hiring and firing and loud exhortations to 'execute' and 'achieve', behaved like a charismatic gang leader. When my former client met his new team he discovered, recalcitrant, hostile staff who did not hold him in high esteem. This aroused emotions that triggered his particular pattern of response which was to *move against*.

Our *threat brain* habits are powerful and, as we saw in Part One, they can easily override other motivations, closing down *safe brain* and compassionate, complex capabilities. The environment my client found himself in was reminiscent of the competitive, callous and dangerous circumstances that defined his youth. In his implicit memory he had stored powerful strategies for surviving these kinds of challenges and their activation potential was strong.

So we see that changing a habit – especially one that has developed to protect us – is not easy. Changing the collective habit of a group is even harder and any attempt to do so should take into account each member's 'back story'. In Part Three you will see how this works and how 'depth coaching' can lead to effective group and system change.

At the turn of the 19th century, William James, the highly influential psychologist and philosopher, argued that all living creatures are 'bundles of habit' that are both innate and learned. Habits, he observed, arise due to the sensitivity of the organism to outside influence.[38] Today, pioneering experiments in neuroplasticity provide evidence to support the idea that our brain is malleable and capable of life-long learning. However, James warned of the *paradox of plasticity* which is this: even though we are highly receptive to experience and our neurons are ready to be stimulated and to form pathways between other neurons, once a pathway has been laid it is, like the channel of a river, easier to use or 'traverse' again. Thus when new information is received it is likely to flow through the pathways already formed. Our nervous system quickly grows into the shape in which it was first pressed. Plasticity enables us to easily make paths yet the first paths become so well used that over time they can entrench our learning. The first cuts are indeed the deepest.

Given our tendency to form and re-use neural pathways, James's advice was, *"to make our nervous system our ally instead of our enemy,"* and to do this we must, *"make automatic and habitual, as early as possible, as many useful actions as we can."*

James advised young people to *"keep faithfully busy each hour of the working day"*, and to remember that:

> *the hell to be endured hereafter, of which theology tells, is no worse than the hell we make for ourselves in this world by habitually fashioning our characters in the wrong way. Could the young but realise how soon they will be become mere walking bundles of habit, they would give more heed to their conduct while in the plastic state.[39]*

---

[38] (James, 1890)
[39] ibid

James's advice might torment parents who struggle to convince their child that a walk in the park or reading a book is more beneficial than an hour on their Xbox. *Could the young but realise.* The trouble is that many can't and don't. So many of our habits are laid down in early childhood and some, even before birth. They are, as we have seen, the result of inherited qualities, biological imperatives and early experience. Our habits start to take root at a time when we lack the cognitive complexity to appraise, evaluate and make informed decisions about what we do. They embed themselves before our sophisticated prefrontal cortex is fully developed and able to help us reflect and act wisely.

A young child who has become used to the physically inert yet mentally fast and hyper-stimulating experience of online gaming will find it very hard to shift these habits later in life, especially if the habit is also associated with a *threat brain* response such as avoiding difficult relationships in the home or at school.

Later, our habits are honed and ossified through peer pressure, cultural conditioning and our maturing emotional responses.

Habits are deep rooted and heavily preserved. There is, however, another and perhaps more significant reason why it is hard to interrupt or break a habit and that is because their influence is mostly *unconscious*. Often we do not notice and/or fully understand our habitual responses. Many of us live our lives on autopilot, doing what we do simply because we have always done it. If, however, we were to become more aware of our unconscious forces we would gain insights and intelligence that could help us act with much greater intention, choice and creativity. Exploring the landscape of our unconscious is how we learn about, reflect on and choose whether to let go or hold on to a habit.

The emergent unconscious

Many of us associate ideas about the unconscious with Freud's pioneering studies and theories. Most of us, for example, have heard about Freudian slips, repressed wishes and messages contained within our dreams. However, our current understanding of the unconscious is more expansive. It includes and adds to Freud's foundational ideas and has been variously described as "adaptive",[40] "new"[41] and "automatic".[42]

I will refer to it as the *emergent unconscious* for two reasons. The first is that that our knowledge of unconscious processes continues to grow. Researchers using new technologies are discovering different ways to explore the inner workings of our minds and bodies. The second is that consciousness is an evolutionary adaptation and through new experiences it is capable of further growth. By 'feeding' it more information from our unconscious body and mind we can support its growth. As our unconscious emerges our consciousness expands.

There are many processes operating at an unconscious level that enable us to get on with our day-to-day lives without having to consciously think about every step we take or every word we say. Many of these processes evolved before we even had consciousness. We were able to digest food, sense changes in our environment and move, for example, before we were able to think about our thoughts, plan, imagine, problem solve and use language. The fact that we are unaware of so many bodily processes is not our fault or an indication of our limited capability: it can be an *advantage*. This is because in any given moment our senses are taking in millions of pieces of information yet it is only possible to attend to (be conscious) of about forty 'bits' of information per second.[43] So our brain *filters* and *selects* and makes unconscious decisions about what we ought to be aware of. There are times when we notice what is going on in our bodies as, for example when we feel sick and need to vomit. However, mostly the somatic unconscious carries out its functions without our being aware.

---

[40] (Wilson, 2002)
[41] (Eisold, 2009)
[42] (O'Connor, 2015)
[43] (Norretranders, 1998)

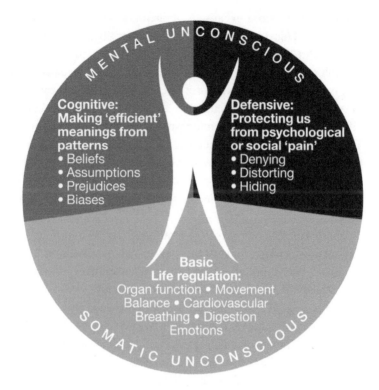

Figure 7: *The emergent unconscious*

Thus the unconscious enables us to conduct our lives efficiently by autonomously carrying out many functions important to our survival and many of these processes are concerned with basic life regulation or homeostasis. Ensuring *sociocultural* homeostasis which takes us beyond basic life regulation and involves our ability as human organisms to survive and thrive with members of our species, is largely achieved through the application and cultivation of consciousness. Empathising with others, working out how to accumulate and store resources, making and using tools and managing my status within a group are all acts that require conscious capabilities. However, in evolutionary terms we are still beginners in this endeavour. Consciousness is a new capability and its development in the service of sociocultural homeostasis is, in

Damasio's words, "*a somewhat fragile work in progress, responsible for much human drama, folly and hope.*" I understand Damasio's *sociocultural homeostasis* as the cultivation of harmonious and healthy adaptive relationships between our inner needs and experience and the environment in which we live. In this sense, it corresponds to the *integration* of our *Trimotive Brain* discussed in Part One and the process of *individuation*, which relates to healing the split between our unconscious and conscious selves, which we will consider shortly.

Although our unconscious processes are very efficient and capable, there are good reasons why we may wish to become aware of some of them. One reason is that our unconscious makes *mistakes* and if we are unaware of these mistakes we may start to feel, think and do things that are inaccurate, unfair and harmful to ourselves and others. Our assumptions and opinions about others are fertile ground for mistakes and deeply influenced by unconscious beliefs. A colleague may unconsciously believe, for example, that black people are lazy – an idea that his mother unintentionally conveyed when she made up bedtime stories involving a much-loved 'golliwog' rag doll. This unconscious belief influences him when he is recruiting new staff and appraising performance, yet he is unaware that his actions are biased.

Another reason is that our unconscious contains intelligence that could, if we were aware of it, be very useful to us. Understanding how it makes mistakes is one thing but tuning in to the *wisdom* of our unconscious body and mind – as we shall discover – gives us a rich store of inherited and hidden knowledge to apply and benefit from.

Some would argue that the unconscious is unexaminable and attempts to reveal its processes are futile. I disagree. I have experienced many occasions on which people, including myself, have become aware of feelings and thoughts that have existed and strongly influenced us, sometimes for many years, without our conscious knowing. Later, for example, we discover how, for most of her adult life, Maggie was driven by unconscious forces that kept her very vigilant over threats to her financial security and social status.

Our emergent unconscious offers two areas for exploration. The *somatic* and the *mental*. These categories are offered as a means to simplify and learn about the unconscious. In reality, and as we have seen, the body and mind are not independent of one another. Bodily sensations affect my mental processes just as my mental processes affect my physical experience. Nevertheless, to gain clarity and to introduce a discussion on the subject, I have found it easier to separate them. The somatic unconscious relates to bodily experiences, and the mental unconscious relates to feelings and thoughts that operate out of awareness. The mental unconscious can be subdivided into a) *cognitive processes* concerned with making meaning out of experience and forming assumptions and beliefs that guide our actions and b) *defensive processes* that hide, distort or deny feelings and thoughts that we cannot own because our sociocultural environment rejects or deems them unacceptable.

The somatic and mental unconscious are interconnected and share some basic defining features: they are non-conscious, fast, unintentional, difficult to control and effortless. Each system in itself represents a vast area of study and speculation. My intention here is to offer an overview of their content and function so that you can reflect on the *breadth and depth* of motivating forces that greatly influence you but of which you are probably unaware. Hopefully your reflections will support a compassionate understanding of how easy it is to become entangled in our own not knowing.

The somatic unconscious – organs, sensations, emotions

An easy way to understand and feel the somatic unconscious at work is to stand with your legs together, ankles and toes touching, arms by your side and eyes closed. Notice what happens. You will feel, in this seemingly motionless position, your body making minute movements. These are balancing and coordinating adjustments, made automatically, to ensure that you don't fall over. Most of us think we have five senses – touch, smell, vision, hearing and taste. Yet *proprioception* counts as a sixth[44] and it allows us to

---

[44] (Brown, 2006)

'know' or 'feel' where all our body parts are in relation to each other, which enables us to co-ordinate them in order to move. We are rarely, if ever, consciously aware of this sensory feedback coming from our muscles and joints – which is where the receptors of our proprioceptive system reside. We only become aware of this unconscious activity when something is wrong. An inability to feel and control our joints may be caused by temporary loss of the proprioceptive system, as for example, when we have been sitting for a long while with our legs folded beneath us we may experience 'dead leg'.

Related and adding to the function of this sense is another unconscious process supported by the vestibular system in our inner ear. This is activated when there is a change in gravity (are we conscious of when that happens?) and when our head moves. Without our vestibular sense we would have difficulty with all *fine* spatial and visual motor skills from turning the page of a book to following the movement of an object, as well as *gross* motor skills such as running, jumping and hitting a ball with a bat. It is thanks to these unconscious activities that we can experience life in a physically and literally centered way instead of a dizzy, vertiginous haze.

We can become more conscious of our body alignment and balance through exercise, in particular, yoga and pilates. In these practices we learn to stretch, strengthen, relax and flex our muscles and joints instead of holding them in the rigid, tense postures that many of us adopt when we sit, stand and walk. The Austrian psychoanalyst Wilhelm Reich observed this rigidity in his troubled clients and understood this as "muscular armoring", a physical condition that results when the flow of emotional energy is blocked and held in the musculature. It is very common for us to experience neck and back aches as a result not of injury, but of emotional stress. In Reich's view, by holding this stress in our muscles, we create tense, rigid body movements and expression.[45]

Body tension is visible to others and can affect the impact of our presentations, public speaking and, most significantly, other

---

[45] (Reich, 1972)

people's confidence and trust in us. You can probably think of people whose own unease, visible in their postures, transmits to others around them. This is partly because we have 'mirror neurons' that pick up on and mimic other people's emotions. These neurons help us develop sensitivity and empathy and may be why other people's moods are 'infectious'.

An immediate benefit of softening and flexing our body through stretching and balancing exercises is that we trigger our parasympathetic nervous system which releases *safe brain* chemicals that soothe and calm. Tai Chi is an excellent example of this 'relaxation in motion'. Later I will introduce a simple, short breathing exercise which stretches and exercises the *internal* organs and has a similar relaxing effect.

Another significant function of the somatic unconscious is to produce emotions. In Part One we saw that emotions motivate us. Emotions, we learnt, are neurochemical reactions in our body, produced by the sympathetic and parasympathetic nervous system, that happen without our conscious control. These emotions activate our *Trimotive Brain* which responds, depending on the emotional stimulation, in different ways (threat, drive and safe) to present, remembered and anticipated experience. Memories of, worries about or actual danger, for example, will trigger our *sympathetic* nervous system, which floods our body with adrenalin and stress hormones getting us ready for the threat response (fight, flee, freeze).

When we become conscious of emotional sensations in our body and the meanings we associate with them we create names for them – names like anger, sadness, fear, joy, suspicion, disgust, boredom and curiosity. In Part One we learned that distinguishing emotion from feeling is important because it is our *naming* of these bodily responses that significantly shapes how we act. I could name the fluttering sensation in my stomach: anxiety, excitement, love or nerves. The way I *choose* to interpret these sensations creates my experience. Life does not merely happen to me, I shape it and give it form through the labels and definitions I apply. Some of this naming goes on at an unconscious level. Sometimes we 'know' we are angry and act on that anger before we consciously understand why we are and whether anger is the most appropriate response. This is because our unconscious has already experienced the emotion, named the feeling and triggered action. It has, in other words, 'reacted'. Consciousness enables us to work with this process and turn it into a considered response. The sooner we notice our emotions the earlier we can intervene in the chain of reactions.

We can become more conscious of our emotions by noticing the changes they bring to our body states. Mindfulness practice helps us notice how our body is reacting to 'here and now' experience. When we are mindful we can delay the naming process, which may result in a more precise appraisal of our emotions leading to greater accuracy and congruence in our feelings, thoughts and actions. We learn to hear and feel our heart beat, the rhythm and depth of our breath, the temperature of our skin, our jaw clenching or our shoulders as they tense. We do this without judging ourselves or trying to change anything – the practice is simply to notice. By noticing our embodied emotions we give ourselves more time to reflect on their significance. *That's interesting,* I say, *I notice my heart is beating fast and my stomach feels unsettled, I wonder what that means?* We hold back from the quick interpretation and reactive response (heart beating means danger – means activate threat response!) and consider the experience in a *centred* way.

Think of the movements a tennis player makes as she prepares to receive a serve. She is in her centre, ready to move to the most effective place on the court to return the ball. If she is 'off centre' and prematurely anticipating where the ball is going to land, she will likely move her balance to one foot or the other and thus limit her ability to respond. It is similar with our emotions. If we lean too quickly into naming the emotion, we may unnecessarily over-activate one part of our emotional system and thus reduce our response repertoire. My first impression of a person is based on the quick naming of the bodily response I immediately have upon meeting them. Whilst these 'body chemistry' responses have something to tell me about the relationship, I would be unwise to rely *solely* upon this type of information.

Usually our experience requires a *combined* threat, safe and *drive brain* response. If an encounter sets my heart racing and unsettles my stomach I can learn to respond in a centered way. I can honour my *drive brain's* desire to explore and stay open to this new experience whilst at the same time acknowledging my *threat brain's* advice to be cautious. I can do this because I have breathed slowly and deeply, instructing my *safe brain* to regulate these physical responses and allowing me to enter the situation with focus and calm.

The mental unconscious

Our somatic unconscious selects sensory information to regulate and motivate physical and emotional functions in the service of our survival. Our mental unconscious enhances this process by filtering and appraising information. Cognitive processes are concerned with what an experience *means* and defensive processes work to keep feelings and thoughts that might cause us problems out of awareness. We will explore each of these processes in more detail below.

Unconscious cognitive processes

The purpose of creating meaning is to improve the accuracy of our assessments and decisions. Without knowing what a sensation means (e.g. dry throat means thirst) I will be unable to take action. This chain of events continues and is aided at each step by meaning. I am thirsty, I see water. Water means a liquid I can take to quench this thirst. Satisfaction of my thirst means I can now walk for longer. These automatic, unconscious *inferences* that create meaning are based on our individual knowledge of the world and our memory of past experience. Meaning is relative and partial and dependent on the particularities of our environment, culture and personal experience.

Many of my cognitive unconscious processes are concerned with taking care of 'routine' functions. If I had to consciously think about the meaning of water, a birthday card, the word 'goodbye' or the purpose of a supermarket my life would be slow, energy-draining and potentially dangerous.

To discover and attribute meaning to a perception, the cognitive unconscious turns to memory for help. In Part One we learned about two memory systems, the declarative, explicit memory and the non-declarative, implicit memory. It is the latter that the cognitive unconscious consults first, for it is in the deep vaults of our implicit memory that information and meaning crucial to our survival is stored. Remember, survival or *the biological imperative* is always the first concern of all our unconscious processes. Meaning emerges when we match a current experience with a stored memory. The association between the two provides the information required to make sense of what is happening.

To enable us to match and associate experience with a stored memory, the cognitive unconscious is very good at noticing patterns – these are repeated and recognisable experiences stored as templates and sometimes referred to as 'mental models', in our implicit memory. *Patterns of experience* inform our core beliefs, assumptions and biases. If those patterns are emotionally charged (failing in exams leads to disapproval and rejection at home) they will be branded into the template and prove very hard to erase.

Being able to respond and take action without full conscious awareness provides many advantages. Aside from the obvious benefits of implicit memory working with the cognitive unconscious to understand the meaning behind basic life skills such as speech, drinking water and running from predators, the 'tacit' knowledge you hold about the cultural norms and values of the society you live in enables you to understand and survive in your local environment. Physicist and philosopher, Michael Polyani[46] describes tacit knowledge as *"inarticulate acts of intelligence"* and when it is absent we may feel confused, isolated, anxious or puzzled as when, for example, we visit a country that is culturally very different to our own.

Sometimes, however, our implicit memories mislead us. If, for example, you have been repeatedly punished as a child for not

---

[46] (Polyani, 1962)

finishing your food you may continue, as an adult, to regard a laden plate with some dismay. Subtle or significant differences, such as the kindly woman who has served you and the cultural expectation that you *don't* eat everything will not override your automatic and unconscious first interpretation of events. The cognitive unconscious works very closely with the somatic unconscious. So, when you see that full plate your body goes into threat (emotions happen automatically). Your cognitive unconscious very quickly appraises this sensory information and associates it with a stored memory of meal times at home. The result is an interpretation of the current experience and situation as awkward, embarrassing or problematic. In China, however, where it is *polite* to leave some food on the plate, your mental model warning you about the potential risks in this situation is inaccurate. Thus our cognitive unconscious can make mistakes by using past information to interpret current events.

Another function of cognitive unconscious processes is to filter and select the right *quantity* of information from a potentially vast store. Research suggests that our explicit conscious memories only represent a fraction of what is held on record in our implicit memory system. The mythical Sherlock Holmes and candidates in the World Memory Championships have excellent memory retrieval abilities and can travel to their 'mind palace' to reproduce reams of incidental detail. For most of us, however, total recall is not helpful.

Consider, for example, brain research on schizophrenia which shows a high percentage of cells in the hippocampus in disarray.[47] The hippocampus, as we have seen, is the brain structure involved in our declarative, explicit memory. It provides memories for conscious recall. Schizophrenics may have problems in filtering memory so that either too much or too little is received, leading to information overload or deprivation. In the latter case the brain starts to compensate for lack of input by manufacturing information in the form of visual and auditory hallucinations.[48] Sherlock Holmes is described as a 'high functioning sociopath'.

---

[47] (Harrison, 2004)
[48] (Swabb, 2014)

Perhaps his extraordinary information-processing abilities come at a price. Quantity of information without *quality* will not serve us well. Ultimately, the cognitive unconscious needs to select and process information that is useful to us. It does this by scanning to see how energised and available it is or, to use a psychological term, how high in 'activation potential'. The criteria for determining this measure are: is it relevant to my survival? Is it habitual and familiar to me (e.g. a core belief)? Will it make me feel good?[49]

These criteria may interfere with the *accuracy* of information selected and the psychologist Timothy Wilson notes that:

> *...the conflict between the need to be accurate and the need to feel good about ourselves is one of the major battlegrounds of the self.*[50]

My cognitive unconscious may inaccurately process my poor performance as skilled in order to preserve my self-esteem and this may be useful to me because feeling good does offer survival advantages.

The benefits of feeling good are of special interest for Mihaly Csikszentmihalyi[51] who is best-known for his research into highly focused mental states. Csikszentmihalyi proposes that optimal experience ('flow') occurs when the information that is fed into consciousness through the activity of the cognitive unconscious is congruent and supportive of a person's goals. "*Useful*" information, according to Csikszentmihalyi, is "*encouraging, optimistic and reassuring*". There is evidence to support this. In Part One, for example, we looked at images showing that the threat response is triggered when our self-talk is critical, punitive and harsh.[52] A brain in threat is limited in its response repertoire. Fighting, fleeing and freezing are not conditions conducive to creating flow experiences or securing us a competitive advantage beyond the battlefield.

---

[49] (Wilson, 2002)
[50] (Wilson, 2002)
[51] (Csikszentmihalyi, 1992)
[52] (Longe, et al., 2010) (Newberg & Waldman, 2012)

According to flow theory, 'disorders' in consciousness occur when information not directly relating to our goals enters awareness and drains us of 'psychic energy'. This 'poor quality' information conflicts with our existing intentions or distracts us from carrying them out. Thus, *controlling consciousness*, argues Csikszentmihalyi, is the way to achieve mastery of both skills and self. A well-ordered consciousness, he says, supports human growth.

I am not convinced that 'order' necessarily emerges from controlling our feelings and thoughts so that they are only or even mostly encouraging, optimistic and reassuring. I think there is much to be gained from inviting our darker experiences into consciousness and I will say more about this in the next section. I am also wary of promoting overly 'positive psychologies' that can generate comparative feelings of inadequacy or shame in those of us who are more often despondent, frustrated and cynical. A typical consequence of only focusing on the positive – particularly in organisations – is that we don't have enough challenging and honest conversations because no one wants to be the person who brings 'bad news', identifies problems or expresses doubt or fear. To do so would mean being seen as 'resistant', complaining, weak and negative and would risk rejection that comes in the shape of poor performance appraisals, being overlooked for promotion and being left out of decision-making processes or Friday night drinks.

Many of us do not live in 'flow'. We are frequently distracted, unfocused, reactive, inattentive and absent-minded. The modern self is, Ken Eisold suggests, *"discontinuous, contradictory and fragmented"*.[53] This inner turbulence is the source of many of our emotional and behavioural difficulties. To understand the nature of this turbulence or *inner conflict* we turn to the activity of our defensive unconscious. *Integrative* order arises when we are capable of acknowledging and living with *all* the qualities of thought and feeling we experience.

---

[53] (Eisold, 2009)

Unconscious defensive processes: protecting, hiding, distorting

The defensive unconscious, sometimes referred to as the 'dynamic', 'old' or Freudian unconscious, is primarily understood to be a collection of processes that keep certain feelings and thoughts out of consciousness because they cause us *significant* pain. The cognitive unconscious processes produce 'helpful meanings' to try and make us more efficient in our day-to-day life and as a result might ignore or filter out information that interferes with our efficiency. The defensive unconscious is also involved in this work but its objectives are more specific. It works to ensure that we are not abandoned, rejected or attacked by our social group and it does this by hiding thoughts and feelings that might be unacceptable or unwanted by them. Our first social group is our family.

Given that a primary function of all bodily systems is to ensure homeostasis or 'life regulation' it is not surprising that a process exists to sift out and keep a lid on our personal Pandora's box, which contains impulses and desires that could interfere with our *sociocultural* homeostasis.

Thus, if the main contribution to life regulation of the somatic and cognitive unconscious is to make us more *efficient* in our physical and mental responses, the defensive unconscious contributes by *protecting* us from experiences which cause us psychological and social pain.[54]

Sometimes we can, through our defensive processes, create an illusion that threat has gone away or does not exist, which is one way of achieving temporary homeostasis and can be useful. For, example, projecting our unwanted characteristics onto other people can relieve inner conflicts that arise from having, but being frightened to have, these feelings. Humour sometimes works as a

---

[54] John Cacioppo and William Patrick in their study of loneliness (Cacioppo & Patrick, 2008), show that psychological and social stress trigger many of the same neural responses as physical pain and affect our immune, cardiovascular and digestive systems, providing further evidence to show how our body and mind processes are interconnected.

defence when it allows us to express or distort difficult emotions or hide from very threatening ones. Robert Lifton, a psychiatrist specialising in post war trauma, puts this well when he says:

> *mockery and self-mockery, irony, absurdity and humour enable the... self to 'lubricate' its experiences and to express the absence of fit between the way the world presents itself and the way one actually feels about it.*[55]

When we are children, usually the only thing we *can* do in the face of threat is to employ defensive strategies – we have not yet matured the physical and mental capabilities that give us more options and choices. In Part One we saw how our childhood defensive routines express themselves in *moving against*, *moving towards* and *moving away* patterns of behaviour which can become habituated as our adult orientation to life. Thus, whilst defensive processes enable us to conform and achieve sociocultural acceptance, as we get older their protective mechanisms, motivated by threat, restrict and limit our potential.

This is because the defensive unconscious is like a magician bending and 'disappearing' unwanted feelings and thoughts. As such, it offers only a temporary, short-lived solution – which is what a threat response is designed to be. Yet our feelings and thoughts do *not* disappear. When banished, they lurk and hide in the tributaries that bisect the landscape of our unconscious. What are some of these experiences that our defensive unconscious wants to disappear? Our covert racism? Our sadistic sexual impulses? The unbearable loneliness we experienced as a child? Lying at a job interview?

The defensive unconscious scans and appraises just like the cognitive unconscious yet its purpose is to sift out and shield us from the dark side of our existence and our character. Which of us really wants to discover that we are racist, sexually abusive, alone and a fraud? Thanks to the defensive unconscious I can convince myself that I am a tolerant person surrounded by loving, reciprocal relationships and achieving great things in my career. I am

---

[55] (Lifton, 1993)

competent, loveable and good, I tell myself, and because I am these things I will be accepted and I will *belong*.

Another truth that the defensive unconscious works hard to shield us from is our mortality. Our bodies and minds which seem so permanent, real and essential will one day decay and disappear into dust. For many of us this is a terrifying prospect and so the denial of our inevitable death becomes a strong – perhaps the strongest – defensive force expressing itself in many 'compensatory' behaviours. The desire to accumulate great wealth or power may well be driven by this hidden fear.

Ernest Becker, a cultural anthropologist and author of *The Denial of Death* wrote:

> *The tragic bind that man is peculiarly in – the basic paradox of his existence – is that unlike other animals he has an awareness of himself as a unique individual on the one hand and on the other he is the only animal in nature who knows he will die. ...he is an emergent life that does not seem to have any more meaning than a non-emergent life... and so despair and the death of meaning are carried by man in the basic condition of his humanity.*

Becker argued that with a degree of ambivalence and self-deception, human beings could not only survive this "tragic bind" but could be capable of achieving great things. He suggested that:

> *repression fulfils the vital function of allowing the child to act without anxiety, to take experience in hand and develop dependable responses to it.*

Becker proposed that our 'refusal of reality' is something we all do to manage debilitating anxiety and only becomes problematic (neurotic) when it starts to have damaging effects on us or the people around us. Psychologists often claim that the extent of damage increases as our distortions become more intense.

Freud had no illusions about our 'creatureliness' and believed we are fundamentally ruled by instinctive drives – just like any other animal. If the defences weren't working, said Freud, we would be engaging in all sorts of animalistic pursuits comprising sex, gorging and fighting. Art, religion and every other aspect of man-made culture are merely ways we prevent ourselves from acting like animals. This is one way of understanding the defensive unconscious.

Carl Jung, however, was convinced that the defensive unconscious had a function beyond serving as a barrier between our civilised and animal selves. He agreed with Freud that we have a 'dark side' which he described as our 'shadow' and he, too, understood this part of the unconscious as a process which manages the refused and unacceptable parts of our self. However, unlike Freud, Jung saw that the shadow also looked after the 'pure gold' of our personality. The defensive unconscious takes care of what we don't like about ourselves and also manages the yearnings, talents and unique characteristics that could not find full expression in the environment and culture into which we were born.

There are stories of those who triumph over what Jung described as the 'cultural process' and retain their 'whole' or true self – this is often the story of artists, inventors, entrepreneurs and musicians who follow their passions in spite of pressure to conform. However the backdrop to their tenacity is a crowded collage of everyone else who left behind or gave up part of their self in order to measure up to imposed goals and expectations.

As we become more 'social' we learn to reject or hide parts of our self that do not fit acceptable norms and in doing so we become 'split' or fragmented. The conflicts we experience are between these split off and divided parts of our self. Sometimes conflict is so deeply buried that we only feel it as a vague sense that something is 'missing' or 'wrong'. For others, the conflict is nearer the surface and interferes with our relationships, aspirations and health.

Jung proposed *individuation* as the lifelong process of becoming the complete, whole person we were born to be. This involves working with our defensive processes and bringing what was previously banished into conscious awareness. What we dislike, fear or hate about ourselves, no matter how dark, can safely re-emerge and productively inform the way we live our lives. James Hillman, the Jungian scholar and analyst, suggests that it is our *imagination* which helps us to work with feelings like shame, hatred and inferiority and this idea is developed in later chapters when we explore practices that support our imaginal capability including, acting 'as if', active imagination and voice dialogue.[56]

The defensive unconscious operates in us all and even though it may not be hiding horrendous truths about our life or motivating us to create works of art, its activities can still have a significant impact on our lives.

Paul, was a successful executive client of mine whom I worked with for several years. In his experiences we can glimpse the ordinary workings of the defensive unconscious.

Paul was the Commercial Director of a fast-growing pharmaceutical company. In our first session he spoke about his father who had taught him the value of discipline, will power and, most importantly, achievement. It's a tough world, said Paul, and winning does matter. If you're not out in front and running you'll get crushed in the stampede. These lessons had stayed with him. Now he worked long hours at the office, responded to company calls and emails at home, and yet never felt satisfied that he had accomplished enough. Paul described his colleagues as less competent than himself and he found it hard to name people he admired except for a few sporting heroes whom he idealised. He recognised that he set very high goals and standards for himself and others and that he became impatient when he saw people give in too easily or complain. Whenever he achieved a goal another one quickly appeared. The horizon was forever receding. It was a bit like being in the gym, he theorised. You set yourself a goal, you work hard to achieve it and then you immediately set yourself another goal. If you interrupt the regime, if you miss a few sessions, then you lose what you have gained in a very short time. So you don't stop.

Paul reflected on his recent promotion to the board and concluded that it was an anti-climax. He thought he would feel some pleasure or sense of achievement yet the announcement left him numb. He didn't like to talk or brag about his successes but equally he found it very hard to tolerate any notion of failure or coming second. He was

---

[56] (Hillman & Ventura, 1993)

also unsure whether people appreciated him or genuinely believed he had talent. He was a suspicious man and mistrustful of easily given praise or loyalty. Once a friend had told him, *your rules of belonging are too strong.* Paul didn't fully understand what that meant, although the phrase had stuck with him.

I asked about his personal relationships and he talked at length about his marriage. He described his wife as moody, demanding and hypercritical. She was never satisfied. His daughter, he said, was like her mother. He described her latest 'campaign' to own a horse. It's a dangerous sport, he mused, and that worried him, yet she always got what she wanted in the end. He told me that he pacified her frequent tantrums with expensive gifts but he secretly resented the amount of money he spent on her. Family life had not, according to Paul, been all it was cracked up to be.

At the end of the first session Paul alluded to some health problems and told me he wasn't sleeping well at night. However, he was quick to dismiss pains in his chest as 'indigestion' and joked that he could self-medicate a good night's sleep with a few pills or alcohol. When I asked Paul what he dreamt about when he did fall asleep he smiled and said he'd like to rev up a Ferrari on a long empty road or, one day, sail a yacht round the world.

In this brief excerpt, you can detect Paul's defensive unconscious at work. It *represses* painful truths about his authoritative father who could only offer 'love' in return for achievement. It helps him *deny* fears about his own inadequacy by directing his thoughts towards goals and standards and obliterating anxiety with drugs. His tendency to *split* people into good and bad enables him to manage the unwanted and feared complexities of relationship and by *projecting* his own critical and disengaged feelings onto his wife he can absolve himself of blame and guilt. Paul might also be seen to act in a *passively aggressive* way towards his daughter by hiding his anger and disapproval behind gifts and acquiescence. *Fantasies* of a better life may protect him from the mundane truth of his own existence whilst *disassociation* from his feelings allows him to rationalise, control and avoid disappointment.[57]

As you can see, Paul's defensive unconscious has many strategies it can employ to protect him from difficult truths about his childhood, his current relationships, his abilities and his aspirations. Yet, in the long term how effective is this process? When reading Paul's notes we would be justified in predicting some trouble ahead. Often we see the first inkling of trouble when what 'should' be repressed starts to become visible and what has been denied or distorted starts to appear in its original and truthful form. Paul struggled to find meaning and pleasure in the life he led and he described frequent disappointments, dissatisfaction and a vague feeling that something was missing.

That something, Jung argued, is his banished or hidden shadow self. The Jungian scholar Robert Johnson suggests that the defensive unconscious has an important role early in life to help us 'join' our family group and society. By hiding our socially 'unacceptable' aspects it protects us from being rejected or abandoned at a time when we do not have the knowledge or resources to go it alone. Johnson says:

> *It is clear we must make a shadow, or there would be no culture; then we must restore the wholeness of the personality that was lost in the cultural ideals or we will live in a state of dividedness that grows more and more painful throughout our evolution.*[58]

Whilst the defensive unconscious helps us to become part of society, once we have emerged from the vulnerable shell of childhood and established ourselves as independent adults these processes become less useful. By the time we reach mid-life a different set of imperatives call. In order to live the second half of life *as we are* rather than how others expect or want us to be, we need to meet our shadow and discover our gold.

---

[57] For some common defence mechanisms see www.bit.ly/Trimotive06
[58] (Johnson, 1991)

Freedom to choose

The somatic and mental unconscious together comprise a complex system of processes that manage and motivate our conscious experiences. So much so, says the neuroscientist and author Sam Harris, that these processes make conscious 'free will' an illusion. However, as humanistic philosopher and analyst Eric Fromm pointed out many years ago:

> *The argument for the view that man has no freedom to choose the better as against the worse is to some considerable extent based on the fact that one looks usually at the last decision in a chain of events and not the first or second ones.*[59]

We have seen that first and even second 'events' happen in the somatic and mental unconscious. It would follow then that if we want to cultivate our 'freedom to choose' we should attempt to become better at noticing how these unconscious processes influence us. Yet, let's pause for a moment to consider this question: *If evolution has created unconscious processes to serve a function why would we want to become aware of them?*

The first answer in support of awareness is that evolutionary design is not always good design. Our unconscious processes are flawed. My somatic unconscious can react with extreme speed when perceiving a snake which in fact turns out to be a coil of rope. My cognitive unconscious can influence my discriminating recruitment decisions. My defensive unconscious can delude me into believing I am the only competent person in the office. Our unconscious processes can be reactive, selective, biased, over-protective and irrational and so being more aware of them might help us correct their mistakes before they have a chance to significantly mislead us.

The second answer is that evolution *also* gave us consciousness. As our brain grows so too does our awareness. Neuroscientist Antonio Damasio defines consciousness as, "*a state of mind in*

---

[59] (Fromm, 2010)

which there is knowledge of one's own existence and of the existence of surroundings[60] and he suggests that consciousness optimises the organism's response to the environment. We can plan for a possible future, delay or inhibit automatic responses, communicate more effectively and think about and solve abstract problems. These abilities give us significant survival advantages.

Although it is unlikely we will ever understand all the mysteries of our unconscious mind we can continue to evolve our ability to notice our impulses, reflect on our thought processes, test our assumptions and imagine the person we wish to be. In becoming more aware we continue to expand consciousness which is, in evolutionary terms, a new ability and probably capable of conferring many more benefits. Freedom, says Eric Fromm,

> *is an attitude, an orientation, part of the character structure of the mature, fully developed productive person.*
> *...the decisive factor in choosing the better rather that the worse lies in awareness.*

Instead of reacting angrily to an irritating colleague, for example, we notice the emotional sensations that trigger our threat and understand them as early anger indicators. At that point of consciousness we have greater freedom to choose what to do with the sensation. Increasing our awareness may simply amount to noticing our emotions a second sooner than we usually do. Or it may go further and uncover the motives of our defensive unconscious or the origins of our biases and beliefs. In each case, we are expanding the content of our conscious thought and, by doing so, enabling a more informed, self-authored life.

Expanding consciousness by paying more attention to some of what is presently unconscious offers significant benefits. However, as you may have experienced, becoming aware of a feeling, thought or behavioural habit does not necessarily mean you can or do change it. Consciousness may increase but it still might not have enough of a controlling hold on our habits, impulses and desires. Professor Paul Gilbert, a consultant psychologist working with

---

[60] (Damasio, 2012)

depression-related illness, noted that even though his patients became more aware of the context and circumstances of their illness they did not necessarily become less depressed. They knew, for example, that they were not to blame for the abuse they had suffered but they still *felt* blameworthy and bad.[61]

Awareness may give us more freedom of choice but it is a not a sufficient condition to liberate us from the problem habits we are caught in. The *quality* of awareness that we experience is as important as the quantity. In the next chapter I explore how self-compassion enables us to develop a 'warm' quality of awareness that helps us to work more effectively with what becomes known. By learning to accept, tolerate and like who we are, we have a far greater chance of learning new habits and letting go of old ones.

---

[61] (Gilbert, 2012)

Chapter Five: Warming up Awareness

A certain kind of awareness

Most of us are aware of a habit we have and wish to stop. We are also very aware of how hard it is to break a habit and we have dealt with some of the reasons why.

Research suggests that most of our efforts at self-reform fail within two years and the reason, I suggest, is that when we relapse our *threat brain* quickly takes over and pulls us back to our tried and tested survival 'solutions'. When I fail at my diet or when, after a few months of being depression free I wake up once more feeling useless, my *threat brain* will be ready and waiting to help me survive the problem. If you feel inadequate, unworthy, weak and vulnerable, it says, I know how to help. I know that I can relieve these feelings by motivating you to spend longer at the office, to drink and eat until you disappear the feeling, to watch TV to crowd out thoughts, to dump your anger on those around you and to encourage whatever habit I have helped you cultivate in order to stay alive.

The unconscious is a creature of habit and strives to maintain 'balance' and efficiency by directing us towards what is familiar and known.

Adam was a stockbroker who became addicted to the adrenalin-filled highs of life in the money markets. He had a cocaine addiction and spent his evenings not at home with his wife and three children but in the 'gentleman's clubs' that populated the City trading district. After one particularly excessive night he received a caution for being drunk and disorderly. He was lucky that the police did not discover the stash of drugs he had hidden in a folded piece of tin foil.

The incident encouraged Adam to seek help and within a few months he decided to join a financial services company which offered regular hours and the opportunity to spend more time at home. Unfortunately, Adam was not able to sustain this new life. He felt 'micro managed' by his new boss and unable to fit into what he felt was a heavily regulated and risk-averse environment. He was referred to me for coaching because of his mood swings, frequent angry outbursts and inability to work as part of a team.

Adam was caught in a *threat-drive brain* loop that made it difficult for him to relax, concentrate and reflect on his situation and what he truly wanted from life. He found it very difficult to tolerate boredom or what he described as 'empty days' and so he used drugs to 'energise' the down times and ensure that there was no opportunity for contemplation or appraisal of his life. Adam's *threat brain* habit was to *move against*, a habit he had developed early in life as a way of coping with his mother's illness and untimely death. Following a messy and painful divorce, she took to her bed, stopped eating and became completely reliant on her elderly mother for care. Adam, who chose to live with his father, was terrified and helpless as he watched her lonely and desperate decline. Eventually he stopped visiting and when she died, he refused to attend her funeral. The anger he felt towards his parents was re-directed into the pursuit of money, glamour, status and power which served a further purpose of obliterating his sad and loving memories.

Another reason why our habits prevail is that we often only address the *symptoms* of our problem. We deal with our compulsion for food by eating less, we manage anger by staying silent and we try to reduce work-related stress by turning our phone off at night. However, below the surface of our behaviour lie the original emotions and motivations which led to our habit in the first place. As in Adam's case, these usually come from our *threat brain* and may be rooted in loneliness, shame, rage and fear. If we want to break out of the reform-relapse cycle we need to acknowledge and find ways to live more peaceably with these feelings. Ignoring them or pretending that they don't exist won't work as they will almost certainly reappear in the guise of new symptoms or 'leak out' in unexpected ways to undermine our change efforts. When Adam began to understand his *threat brain* habits – in particular the source of his anger – and learned to soothe and regulate these responses, he became more able to interrupt his destructive tendencies before they caused him and others harm.

Whatever the method or school of thought, all coaching and development encourages people to remember, notice and observe, inquire, test their assumptions and engage in reflective practices such journaling, peer review or mentoring. These are the ways in which we broaden our experience and grow our awareness. However, if what we remember, notice or discover as we inquire and reflect fills us with confusion, dread, shame, guilt or disgust, our *threat brain* will activate and potentially shut down our ability to learn. A brain in threat will not help us grow the kind of awareness which leads to freedom of choice, liberation from problem habits and the maturity of character that Fromm and most developmental practitioners describe.

To cultivate *this* kind of awareness we need to minimise or soothe our threat responses as we learn and discover more about ourselves. When we fail or when alternative truths hurt – as at some point they will – staying centred, calm and relaxed will help us flow with the experience and will propel us safely downstream where awareness eventually opens out and merges with new possibility. Like a river meeting the ocean the narrow channel of our habitual mind can, in time and with effort, find greater depth and space to express itself freely.

Warming up awareness was a phrase I first heard Professor Paul Gilbert use to describe the preparatory process that accompanies learning and change. Warm awareness supports three important brain states essential for learning: *curiosity, courage* and *persistence*[62] and behind these states are the emotions of safe and healthy *drive brain*.

In many organisations, warm awareness is in short supply. We are often in threat through fear of redundancy, bullying, overwork, lack of knowledge, resource deficits and relationship conflicts. In

---

[62] (Collins, 2016)

these conditions, learning new skills or developing ourselves is hard work. As energy-conscious organisms we will de-prioritise these activities to conserve resources whilst our body and mind is dealing with more immediate problems.

Unfortunately, many leaders do not see or understand the consequences of *threat brain* and thus apply 'solutions' that fail to achieve their intended results. This is not their fault. It is mostly the result of a cultural pressure or norm to manage problems by doing, achieving, consuming and accumulating more. This creates a typical and exhausting *threat-drive brain* 'loop' that most of us can identify with.

Recently an organisation I work with announced a huge redundancy programme which involved a significant number of employees having to give or receive difficult news. At the same time the leadership team launched a well-meaning initiative to bring together the left over and disparate parts of the business. However, most people were unable to fully take in or respond to management messages relating to these new projects and this seriously affected their successful delivery. An approach which first attempted to soothe individuals and groups – for example leaders having more face-to-face conversations about topics that matter to people – and *then* introduce plans for change or strategic development would have more chance of success. Self-awareness, which grows out of curiosity, courage and persistence and which sustains innovative and collaborative working practices will not flourish without a practice that soothes the threatened brain. This practice or orientation to life is self-compassion.

A golden thread

I am not a stranger to the threat-drive loop. Towards the end of my doctorate research, I experienced the painful end of a long and significant relationship. At that time the challenge of sustaining focused study along with single parenting and difficult consulting assignments felt overwhelming. Previously I had always managed to find a store of energy or 'drive' to propel me through problems, but this time I was depleted. Something had to give, so I decided to propose, at my midpoint assessment, a break from the programme. I couldn't see how I would find the focus, discipline and creativity I needed to research and write when what I most wanted to do was sleep.

During this meeting, attended by internal and external examiners, I was asked to describe my most recent research activities. I found myself speaking about my conversations with Professor Paul Gilbert whom I had contacted after reading his book, *The Compassionate Mind*. I felt his insights were relevant to the corporate and organisational problems I was working with and I wondered how his approach could be adapted for use in leadership development and coaching. I shared with the panel my belief, based on my years of professional practice, that increased self-awareness – often taken as the start and end points of personal development – has limited application unless that new-found awareness is accompanied by a practice which supports the individual to live with what becomes known. That practice, I suggested, was self-compassion.

The panel listened attentively. What they heard between the lines of this professional account was my *own* story, not in words but in the tone and mood which imbued the session. I was distracted, self-critical, lacking confidence and depressed. At the end of the meeting, after an intense inquiry partly relating to my health and wellbeing, the panel challenged my decision to postpone. In fact, they strongly encouraged me to continue my research but to approach it differently. If my research was about self-compassion and growth, they asked, how would my understanding evolve if I were to apply the practice in my own life? The panel had glimpsed, before I had, the golden thread of my research which had started as an inquiry about the meaning and impact of doing 'good work' but became an exploration about how self-compassion could enable personal health, resilience and productivity.

Talking to myself – the value of voice tracking

Up until then I had not experienced myself as particularly *uncompassionate*. Although I set high standards for myself and others, I generally thought this was a good thing. I did not see or understand my drive and desire to achieve as motivated by anything other than a will to contribute in the world. I barely recognised the feelings of threat and insecurity that often motivated me and which inflamed my *drive brain*. Like my executive client, Paul, I didn't notice how hard it felt to acknowledge or take pride in my successes or how my self-criticism might project itself upon others. It was only when Chris, my research supervisor, suggested I track my critical and compassionate inner voices by listening to audio tapes of our sessions that I clearly heard the voice of my inner critic and noticed how it dominated my internal conversations.

My inner critic is very intelligent. You probably wouldn't want to get into an argument with her. She likes to solve problems quickly, does not tolerate weakness and failure and is impatient when I procrastinate or struggle. I can appreciate her for supporting and encouraging my aspirations and successes and for pushing me on when I have wanted to give up. However, my inner critic has also made it hard for me to notice and turn towards my vulnerability and pain, to rest, to nurture relationships and to hear other voices within me whose intent and perspectives are quite different.

Listening to recordings of your voice in conversation is a practice I encourage my clients to try. James was one such client. At first he had very little self-compassion which was clear in his first comments about our recorded sessions. *"I don't like the sound of my voice"*, he said, *"when I hear myself speak I want to say to myself, pull yourself together! Stop projecting such weak, negative, sad, helpless images This is not who you are!"*

At times I could hear a whisper of James's self-compassionate voice, *"I almost feel sorry for myself listening to it"*, he once said. However, he was usually very quick to silence the compassion. *"It's just self-pity, isn't it?"* he asked.

As we will soon see, self-compassion is neither self-pity nor self-indulgence. It is, however, a way of experiencing ourselves that is easily diminished or disappeared by internal and cultural forces which promote excessive or toxic *drive brain* motivations and which label self-compassion as 'weak' or 'soft'. In a recent study,

Paul Gilbert and colleagues[63] found that people fear compassion, feeling it will undermine their motivation and diminish ambition. You too may have had that feeling when you started to read about self-compassion in this book. When I started to listen to my own inner critic I realised that this voice was familiar to me. As a child, I remembered hearing it coming from the corner of my bedroom ceiling as if, like Gollum the Hobbit, it lived there in angry exile. Back then, in the dark nights, it had me cowering under my sheets and apologising for bad things I was supposed to have done. I thought the voice had long gone away but I was wrong. I had just internalised it and become used to it.

What is self-compassion?

Discovering the absence of self-compassion in my internal conversations encouraged me to experiment with practices that might help me develop this voice. For two years after the faculty assessment I attended workshops and courses on self-compassion and I brought together a 'Spirit Circle' which, as Christina Baldwin suggests, generates an "alchemy of collective wisdom".[64] This group was attended by a wide array of friends and colleagues invited to inquire and talk about what mattered most to them. Self-compassion – the absence, desire for and experience of it – became a recurring theme.

In these research years, I also met and learned from experienced clinicians such as Paul Gilbert, Christopher Germer and Kristin Neff and began to apply their insights to understand what was happening to me. Eventually I began to sense and experience the potential of this rare quality 'self-compassion' and I witnessed personally and with clients the self-respect, resilience and willingness to collaborate that it cultivated. These outcomes seemed especially important in organisations that felt threatened and weakened by internal and external pressures.

Kristin Neff is a professor in human development at the University of Texas. She pioneered research into self-compassion

---

[63] (Gilbert, et al., 2011)
[64] (Baldwin, 1996)

in the early 2000s, proposing that self-compassion comprises three qualities; *mindfulness, kindness* and *common humanity*. Based on my own experiments and the contributions of my organisational clients, like James, who were responsive to the subject, I was able to explore each of these qualities and develop a useful coaching and organisational development approach to encourage and sustain those qualities. In doing so, I am convinced that beyond the clinical and mental health context, self-compassion has significant applicability. In ordinary workplaces people easily recognise the threat-drive loops that hold them in unwanted habits and are keen to discover how to interrupt their own spinning wheel. I will share some more of their stories in Part Three.

Self-compassion – Core quality 1: Mindfulness

Mindfulness requires us to be *sensitive* to our experience. In other words, we must first *notice* what is going on in our minds and hearts. Mindfulness is noticing and accepting our thoughts and feelings in the present moment without judging, analysing, distorting or denying. Neff describes mindfulness as:

> *Being aware of present moment experience in a clear and balanced manner so that one neither ignores nor ruminates on disliked aspects of oneself or one's life.*

She goes on to say that mindfulness prevents:

> *...being swept up in and carried away by the story line of one's own pain.*[65]

One of the reasons why habits are so hard to break is that we have become used to telling and re-telling the same story about why we do the things we do and often those stories serve to justify, rationalise and entrench our actions. We like to be consistent, even if that consistency involves perpetuating our own problems.

As I researched self-compassion through my own experiences I began to see how I had become swept up in a storyline that involved, in particular, very inaccurate beliefs about my close relationships. I

---

[65] (Neff, 2011)

also noticed, as I surfed the Internet, paced the floor, became distracted by my inner critic and took painkillers to loosen the knot of anxiety in my stomach, that mindfulness was not something that came easily to me. I found it hard to stay in the present, I noticed my mind constantly wandering to future plans or past experience and I saw how busy, preoccupied, analysing, evaluating and judging I could be. Mostly I judged and condemned myself and this realisation saddened me. In those darkest moments of my own small but significant life crisis, I felt powerless, alone, afraid and locked in my *threat brain*. The more I read about mindfulness, the more I wanted to *be* mindful – but it was difficult. Realising I needed help to get started I decided to join a local mindfulness based stress-reduction course (MBSR).

MBSR is a widely available programme based on the teaching of Jon Kabat-Zinn.[66] The course I attended was an 8-week programme involving a 4-hour session every Saturday followed by a disciplined homework regime. We were given audio tapes, workbooks and guidance on how to develop our meditation practice so that eventually we would be meditating for up to an hour a day. My class was attended by people who were stressed, depressed, unwell, anxious and, like me, seeking relief from emotional and sometimes physical pain.

During each session, most participants shared concerns about their inability to meditate or detach from their problems. There were often tears and self-condemnation relating to perceived personal failure and inadequacy. Within a few weeks several people dropped out. Like everyone else I had moments and days of feeling incompetent. I too had not been able to sustain the long meditation practices at home and sometimes, in the sessions, was overwhelmed with anxiety, cramps or mundane, distracting thoughts as I sat uncomfortably cross-legged on my cushion.

I wondered how self-compassion could help my mindfulness practice and advice from a seasoned practitioner, Russell Kolts, was extremely helpful. Kolts specialises in working with clients who have anger management problems, in other words, people whose

---

[66] (Kabat-Zinn, 2001)

threat brain is very active. When working with anger and other *threat brain* responses, Kolts suggests that *very* short bursts of meditative mindfulness practice can be far more effective than pushing oneself to achieve the much longer times suggested in many books and courses. It was certainly the case for me. A few minutes, several times a day, of deep breathing and focusing attention helped me to quieten my daily agitation. This 'little but often' approach generated regular moments of quiet calm and made me feel as if I were 'succeeding' which in turn helped to soften my inner critic and the potentially threat-triggering feeling of inadequacy and failure.

Sometimes we are not ready or able to use mindfulness to lift ourselves out of threat. Sometimes we need a practice that enables us to be with our pain. Being a 'compassionate mess' involves accepting our current state without either sinking or swimming. Compassion enables us to float, alive but perhaps inert and broken for a while, until we are ready to take action.

I agree with Neff that mindfulness practice is a component of self-compassion, yet it is more effective when practised in a gentle and forgiving way. Being mindful in today's busy, noisy, driven world is not easy. We need to recognise this and simply do the best we can, when we can.

This brings us to Kristin Neff's second quality of self-compassion which is *kindness*. If we are not kind to ourselves any new experience that may benefit us becomes much harder to practise because we become easily distracted by our negatively charged feelings and thoughts, especially in the beginning when we feel we are failing, incompetent and getting nowhere.

Self-compassion – Core quality 2: Self-kindness

Being kind to ourselves is much harder if we learned early on that we are not worthy of unconditional love and have grown up believing that we do not *deserve* happiness, love, good work or friends. Paul Gilbert argues that the concept of 'deserving' is unhelpful. Deserving is linked to reward and punishment and can create a highly polarised, 'black and white' way of viewing the world. For a moment stop and consider your own ideas about who 'deserves' what. Can you see how your beliefs might support unhelpful feelings of entitlement, shame, or judgement?

Eric Fromm in *The Art of Loving*, writes:

> *To be loved because of one's merit, because one deserves it, always leaves doubt.... 'deserved' love easily leaves a bitter feeling that one is not loved for oneself, that one is loved only because one pleases, that one is, in the last analysis, not loved at all but used.*

When we are kind to ourselves we are concerned not about what we 'deserve' but about what we *need* and what would be helpful to our growth. Benjamin Zander, Conductor of the Boston Philharmonic Youth Orchestra, awarded all his music scholars at the New England Conservatory an A grade *before* the course began. The only condition was that during the first few weeks each student had to write a letter, using their imagination and positivity, to describe how they got their 'A'. Zander's rationale was:

> *When you give an A you find yourself speaking to people not from a place of measuring how they stack up against your standards but from a place of respect that gives them room to realise themselves.*[67]

Imagine what might happen if this was how you conducted your performance appraisal processes!

Often our first attempt at, or interpretation of, kindness is *self-indulgence*. We give ourselves permission to drink the whole bottle of wine, watch TV all weekend, sleep until midday and spend to our credit card limit. When my faculty advised me to conduct my research with self-compassion my first thoughts were, that's impossible! I won't get out of bed, I'll watch box sets all day and prune my garden. I'll never get down to any research being *self-compassionate*. I was, of course, confusing compassion with indulgence.

---

[67] (Zander & Zander, 2000)

Self-indulgence means doing whatever we want without thought or concern for the potentially harmful effects of that indulgence. Often we *indulge* because deep down we don't like ourselves and we don't care about the harm our behaviour may cause. When we are kind to ourselves we start from the premise that we are worthwhile, worthy of love and that we *matter*. Our existence on earth *counts* and no matter what we achieve, or whatever imperfections we harbour, we are essentially whole, acceptable and enough.

There is growing evidence to show that people who are self-compassionate are *more* motivated than those who are not. Self-compassion enhances learning behaviours including willingness to take risks and learn from mistakes, greater initiative and clarity around personal goals and fewer self-handicapping strategies such as procrastination and pessimism. [68]

The kindness component of self-compassion softens the judging, critical, sometimes self-loathing voice of our inner critic. Our kind voice will thank our inner critic for trying to help but will ask, with warmth, for it to quieten down for a while so that other voices inside us can speak. Our inner critic will eventually respond to this kindness.

In her second autobiography,[69] the British author, Jeanette Winterson, described her painful and long journey towards befriending her inner critic whom she describes as a "savage lunatic". Winterson's strategy was to give her 'lunatic' one hour of her time a day. They went walking together:

> *Our conversations were like two people using phrasebooks to say things neither understands... her conversational style was recriminatory (blame, accusation, demands, guilt) ... her preferred responses were non-sequiturs. ...occasionally the creature appeared when I was reading, to mock me, to hurt me, but now I could ask her to leave until our meeting the following day and, miraculously, she did.*

---

[68] (Breines & Chen, 2012)
[69] (Winterson, 2012)

And then after months of walking, talking, fighting and forgiving there is a breakthrough,

> *I said something about how nobody had cuddled us when we were little. I said 'us', not 'you'. She held my hand. She had never done that before; mainly she walked behind shooting her sentences. We both sat down and cried. I said, 'we will learn how to love'.*

When Winterson brought kindness and warmth to her conflictual inner dialogues she made a breakthrough that opened the way not just to self-love but to love of others. Learning to walk with our inner critic may not be the sort of change we hope for or expect. Yet it is one of the most crucial relationships to cultivate for those of us yearning to discover what is possible in ourselves beyond striving, achievement and disappointment. Kind self-talk soothes our *threat brain*, quietens the critic and enables us to stay open and responsive to new experience.

Kindness to self is one of the most difficult practices to master, especially for people who have gained considerable outward success by *not* being kind to themselves. When I started my research I had not realised just how prevalent and also how *hidden* the *threat-drive brain* loop is for people in organisational life. Hidden, that is, until they burn out, leave the company or become disengaged and 'resistant'.

Leaders who set the cultural tone in organisations where we spend so much of our lives need to learn that kindness does not weaken a person. It grows mature capabilities that enable creativity, new learning and a positive approach to work. When we are kind and tolerant of ourselves and others we convey resilience and strength that others notice and respond well to.

The third component of self-compassion draws attention to the idea that compassion – meaning to suffer *with* – is a relational and social experience. Cultivating a healthy relationship with ourselves through developing a mindful and kind approach to our experience ultimately enables us to live well in a world of other people. Perhaps one of the most significant outcomes of self-compassion is that we are able to feel compassion for and give love to *others*. In doing so we can step out of threat-based relationships characterised by competition, avoidance or compliance, and reclaim our need and willingness to be part of reciprocal and enduring relationships.

Self-compassion – Core quality 3: Common humanity

We are not alone in our struggle. Neff's third component of self-compassion involves recognising that we are part of a mysterious, complex and connected universe and enables us to re-frame our feelings of inadequacy in order to accept our imperfections. Neff writes:

> When we are in touch with our common humanity we remember that feelings of inadequacy and disappointment are shared by all. This is what distinguishes self-compassion from self-pity. Whereas self-pity says 'poor me' self-compassion remembers that everyone suffers and it offers comfort because everyone is human.

Common humanity is a subject of profound interest to a wide range of people, some of whom have had lasting influence in the way we think about our lives and our organisations. In this section, which deals with shared human experience, it feels appropriate to include some other voices that have contributed to this conversation.

The French philosopher, Jean-Paul Sartre, believed that self-contemplation could not exist separately from engagement in the world of others. He called this 'inter subjectivity' – in learning about ourselves we necessarily learn about and from others. In his famous 1945 lecture, *Existentialism is a Humanism,* he argued:

> I cannot obtain any truth whatsoever about myself except through the mediation of another. The other is indispensable to my existence and equally to any knowledge I can have of myself.[70]

Sartre was defending Existentialism against accusations that it was an excessively subjective philosophy concerned only with individual

---

[70] (Sartre, 1946)

choice. Although he did not believe in a universal human nature or 'essence' he did propose a common human *condition* that remains the same no matter the cultural, historical or economic variants.

What never vary are the necessities of being in the world, of having to labour and to die there.

Sartre saw that a common *purpose* united humanity and that purpose was how to live and die well.

Our lives are not unique. We inherit shared human characteristics and capabilities and we learn how to feel, think and behave like others in our community. When I reflect on the hundreds of individual stories I have heard in my consulting room over the years I can, like Sartre, distil the core themes to relationships, work and loss. These are our 'existential' concerns and we share them with every other human on the planet. Furthermore, our will to survive is shared with all life on earth. Last week, when walking along the South West coast path in a particularly exposed part of the country, I saw a tree clinging perpendicular to the cliff face. It was held to the rock by its roots, suspended above the sea like a burnt-out bridge. Against the odds this tree had managed to survive.

Beyond Neff's idea of common humanity, then, is a wider common *ecology* of which we are also a part. Understanding ourselves as part of this complex living system or web of life, is, according to physicist Fritjof Capra, the most critical challenge of our time.[71] In Part One we learned how individual brain cells (neurons) are activated by experience and join other neurons to form networks or templates which represent what we have learned and what we know. In the same way, we can think of social groups, including the organisations in which we work, as being made up of networks. In this case the individual 'cell' is a person who forms relationships with other individuals to create social networks which represent the forms of organised living we know as families, societies, governments and industries. Together these social networks comprise the ecology of human life. The knowledge

---

[71] (Capra, 2002)

management theorist Etienne Wenger called these networks *communities of practice* and noted how significant they are in today's global economy.

> *Firms that understand how to translate the power of communities into successful knowledge organisations will be the architects of tomorrow.*[72]

The 'power of community' of particular relevance here is the will and energy of people to voluntarily share not just their knowledge but a wealth of personal and social resources for the good of the whole. This *compassionate engagement* – we could call it collaboration – flows from individuals who are not constantly living in threat and/or who have developed ways of managing threat.

Victor Frankl, writing about his experience in the Nazi concentration camps, observed that prisoners who retained a sense of *purpose* and *meaning* in their lives were able to cope with threat and act with compassion and care despite the horrendous conditions.[73] Clarity of personal purpose emerges when we make time to reflect and connect with what is truly important to us. It is a *safe brain* capability that regulates and takes us beyond threat.

Extending the ecology metaphor further we imagine people reaching out not just to fellow humans for relationship but also to nature and to other living organisms that share this earth. This is not a radical or 'new age' concept. It is surely common sense to form reciprocal relationships between life-giving or life-enhancing entities. The water I drink and the air I breathe are as essential to me as my neighbour whose contributions in the world help me in mine. Together we form and sustain the living system.

The value of this perspective for organisations is explored by Peter Senge and colleagues who advocate that leaders should emerge from their 'bubble' – a metaphor used to describe the partial yet powerful beliefs that foster blind spots and group think – and recognise,

---

[72] (Wenger, et al., 2002)
[73] (Frankl, 2004)

if life beyond the bubble is really about coming home to our humanness, the flourishing it promises is unlikely so long as we hold that humans are somehow separate and superior to the rest of life.[74]

Unfortunately, contemporary culture does not often support this interconnected *living systems* perspective. We are treated and treat ourselves like mechanical parts. Many of the metaphors and guiding principles we use to describe our daily lives, particularly at work, are machine based: it's running like clockwork, we need a quick fix, he put a spanner in the works, I need an MOT, let's take a pressure check, dial up, find our leverage points.

Management theorist, Gareth Morgan, has written extensively about how our metaphors influence the way we see, think and act. He observes that,

the use of machines has radically transformed the nature of productive activity and has left its mark on the imagination, thoughts and feelings of humans throughout the ages. Scientists have produced mechanistic interpretations of the natural world and philosophers and psychologists have articulated mechanistic theories of the human mind and behaviour.[75]

Our lives, like machines, are standardised, highly specialised (e.g. we develop skills and expertise within a narrow field), measured, evaluated and calibrated against rigid cultural norms. We are locked into prescribed routines, surveyed and regulated by rules or 'operating' instructions. Given this it is unsurprising that, like machines, we have difficulty responding effectively to changing circumstances or that we 'break'.

A machine does not act spontaneously and novelty does not emerge from the designed, programmed and controlled mechanical invention. A machine does not reflect or think or have any conscious ability to shape its destiny. Being human means using our

---

[74] (Senge, et al., 2008)
[75] (Morgan, 1997)

uniquely conscious self to reflect on our experience and adapt our behaviours in the light of new learning and foresight. What we lose when we are 'de-humanised' is our capability to respond with insight, imagination and creativity to the challenges we face.

Years ago, as a trainee psychologist, I was disturbed by the mechanistic approach to human suffering. Since then I have observed the machine metaphor play out in many different contexts, not least in organisational life. The result is fragmentation, isolation and a pervasive belief that we suffer alone. That so much of modern culture has come to be this way is not a cause for self-condemnation but an invitation to bring compassionate attention to how we separate ourselves from each other and from our environment.

Karl Marx is perhaps the best-known exponent of the concept of alienation or *entfremdung* (estrangement). He described the social alienation of people from aspects of their human nature and understood this as a consequence of society being divided into classes and other hierarchies. Marx noted how the organisation of work, in particular the division of labour, separates a person from the *product* of their activity, renders them a mere cog in a machine and ultimately destroys the meaning of labour and, given how important labour is to a person's soul, the meaning of life.

Ros Douthat, writing in *The New York Times* in 2014,[76] noticed a revival of Marxist ideas in response to global financial crises, gross inequalities in the labour market and growing consensus that material wealth has a finite correlation to emotional health. In other words, the accumulation of resources does not, beyond a certain level, make us any happier or productive. Yet a few years later, the American election was won by Donald Trump, a businessman whose main interest is to promote the material wealth of his nation and any means, it would seem, might be justified to achieve this end.

Although we have been talking about the *Trimotive Brain* as an individual motivational system we could, metaphorically, apply *Trimotive Brain* concepts to understand the motivations that drive groups and societies. In the 2016 US election results we might see a

---

[76] 'Marx Rises Again', *The New York Times*, April 19th 2014

'national consciousness' sabotaged by its *threat brain*. We see the dark side of this living system, so long glossed over and denied, emerge with rage and fury. The USA, like Germany in the 1930s and the UK during Brexit, might be seen to have given way to its survival impulses because its *safe brain* capability was not strong enough to pull it back to centre. Once again we see the spinning threat-drive loop, this time within and across nations. Fears relating to the unstable economy, social inequality and terrorism conjure ancient memories of the predator and of scarcity. The contemporary survival response, fuelled by *threat brain* fears, is the *toxic drive* to accumulate, compete and achieve more. Conversely the latest world happiness report[77] claims that *"mutual trust, shared purpose, generosity and good governance"* are the key factors behind individual and social well-being. These could be understood not just as personal but also as collective, 'social *safe brain*' characteristics.

Recognising our common humanity requires us to recognise ourselves as living organisms. This involves recognising that living systems require certain conditions for growth. If your life feels stunted, diseased or wilting it is unlikely to be your personal fault for you do not live or work in a world devoid of others. We have co-created the conditions of our lives and work. We till and share the same soil. If one of us is struggling it means others are or will be too. A quick skim through human history helps us to realise that everybody has or will suffer hardship and loss and that everybody makes mistakes, harbours regrets and worries about their shortcomings.

Summarising the importance of common humanity, Neff says:

> *When our sense of self-worth and belonging is grounded in simply being human we can't be rejected or cast out by others. Our humanity can never be taken away from us, no matter how far we fall. The very fact that we are imperfect affirms that we are card-carrying members of the human race and are therefore always, automatically, connected to the whole.*

---

[77] (Helliwell, et al., 2017)

Self-compassion involves being mindful, kind and accepting of our human condition. We realise that the feelings, thoughts and behaviours which frighten, disgust or anger us are a result of the way our brains have evolved to enable us to survive. The way we live in, adapt to and manage our physical and relational environment is strongly influenced by these complex, enduring and difficult-to-control forces. When we bring a warm, self-compassionate *quality* of awareness to our experience we are less likely to be overwhelmed by feelings of threat and less likely to defend our individual welfare over others.

In the next chapter I will describe some practices and activities that help us cultivate self-compassion. Before that though, a gentle reminder that change, growth and letting go of our habits goes through phases which include exhilaration, hope and despair. Sometimes we circle our problems for years. The theologian Thomas Moore suggests that looping or circling may be a necessary and helpful experience. By *"repeating both the glorious and the defeating themes that are embedded in our soul"*[78] we come to know ourselves more deeply in the end. Whilst we can learn to be more self-compassionate, the learning takes time and is likely to involve disappointment and disillusion along the way.

Stages of self-compassion – wait, give up hope, keep the faith

Christopher Germer, a clinical psychologist specialising in compassionate mindfulness practice, observes three stages in the growth of self-compassion which he describes as infatuation, disillusionment and true acceptance. In the infatuation stage a person who has discovered self-compassion can experience intense relief at being given or feeling the permission to care for, like and accept who they are. In some ways, it is like falling in love with one's own self. Admiration, appreciation, trust, forgiveness and respect are directed inward and trigger the parasympathetic nervous system to release feel-good hormones. This was my own experience

---

[78] (Moore, 2001)

and one I have subsequently heard clients talk about when they first learn about and start to practise self-compassion.

James, whom I talked about earlier, wrote:

The struggle to be a better person just melted away. I started to like myself and be interested in this person, 'me', who had qualities and strengths I had never acknowledged. I felt moments of real joy. Just being alone, appreciating the life I have and realising it doesn't have to be so hard.

Another client, Mark, observed:

In our last discussion you said, 'you are okay'. Something so simple has been unbelievably helpful. I have adopted this as a mantra that I leverage when I can feel my demons lurking. I am on the road and have been sleeping, managing stress levels, with the simple truth, I am okay.

The first experience of self-compassion often draws its energy from our desperate need and wish to *feel better*. When we feel the lightness of living that self-compassion brings we may be tempted to believe our problems are over. However, suffering and pain are inescapable human experiences and when they resurface it can feel as if self-compassion hasn't worked. This is when we fall into what Germer calls *disillusionment*. People re-experience or 'relapse' into their problems and sometimes, because they have tasted life without them, the return of the problem is felt with much more intensity. Feelings of grief, hopelessness, cynicism and anger define this stage and it is now that many, if not most, people give up on the idea of change.

Germer calls the final stage of cultivating self-compassion *acceptance*, which he describes as a 'ripening' of practice:

The instinctive effort to avoid discomfort may linger somewhere in the background, but we've seen through it. We give ourselves kindness for its own sake.

In other words, we have regulated our *threat brain* motivations, attained some measure of *safe brain* calm and from there can draw upon a deeper wisdom to practice self-compassion, not necessarily to make ourselves feel better but simply to take care of ourselves because we feel bad. It is, as Germer notes, the shift from seeking cure to *taking care* and is a merciful response to our human condition.

When I started to practise self-compassion I had to learn patience not because I necessarily *wanted* to but because hurrying did not work. There are times when we cannot force ourselves to feel better, do more or pretend that we are in control. The period leading up to acceptance could be described as *waiting*. This is not an inert state and in the next chapter I will share some of the things you can do whilst waiting. The purpose of waiting is to give up the struggle which arises in the first stages of infatuation and disillusionment. Waiting is more fertile if we *let go of hope*, which is our attachment to how we want life to be. There may be sadness and grief that accompanies the giving up of old dreams and beliefs and we need to be kind to ourselves as our skin sheds and new life starts to emerge. The antidote to disillusion during this time is to *keep the faith*. We reassure ourselves that whatever happens will be the right thing (even if we don't fully understand it at first) and we come to trust in our ability to learn, grow and find joy again. Dina Glouberman who describes this process in her book, *The Joy of Burnout*, uses the mantra '*wait, give up hope, keep the faith*' which can be understood as, be patient, be open to what happens and trust.

Waiting takes us to the resting place of acceptance when, almost without our noticing, old habits loosen their grip and let us go. It is indeed the case, as T.S. Eliot observed, that "*the faith and the love and the hope are all in the waiting*".[79] It is an important word, used intentionally to challenge the speed of change that is so often expected of us and to emphasise the slow, contemplative period that precedes and accompanies the emergence of novelty, innovation and new ways of being in the world.

---

[79] (Eliot, 1936)

Chapter Six: Waiting – doing a little, often

Keep it Simple

Self-compassion soothes the threatened brain and enables us to cultivate warm awareness. It is this kind of awareness that enables us to appraise and understand our lives as part of a flow of events that has carried us, willing or not, in its current. We do not choose our genes, our parents or our formative experiences. We did not design the unconscious processes that influence us or the social world that clips and prunes our growing form. Nevertheless, we do have to live with the consequences and we have seen how this can sometimes cause us problems. With warm awareness we can learn some useful things about ourselves that might make a positive difference to the way we think our life is, must and could be.

It takes time for awareness to warm up and while we are waiting we may be tempted to deal with our problems by increasing our *drive brain* activities. Sometimes this helps, as for example when we deal with our fear of ageing by taking more exercise and eating well. However, sometimes, as we saw in Part One, it creates a *threat-drive brain* loop which compounds our difficulties. Usually this happens when *safe brain* is inactive and we do not think about, reflect on or deeply consider the purpose and consequence of our actions. This is why so many reactive 'solutions' fail. Rarely does looking up ex partners on Facebook, cosmetic surgery or giving up our corporate job to run a bed & breakfast in Devon solve our deeper concerns. We would do better if we recognised and soothed our *threat-drive brain* loops and encouraged some *safe brain* stillness and wisdom. When we are centred and quiet we are able to hear other parts of our self speak. Our awareness is attuned not to options and choices – which is where *drive brain* attention is drawn – but to values, yearnings and longings. Later, we can translate these deeper needs into choices and actions but first we need to listen carefully in order to hear and understand them. This is how *safe brain*, motivating us to pause, reflect and wait a while, influences *healthy* drive.

Freud proposed that between the unconscious and conscious mind was the *'preconscious'* which contains thoughts and feelings that *are* accessible if we pay careful attention to them. In extending this idea I suggest that there are aspects of our somatic and mental unconscious which are preconscious and which can become known to us through a few basic practices. The aim of these practices is to help us surface new knowledge about ourselves. At first we may not understand the meaning of what we discover but with patience and guidance these revelations combine to form the outline of a new story about ourselves that may alter the way we feel and behave.

We need not approach these practices as part of a 'relentless pursuit of self-development'. We do not have to become masterful interpreters of our dreams, expert meditators or become entangled in philosophical arguments about whether we have free will or not. We don't even have to change. Approaching our problem habits and 'blind spots' with self-compassion requires that our new practices don't feel too onerous, strange or punitive. A kind, mindful, forgiving and playful spirit will keep our *safe brain* engaged and ensure that we are not de-railed by *threat brain* emotions. Learning does not have to be difficult to be worthwhile. The simple truth is we can all extend our conscious capability if we are willing to experiment and practise and in doing *a little, often* we will start to experience our lives as more fully our own. This is what it means to be comfortable in our own skin.

Although we can cultivate warm awareness in many different ways, the methods I outline below are those that my clients have found easy to engage with and to incorporate into their daily routines. These core practices help us become more conscious of our somatic and mental unconscious and they distil down to three activities: paying attention to our breathing, testing our assumptions and writing about our experience. In between practising it is helpful to sleep and rest a lot.

From somatic unconscious to somatic awareness

We have seen that the somatic unconscious regulates our physiological functions such as breathing, blood circulation and the emotions arising from our *threat brain, drive brain* and *safe brain* systems. We can become more conscious of what is happening in our body. We can feel, for example our heart beat through our chest or our pulse. We can pause to notice the rhythm and depth of our breathing and we can notice the sensations in our stomach and hear the noise it makes. We can then begin to observe how these physiological reactions interact with our motivation systems to produce feelings which we recognise as threat, drive or safe.

Becoming more aware of what our body is doing has many benefits. We may be able to detect ill health or imbalance at an earlier stage, we may become better at responding to and meeting our physical needs and we may be able to gain more control of our impulsive emotions.

The first step in developing warm awareness is the ability to stimulate a relaxed bodily state. When we are relaxed we are more likely to be able to extend and control our attention. Often people worry that a relaxed state will make them feel sleepy rather than alert. This is often true when we first start to practise. The physiological changes that occur as we relax and trigger the parasympathetic nervous system may well make us drowsy, particularly if our body is much more used to functioning on drive-based 'highs'. However, when our body gets accustomed to being calm and the 'doses' of oxytocin and endorphins become more regular, we will find that relaxation enables us to think more clearly and to renew depleted energy quickly. A 'power nap', for example, provides a short burst of deep rest that has lasting implications throughout the day. Power napping becomes easier when we are not in a 'dis-integrated' state. When our *threat brain* and *drive brain* are overactive, sleep states are either very difficult to induce or extremely hard to surface from.

Deep breathing and rhythmic breathing

The most basic and effective ways to stimulate relaxation are deep breathing and rhythmic breathing. Slow, measured breathing stimulates our vagus nerve which controls the parasympathetic nervous system and activates the relaxation response. Signals are sent to the brain and body suggesting the environment is threat free.

We do not need to go on a course to learn how to breathe in a deep and rhythmic way but in order for it to make a difference to our body states it helps to practise this kind of breathing a few times a day. When we begin to do this we will probably notice our breathing is 'shallow' (high up in the chest) and that we often hold our breath. These short, sharp ways of using the breath are much more appropriate when we are in danger, as they facilitate the hyperalert fight-flight reaction. Shallow or held breath is linked to higher levels of stress and anxiety.[80]

The next time you feel tense or anxious, first try *deep breathing*. This means drawing your breath slowly through your nose and 'directing' it down into your diaphragm so that you feel your stomach expand like a balloon. When you breathe out, again through the nose, contract your navel towards your spine and feel it pressing the air out of your stomach. As you exhale imagine you are releasing the tension in your body through the outward breath. At first you may find it difficult to draw your breath deep into your body and it may feel uncomfortable to expand your stomach as the air enters – your diaphragm muscles may not be used to breathing in this way and may need time to strengthen. Keep practising and you will soon feel the reassuring calm that arises from deep breath.

Rhythmic breathing is based on the natural flow of your breath. It helps us reduce stress by ensuring regular and continuous air flow at a steady pace. It helps us avoid breathing too fast or holding our breath. Start by taking a few regular breaths in your normal way. Then alter your in-and-out rhythm so that you begin breathing in for the same number of counts as you breathe out. In-between the in and out breath, pause for two counts. Find a number that works

---

[80] (LeDoux, 2015)

for you as each person has a different length of breath that feels right. For me it's four counts in, pause for two, and four counts out. With this kind of breathing – sometimes called 4-2-4 breathing – you don't need to direct breath all the way into the lower diaphragm but it helps to fully fill your lungs. When you do this you will feel your chest and ribcage expand and contract.

These two methods of breathing (deep and rhythmic) will bring a number of noticeable benefits in your body functioning. Your muscles will become more relaxed and you will experience fewer back and neck aches. Oxygen delivery will improve, which increases your mental concentration and physical stamina. Your blood pressure lowers because your muscles are letting go of tension causing blood vessels to dilate and endorphins are released which provide natural pain relief and a sense of well-being. You will also benefit from improved digestion as deep breathing stimulates the lymphatic system to detoxify and cleanse your body.

Deep and rhythmic breathing are the foundations of mindful meditation practice but you don't have to be a meditator to be a better breather! When you practise these breathing techniques you will naturally become more alert to other body processes and states. This awareness, warm because it is relaxed, will compel you towards self-compassionate action when your body is in pain, exhausted, hungry and in need of physical comfort.

From cognitive unconscious to cognitive awareness

Vertical descent inquiry

The cognitive unconscious selects, appraises, filters and makes meaning out of information arising from experience. To do this it consults the store of memories that contain core beliefs or 'mental models' about our world. These core beliefs are resilient, deeply embedded and difficult to change and some of them have reached their 'sell by' date. This means they are no longer accurate or helpful guides in our adult life. Becoming more aware of our core beliefs lets us reflect on how useful and relevant these beliefs are and is the first step towards letting go of those which no longer serve us well.

Vertical descent inquiry is a process of questioning intended to reveal core beliefs – not just what they are but, more importantly, what *meaning* they hold for us. When James told me he felt angry when his boss criticised him I used this process to help him become more aware of the core belief that might be triggering his threat response.

I started by asking him what criticism meant to him. He replied, *'it means my boss does not value me'*. A vertical descent inquiry probes the meaning at each level of sense making and in doing so eventually arrives at, or gets close to, a core belief. In James's case this core belief was, *I will always be alone.*

Figure 8: *Discovering core beliefs – Vertical descent inquiry*

You can practise vertical descent inquiry on your own or with the help of a coach or friend. Start with an experience that has triggered an intense feeling in you, as strong emotions are usually an indicator that a core belief is at work. Then ask yourself, and make notes about, what that experience means to you. Keep asking the meaning question until you can't go any further. You will get closer to your core beliefs. This inquiry takes time and practice because most of us are not used to noticing or analysing the meaning of events in our lives. Just like learning to breathe deeply, we need to learn to think deeply.

Here's another example, this time from Charlotte, a Human Resources professional;

I feel a strong attraction to a man in my office.

What does attraction mean?

Attraction means intimacy, being close.

What does intimacy and being close mean?

It means being understood.

What does being understood mean?

It means I can say what I really think and feel and not be rejected.

What does rejection mean?

It means loneliness and isolation.

What does loneliness and isolation mean?

It means I have done something bad.

What does doing something bad mean?

Being bad means not pleasing people.

What does pleasing people mean?

It means I will be cared for.

What does being cared for mean?

It means I will be safe.

In this second example, Charlotte potentially uncovers a core belief which suggests she can achieve intimacy and security by pleasing others and by diminishing her own needs. By becoming aware of this possibility Charlotte can more easily notice this tendency in herself and the outcomes it generates.

Douglas Stone and his colleagues from the Harvard Negotiation Project suggest that our identity, or sense of who we are, pivots on core beliefs that answer three fundamental questions relating to our self-image; *am I competent*? *am I a good person*? and *am I worthy of love*?[81] When you practise vertical descent inquiries you may notice that these concerns appear often and in various guises across a number of your core beliefs. This is not surprising given how important attachment and belonging are to our survival.

These inquiries may look simple but core belief archaeology requires time, energy, patience and commitment. Yet it is one of the best ways to become conscious of our hidden assumptions and taken for granted 'truths'. Also, remember, this process is about discovering *personal* meaning and truth which implies that whatever emerges for you counts as 'truthful'. If pleasing people means that you will be cared for, that is your truth and it matters. If you start arguing with yourself (or your coach) about the 'true' definition of care or whether your sense-making is accurate, you will end up swapping opinions, casting judgements and evaluating. This is likely to set your *threat brain* going because 'being wrong' suggests you may have to give up this belief and at this stage in the process you are probably not ready to. It doesn't matter what the Oxford English dictionary or a well-meaning friend advises us. No matter how strange or inappropriate our personal truths seem to others, they have a logic of their own and a strong motivating influence in our life. The question is not whether the belief is true but whether it is still helpful to us.

Acting as if

Acting 'as if' your core belief is *not* true is a way of testing your favourite hypotheses about the world and exploring how useful your beliefs are. If, like James, your core belief is that you will always be alone, try acting as if that belief were not true. For a day, a week or

---

[81] (Stone, et al., 1999)

more if you can, imagine that people are keen to get to know you, be friends with you, go out with you, work with you and so on. How might you wake up and behave in the world each day if this were true?

The first thing you will probably notice is *anxiety* because your core belief 'I will always be alone' once served an important function. It was probably the safest way of understanding your world as a child. It was a belief that helped you cope when people were hostile or rejecting and it allowed you to anticipate, prepare for and employ strategies to deal with it. You learned how to be alone, how to value your independence and how to form superficial relationships that were easy to let go of.

So, when you start acting 'as if' your beliefs are not true, minimise your anxiety by relaxing your brain and body using the breathing techniques and kind self-talk. *Yes, you say to yourself, I probably will always be alone but just for today I'm going to pretend that's not true.* The 'just for today' and 'pretend' words slow the pace, don't prematurely commit you to change and create a compassionate inner dialogue that goes something like this:

Threat brain (represented by the voice of our inner critic):
This is a stupid idea. Being alone is much better. If you get close to people they will let you down and hurt you.

Safe brain (represented by the voice of our self-compassion):
That's probably true but just for today let's pretend it isn't.

Threat brain: You'll get taken advantage of. You'll make a fool of yourself.

Safe brain: That might happen but don't worry, if it feels too difficult I'll stop.

Threat brain: Just for a day, right? You won't be going out with these people? You'll be home at the usual time?

Safe brain: Yes, just for a day.

Alcoholics Anonymous encourage their members to 'fake it until you make it' and to focus on just 'one day at a time'. Each day simply go through the motions (you don't have to like it or believe it) until gradually your self-image and assumptions about the world begin to change. I am working with a client at the moment who is terrified of committing to her relationship, however, as she acts 'as if' she is not terrified she is noticing something new. She is experiencing trust. By not running away from the triggers that usually frighten her, such as making holiday plans or arranging for their families to spend Christmas together, she is enabling her partner to gain confidence, to open out to her and to become more available. His behaviour, in turn, encourages her to move closer to him.

Research supports this approach and shows that *virtuous* circles begin to emerge as you practise the behaviours you would like to have.[82] Pretend to be courageous, compassionate, kind and patient and eventually you will find these behaviours become easier until, one day, without thinking about it, the courage and the kindness are spontaneous.

Acting 'as if' *safely* invites habit into our conscious experience where we can play, experiment and reshape it if we wish. In this process we create more up-to-date and accurate responses that, once practised and familiar, sink back into our unconscious to become integrated and automatic. This time, however, the re-worked habit is more useful and healthy and contributes to our well-being.

Practice, Practice, Practice

Revealing a core belief and acting 'as if' it were not true are two basic methods for getting to know your cognitive unconscious. Neither approach requires that we understand 'why' we have this belief. If I discover a core belief that tells me that I should be competitive and ruthless and I don't like that about myself, I don't need to undertake a causal analysis before I take steps to change my behaviours. They are, therefore, a good set of practices for people who like to be 'doing' whilst learning. The difficult part is the discipline required to keep rehearsing and repeating a new behaviour.

If it takes ten thousand hours to *master* a skill it probably takes five thousand to be good at it and may be three thousand hours to be good

---

[82] (Wilson, 2011)

enough. Three thousand hours, equates to 375 days of practising 8 hours a day. Add to that some time off and a few relapses and you are looking at *two years* before a core belief starts to dissolve and a new belief, supporting new behaviour emerges. This is another reason why changing a habit requires patience and compassion.

From the defensive unconscious to defence awareness

The core beliefs that we get to know through exploring our cognitive unconscious processes are, perhaps, easier to access and work with than core beliefs residing in our defensive unconscious.[83] This is because the primary purpose of the defensive unconscious is to hide or distort information and to blind us or numb us to painful truths. These unconscious processes operate through the deeper memory structures of the corpus striatum. Habits incubated and grown in this shady underworld resist interference and, if exposed, can leave us feeling inadequate, bad and unworthy of love. This is why most of us avoid digging too deeply into our dark side: we don't want the roots of our carefully crafted persona or identity to be exposed.

It is, of course, a personal choice whether and how far you want to travel into the unconscious realms of your experience. For many people, working with tangible objectives such as increasing physical awareness and health or committing to one or two new behaviours is enough. For others, unease, emptiness, destruction and longing are powerful experiences which motivate them to seek deeper understanding. When this happens a more artful method of discovery is required in order to bring to light that which is used to living in the dark.

Dog in the cellar

Our defensive unconscious is trying to protect us by hiding, denying or distorting parts of our self which are 'unacceptable'. If we were to show this side of our nature we might repulse, shock or even amaze others. We will stand out, seem different and may risk

---

[83] See Chapter 4 for a summary of unconscious processes.

rejection. To prevent this, the defensive unconscious withholds the darkest and probably also the brightest in us. If, however, this part of us leaks or bursts out - and this can happen when we are very tired, stressed or upset – it usually causes us problems. We get into arguments, are unkind to others or say and do things that contravene social norms and what others expect of us.

A highly creative person I know used to work as financial director for a law firm. She was always getting into trouble during board meetings because she was so frustrated by what she felt were "repetitive, mundane and superficial conversations". Her reaction to the ordinary challenges of corporate life were often extreme. On good days her dark side would appear in sarcastic comments, and disengaged behaviours. At other times she would become aggressive and highly disruptive. One habit she had was to get up and walk around the board table so that she could lean into people whilst speaking and "make her point strongly".

Tension continued to build between her and other board members until one day, following a vicious verbal attack against a colleague, the chairman severely reprimanded her in front of everyone in what she described as an "horrific showdown". She went on sick leave for stress-related illness and never returned.

A few years later, having undertaken, with the support of a therapist, a period of intense and painful self-reflection, she decided to set up as a freelance photographer. As a child, she had been heavily discouraged from pursuing 'arty' subjects and despite her love of photography – which wasn't even recognised as art – she found herself training to be an accountant. When her visually creative talents were finally allowed expression she became a much calmer, happier and kinder person. I still see her dark side bubble up from time to time but it isn't dangerous. Mostly I see her darkness emerge safely in the photographs she produces which are moving portraits of the isolation and division she sees within her East London community.

Imagine that this dark part of you is a dog who, long ago, when he was a small puppy, got locked away in a deep, dark cellar for 'bad' behaviour. Occasionally he was let out of the cellar but every time he was out he got into trouble and was dragged back down. This confused him. The people in the house were always yelling at him. He didn't like this. What could be so wrong about making holes in the garden, chewing the furniture or barking with joy? Often the cellar, where he began to spend most of his time, felt safer.

Sometimes you could hear his lonely howl and now and then you'd sit with your back against the cellar door whispering to him. You wished you could be friends but life was getting busy and you needed to move on. Eventually you forgot about your puppy even though sometimes, late at night, you still heard him whimper.

The puppy stayed in the cellar and grew into a feral and frightened dog. His growl and bark became fierce and loud and impossible to ignore. At times this caused you problems. Other people could hear and did not like the noise he made. One day, many years later, you start to feel strong pangs of guilt and loneliness and/or you begin to experience the anxiety and confusion that so often accompanies mid-life. You realise you miss the puppy and you want to know what became of him. You decide it is time to go back and open the cellar door. You have good intentions, maybe you and he could become friends at last. Or, perhaps you are *forced* to deal with him because, as in the case above, his noise has become too frequent and too disturbing to ignore.

Unfortunately, when you do finally open the door the animal leaps out at you, frothing at the mouth and baring his teeth. You are terrified, you feel he wants to harm you. With all your energy you manage to push him back inside the cellar and slam the door. Your *threat brain* is pulsing, you feel scared, ashamed and disgusted. You do not want to repeat this experience so you decide to forget about the dog and forget you ever had a puppy. From now on you learn to live with the noise and unease and when you hear the dismal barking and scratching of claws you shut your ears and, with a weary heart, carry on as if he were not there. Or, again, like my finance friend, you allow him to escape, wreak havoc and return at leisure to his den.

This is one version of the story. It is what happens when we remember but try to forget or when we notice but try to ignore. The other version is that we open the cellar door, the dog attacks us (or others) but this time, once we have secured him back in, we take time to soothe ourselves and to reflect on the experience. Although nervous and uncertain we recognise that this animal has a right to be out of his prison. We remember the puppy he once was and the fun we had together. We feel sadness and compassion and we accept it is not our fault that he got locked away. As well as feeling fear, we are curious and we wonder how we could slowly get to know our dog again and perhaps even befriend him.

Opening the cellar door slowly and knowing how to gradually ease our mad dog out into the world takes skill and courage and often benefits from the help of an experienced guide. This person – a coach, a therapist, a loving and skilled friend or partner – will not be afraid of this energy that rages in you. They have seen and worked with it in others and, more importantly, in themselves. They know that these broken, lost parts of the self can be brought back into the light and can contribute to your life. This person will also know whether the time is right for you to begin this exploration. You will need self-compassion because without the help of *safe brain* you will be derailed by strong, threat-based emotion.

In Part Three we will see how Maggie, Carl and Ronnie were helped to meet their dog and discovered, in doing so, a more companionable way of living together. This becomes possible when we have calmed the rage, anger, shame and hatred that this banished and abandoned part of our self understandably feels. The poet Rainer Maria Rilke expresses this clearly,

> *Perhaps all the dragons of our lives*
> *Are princesses who are only waiting to*
> *See us once, beautiful and brave.*
> *Perhaps everything terrible is in*
> *Its deepest being something*
> *That needs our love.*[84]

---

[84] (Rilke, 1985)

Free fall writing

You can gradually get to know the character and idiosyncrasies of your dog, or dragon, and over time start to appreciate the power and presence it has in your life. A very good way to begin is to practice a method of writing called *free fall*.

Natalie Goldberg, author and a teacher of writing practice, suggests that this method enables us to reach our 'first thoughts' which are uncensored by the multitude of personal and social norms and expectations that control, shape and constrain our thinking. These first thoughts represent some of what is hidden in our cellar.[85]

To practise free fall you will need a notebook and a pen that won't run out of ink in mid flow. There are also a few basic 'rules' to support this method:

- Write for a minimum of 3 minutes (time yourself)

- When you start writing DO NOT stop

- Don't worry about spelling, grammar, neatness, logic, meaning

- Follow your energy no matter how scary, revealing or unacceptable

To begin, find somewhere to write comfortably and without distractions. Turn your phone off, close the door. Later, when you are more used to this practice you will find it easier to write in a café or crowded train. Before starting, use deep breath to relax and 'open' your thoughts – remember *threat brain* narrows our range.

When you are ready, choose a *stem phrase* to help you get going. The stem phrase can be totally abstract such as:

Green cake...

Robot war...

Chimp...

---

[85] (Goldberg, 2005)

Light finger...

Clouds...

Or the stem phrase could be loosely related to something on your mind:

When we argue...

John assumes...

This project...

What if...

I am...

The deadline...

Children are...

You can 'pluck' a stem phrase randomly from a book or magazine. Simply open whatever is nearest to hand and pick out the first few words you see. Or, you can be more intentional, and note down a stem phrase that has some meaning to you right now. It doesn't matter too much what your stem phrase is because the purpose of free fall writing is to let your hand and pen take you wherever they need to go – more on this shortly.

The stem phrase may initially guide your thoughts but the more you practise free fall the more you will see that your 'first thoughts' – the ones you are trying to reveal – are rarely concerned with what is foremost in mind or, if they are, they have some very different opinions and feelings about it.

The main purpose of using a stem phrase is to provide a method for *blocking your inner critic*. The inner critic hates free fall writing. Free fall is a waste of time, stupid, irrational, pointless, messy, dangerous. It is something for 'arty' people, children or the mentally unwell. Your inner critic does not want you to do free fall writing because, being a voice of your *threat brain*, it worries that you will expose your ugly side or appalling literary skills, and live to regret it. Or you will become incoherent and uncompetitive, overwhelmed with emotion and may even start having new ideas about how to live. Remember, the inner critic has a very clear picture of how you 'should' be and what you 'must' do in order to fit in, avoid danger and survive. It has no time for 'distractions' that may weaken or complicate your current strategy.

When you practise free fall writing, your inner critic will intervene by 'blocking' you. This means you will find it hard or impossible to think of anything to write or your head will be so filled with its voice that you end up writing a neat, tidy essay just to appease it and prove everything is in order. When this happens, when you want to stop writing or you want to control the flow by crossing things out, pausing, analysing and 'starting again', DON'T! *Don't give in to your inner critic.* Instead, when you feel these things use the stem phrase as your ally. Keep writing the stem phrase over and over and over again until you *bore* your inner critic away.

Green cake, green cake, green cake, green cake, green cake, green cake,

you write until suddenly a new thought appears.

Green cake, icing sugar sixth birthday party scraped knee broken swing mum shouting angry from the top of the garden. Where are my friends? Cat with one eye looking at me – why alone on my birthday – it's my party and I'll cry if I want to but if I do cry now I'll cry every day – maybe I do cry every day – crushed daffodil – only six green cakes standing on the wall green cake green cake…

So you practise your free fall, which is like breathing practice for your deep feelings, and you collect these pieces of writing in a journal and resist reading them through too soon. If you do, you will probably miss the gold, the gore and the hidden meanings because your logical brain will try to impose itself onto these fragments. Later, though, the fragments grow into a body of work that can stand up to logic and superficial interpretation.

Once you have been free falling for a few months and you have a journal full of your scribblings, the next step is to take a highlighter pen and read through your writing with as much non-judgement and curiosity as you can muster. Each time a phrase, sentence or word stirs a strong emotion, memory or intense curiosity, highlight it with your pen. When you have gone through all the writing in this way, go back and make a list of all the highlighted sentences and words. Take your time to ponder this list. Spend time reflecting on meaning, and noticing patterns and themes. Something will emerge and, if it doesn't, you can take this list and your work to a coach, a therapist or someone who is more practised at reading and inquiring into the language of the defensive unconscious. Or you can keep writing. Don't hurry. Remember your angry dog is not going to eat out of your hand straight away. Sometimes it takes years to get close.

As you develop this practice you will probably notice that your thoughts want to move faster than your pen can manage. Some people deal with this by typing so that they can write more quickly. I don't recommend this. The way you make letters on a page forms part of the 'message'. Whether those letters are messy, large, small, slanting, written in circles, lines or randomly dotted about the page, they will later remind you about the quality of your feelings and thoughts. Typing onto a screen not only makes this invisible but also provides unhelpful auto-corrects, spell checks and formatting which will sterilise the personality in your written hand.

Research suggests that writing activates a unique neural circuit in our brain that makes learning easier perhaps by improving our focus (our eyes do not switch from key to screen) and by slowing the thought process.[86] If the urge to write faster arises, let it. See what happens. You may find you invent new words, collapse words into each other, develop a shorthand or circumvent unnecessary detail. Your pen may help you get to the point a lot quicker in the end.

When we are in threat and closing in on ourselves, free fall writing – like breathing – can help regulate our emotions. Although the last thing you may feel like doing when you're angry or scared is writing, free fall can be an excellent antidote to threat. Free fall demands nothing from you other than that you move your pen and form the words that come to mind. You can wet the page with tears, stab holes into the paper, let your dog howl out loud as you scrawl

---

[86] (Konnikova, 2014) (Mangen & Velay, 2010)

away. Using free fall in this way is a cathartic and safe way to release or dilute toxic energy and an invitation to our unique, whole, possible self to speak.

If what you have written feels deeply private, find a secure place to store it away from prying eyes. Or, in some cases, you may feel it has done its work and it's OK to burn or bin it.

There are other 'artful' practices, some of which we will explore in Part Three, which help us surface our defensive unconscious but free fall is a very good way to start. Clients who connect with this practice are usually those who are ready to enter a deeper self-exploration and who are willing to engage in an emergent process without any certainty of outcome. Those who find it difficult are often highly controlled by their inner critic, locked in a *threat-drive brain* loop which needs quick, tangible results to feel competent and worthy – or they may have simply become completely detached from the power and the use of the written word. This does not mean they are less creative, more logical or less 'advanced' than those who are willing to take up the pen. It simply means that the forces that get in the way of expressing first thoughts are particularly alive in them. Nicholas Carr in his book *The Shallows* writes about how digital technologies are changing our brain and making it harder for us to engage in 'old skills' such as reading books and writing.[87] Yet in Part Three we will see how once we have some warm awareness, most of us are willing to read, write, experiment and play.

Free fall writing is a practice that blocks our inner censor and helps us to access our first thoughts. In doing so we gain a window onto the world of our unconscious. Somewhere in that landscape, if we continue to write, will appear the silhouette of our 'shadow', banished, disowned or 'dark twin' self. If we look closely we may also see the golden aura surrounding the silhouette and learn to recognise it as the gold in our soul.

---

[87] Foer (2017) makes the related point that these technologies have pressed us into conformity and set us on a path to a world without private contemplation, autonomous thought or solitary introspection.

By now

You have learned a lot about how you developed into the person you are today, guided mostly by evolution, environments and experiences beyond your control. To add to this you have seen how significant your unconscious processes are in motivating and influencing your decisions. All this created the first edition of our life story.

However, you have also seen that it is possible to 're-author' your life by getting to know more about your unconscious selves. The new 'material' we discover by focusing on our body, our thought processes and our defensive routines can provide ample inspiration for creating a different story about ourselves. Using our breath to calm and relax ourselves is one of the first steps in preparing ourselves to notice, inquire, reflect and learn about who we are. When we are in this receptive state we can experiment with methods such as 'vertical descent inquiry' and 'acting as if' to discover the unconscious beliefs and assumptions that guide us. With a measure of self-compassion we may also feel courageous and curious enough to explore the dog in our cellar and free fall writing can help us prise open the heavy door and face what lies within.

We live through and by our stories so taking the time to 'read' them carefully and then edit, revise and update them is time well spent.

PART THREE:

PANNING FOR GOLD

Depth coaching – working with threat

Early on in our evolution we responded to threat by attacking (fight), escaping (flee) or submitting (freeze). These three responses still underpin our threat reaction but over time they have become much more complex. Even though we may be in less physical danger, our *threat brains* are just as active. This is because we have *consciousness* which enables us to imagine, anticipate and remember threat and in doing so increases the opportunities for *threat brain* to activate. Now we can *psychologically* live in threat even though no immediate danger exists. In addition, our dependency on and affiliation to *social groups* has given us new problems to worry about. We fear losing identity, status, wealth and belonging and the approval and acceptance of others. To cope with all this, our body and mind has evolved complex responses to help us succeed in our human environments.

In Part One we learned about three 'survival solutions' that represent human patterns of behaviour that arise in response to threat and which are no longer concerned only with basic survival. These solutions are a way of responding to experiences that could undermine our psychological and social 'life' which now represent a risk to our survival as great, perhaps, as the hungry predator once did.[88] The three survival solutions that I introduced in Part One

---

[88] WHO report 2017 suggestes that depression is the leading cause of disability and ill health worldwide: www.bit.ly/Trimotive07

were *moving against, moving towards* and *moving away* and they represent a much more complex threat response. No longer do we simply attack, run away or become still.

Moving against, which corresponds to the fight response, involves gaining mastery over people or circumstances. When we get stuck in this habit we perceive the world as highly competitive and ruthless and to survive it we dominate, control and aggressively overcome obstacles that might get in the way of our achievement and success. *Moving towards,* is a behavioural pattern which lies at the opposite end of the 'fight' spectrum and corresponds to the submissive, freeze response. We believe that other people will either protect us or be persuaded not to do us harm, so we direct all our energy towards securing their attention, love and approval. When overused, this involves appeasing, placating, complying and sacrificing or 'freezing' our own needs and wishes. *Moving away,* is all about creating an 'island' mentality and existence that enables us to survive *in spite of* others. It is a reassuring strategy because no matter what others do or don't do we remain unaffected. In unhealthy *moving away* we stop striving, expecting or seeking. We become pessimistic, cynical and resigned to our fate because it is easier that way. Our lives are without pain, perhaps, but also joyless. Remember, these descriptions represent our *threat brain* when it is unregulated by *safe brain* and have become our primary orientation to life. When used flexibly and in moderation these same solutions can be healthy. *Moving against* becomes confident, assertive and proactive. *Moving towards* becomes collaborative, consultative and adaptable. *Moving away* becomes autonomous, impartial and focused. In the following chapters our focus is on how to recognise and what to do when our *threat brain* response becomes a *problem* habit.

The three patterns comprise our *threat brain* response repertoire and we have probably tried them all out in our childhood attempts to discover the best way to survive our particular environment and circumstances. However, most of us develop a *threat brain* 'habit' where one of the three patterns dominates our response under stress. Underneath our core response the alternative strategies are available and we may resort to them when our primary solution is not working.

In considering *unhealthy threat brain* habits we see that it is not uncommon, for a bully to disintegrate in to a gibbering, pleading wreck when he meets an even more violent and aggressive 'predator' (switching from *moving against* to *moving towards*). Or we can probably think of people whom we have known to be meek, mild and selfless who suddenly turn on others and become demanding, complaining and bitter. Sometimes we refer to this as the 'passive aggressive' tendency, which describes the swing from *moving towards* to *moving against.*

My intention in the following chapters is to explore these three *threat brain* habits in more detail through the coaching stories of Maggie, Ronnie and Carl.[89] Understanding and regulating our *threat brain* habits is the starting point for developing resilience that arises from motivational integrity. From this centred state we develop greater consciousness of our motives and actions and of the impact they have on our self and others. Whilst we may not immediately change our habits, warm awareness of what we are feeling and doing reduces threat and makes it more likely that, if we wish to change, we will.

We have learned that habits are deeply rooted in our inherited and first lived experiences. We have also seen that to understand and interrupt these habits we have to dive into that past, see how it reappears and directs our unconscious processes and safely draw what we can to the surface of our experience. From there we can apply *compassionate* conscious reflection and active experimentation to adapt and evolve and increase our potential for experiencing and acting through our whole and possible self.

In sharing these stories I also hope to make a case for the value of *depth coaching* which includes an exploration of the unconscious forces influencing behaviour and sustaining the habits we wish to change. Depth coaching seeks to support profound and lasting change and to nurture healthy drive motivations by ensuring that goals and objective are informed not by *threat brain* motives but by the conscious, compassionate and wise motives emerging from *safe brain*. In organisations there are often low tolerance for methodologies which support the slow, emergent, unpredictable

---

[89] Their names and some details have been changed to protect their identity.

and nonlinear progression of human growth and change. The demand for 'objectives', 'outcomes', 'tangible results' and 'fast execution' attached to most development programmes sometimes provide useful structure and goals yet they can also suck the life blood out of experiment, play and depth, and create learning experiences that are superficial and soon forgotten.

The 'transformation' that organisations – and individuals – want from their development programmes will only come about when *consciousness* is expanded– in other words when people in the organisation begin to feel, think and behave with greater insight, accuracy and wisdom. This is achieved when we travel to the edges of what is known to us and courageously take a few more steps. Of course this provokes anxiety and, as we shall see, various expressions of reluctance. Yet we have seen throughout this book that we become more complex, conscious human beings through new *experience*. Carl Rogers, one of the founders of humanistic psychology, wrote:

> *Experience is, for me, the highest authority. The touchstone of validity is my own experience. No other person's ideas, and none of my own ideas, are as authoritative as my experience.*[90]

Just as we cannot know if something tastes good unless we have sampled at least one bite so we cannot know for sure if a method is useful unless we have engaged in it. That one bite may put us off finishing the meal but at least we have a real sense, an experience of what it is, what it offers and whether or not we want it. We cannot look to our neighbour, observe his process and extrapolate from that. We cannot find the answer in a book. We must participate through experimentation and practice to know what may be possible, useful or wanted.

If you accept, or are at least interested in the proposition that there is value in expanding our consciousness and that the unconscious exerts a strong influence on us, AND if you feel courageous and confident enough to take steps into the unknown, then the methods described in the following chapters may be worth a try.

---

[90] (Rogers, 1967)

Chapter Seven: Maggie – Moving Against

Maggie worked for a global telecoms company and was offered coaching as part of her organisation's talent management programme. She was single, ambitious, dedicated to her work and described herself as a 'pragmatist', yet underneath her elegant, corporate composure I sensed someone windblown and wild.

She was a beautiful, 39-year-old of Scottish and Italian descent with glassy blue eyes and a mane of dark hair that shone like polished mahogany. For work she twisted this feral feature into a single coil draped over her shoulder. During our work together I learned about the significance of Maggie's impeccable appearance and how it played a role in sustaining some of her *threat brain* habits.

When Maggie arrived for the first coaching session she brought with her several notebooks containing written commentaries and reflective thoughts about her staff. She wanted to become a better mentor. Great leadership, she believed, was all about developing and inspiring your people.

Childhood challenges – discovering patterns

Usually in the first session I invite clients to talk about their childhood. I ask them to say a little bit about their family of origin and the biggest challenges they faced as a child. This is not because I want to make a diagnosis, offer an interpretation or discover pathologies. It is because childhood stories are like a wallpaper pattern. As the roll unfolds the pattern repeats. The solutions I invented to survive my childhood reappear to a greater or lesser degree in my adult life as habits. This becomes a problem for me if my adult experiences call for a different approach and I don't notice or I am unable to respond. It becomes a problem for me if I am caught in a loop of recurring yet limited primary emotional and behavioural responses.

Sometimes being asked to talk about childhood comes as a surprise to clients who have imagined coaching to be a version of their management one-to-one meetings. So I explain that the purpose of these questions is to reveal patterns and to make sense of how experiences from our past unfold into and influence the present. Understanding the source of our feelings and thoughts can be useful when reviewing current strategies and considering future options.

The stories people tell always spark my curiosity, yet at this stage in our work together I don't probe deeply into their content. It takes time to nurture the quality of relationship that is open to deep inquiry. My initial contribution is to listen without judgement and to appreciate a person's courage in facing up to and surviving their challenges. In coaching, where the majority of clients are ambitious achievers, childhood challenges are often brushed off and made light of because they are not traumatic or extreme. However, as we learned in Part One, we don't need to have been abused, severely neglected or abandoned to develop survival strategies. When we are children *many* events are experienced as threatening. Moving school, divorce, conflict in the home, sibling rivalry, loneliness and failing to measure up to prescribed standards and goals are common, 'ordinary' challenges that significantly influence our developing habits. To recognise this is a very helpful step towards understanding why we react and respond as we do.

In a compassionate inquiry, personal pain, disappointment and sorrow are not judged or evaluated in terms of their severity, which is often the intention when a diagnosis or treatment is sought. The purpose of the inquiry is to surface and honour the *totality* of a person's experience and to travel beyond the polarised 'good' and 'bad' self-ratings that sustain our divided self, in order to discover the intelligence residing in our somatic and mental unconscious. Compassionate inquiry involves slowing the pace, gently inviting vulnerability, listening deeply, appreciating, calming and sharing beliefs. It is an excellent way to develop trust and depth in the relationship and it stimulates our *safe brain* capability.

When the purpose and tone of the inquiry is held within a compassionate frame, it is surprisingly easy to talk about childhood patterns and to see how they recur in our present-day experiences. Usually people enjoy discovering and expanding their self-knowledge in this way. It can be a simple yet very meaningful insight, for example, to notice that your tendency to avoid conflict as a child still plays out in your adult relationships.

A pattern, whilst sharing some similarities, is not the same as a label ('alcoholic'), a profile (ENTJ, from Myers Briggs) or a diagnosis (bi-polar depression). The latter offer precise and standardised characterisations of a person or problem and are often accompanied by pre-established development or treatment 'pathways'. A pattern simply reveals a repetitive occurrence. When we work with patterns we are attempting to discover what energises their recurrence. In other words, why does this pattern persist? What meaning, function and use does it serve?

Borrowing from the biological sciences, my working assumption tends to be that we are intelligent, adaptive beings and that our habits (highly repetitive patterns of feeling, thinking and behaving) serve a function and purpose. There are exceptions to this and we considered some of them in our exploration of how the somatic and mental unconscious can make mistakes. Nevertheless, the premise of compassionate inquiry is that the *original* purpose of our habits was to help us get on in life. So we might ask, how did avoiding conflict help me? What was the purpose of my strong competitive drive? How did my habit of taking charge support my goals and ambitions?

The *moving against, moving towards* and *moving away* patterns reveal clusters of feelings and behaviours that tell us something about our preferred *threat brain* habits. Given that most of our problems arise from a brain in threat, being able to identify this particular pattern in our lives is very helpful when we are trying to understand and regulate threat responses.

To reveal patterns both coach and coachee engage in an investigative process which involves listening, observing, inquiring, reflecting, lingering in curiosity, sense-making and experimenting. In Part Two we explored some basic practices that support this process: tuning into the intelligence of our bodies, surfacing and testing (or experimenting with) our assumptions and beliefs and getting to know our hidden or 'shadow' self through writing. Through these kinds of whole person or 'systemic' inquiries, different versions of our history begin to emerge, be explored and tested. In the stories that follow we look at how these basic practices can be developed to support a deeper inquiry through depth coaching.

Maggie's story

Once I had offered a clear purpose for exploring childhood challenges and stories, Maggie was keen to get started. Her enthusiasm to 'get on with it', as we shall see, was one of the strong forces that contributed to her *moving against* pattern which ran through many of her stories and choices.

Maggie's conscious motive for our sessions was to solve the problem of her team and she said she would do whatever it took to achieve that. However, as the sessions progressed it became clear that there were many unconscious forces operating in Maggie's life that were interfering with her plans. To surface and include them in her new adult narrative helped Maggie to 'detoxify' her *drive brain* motivations – which were fed by *threat brain* concerns – and to make significant changes in her life.

Maggie grew up a in a working-class family on the outskirts of Glasgow. Her Italian father was a violinist who, having given up all hope of an orchestral career, offered music lessons at the local schools. Her mother worked as a part-time cleaner and seamstress. Maggie had a brother and a sister who were close in years. Maggie, the youngest, was twelve years their junior. Maggie often felt like an only child, especially when her siblings left home – her sister to marry and her brother to work in a distillery on the west coast of Scotland.

Maggie's greatest childhood challenge was living in the midst of constant conflict between her parents. Her mother was a practical woman preoccupied with worries about money and the opinion of neighbours. Their house was spotlessly clean and Maggie was always immaculately dressed in clothes her mother made late at night on an old Singer sewing machine. Maggie remembered feeling comforted as a small child by the sound of the needle pumping stiches. However, as Maggie grew older, these clothes became an embarrassment. Her mother's designs had not kept up with the times and wearing them became, for a while, a deep source of shame.

Maggie's father was not practical. He still harboured dreams of becoming a musician and when he was not teaching he played the fiddle in a folk group that toured the local bars. Usually he returned very late at night. Maggie knew this because her mother sometimes allowed her to stay up and watch television. They would cuddle up on the sofa together and Maggie remembered a confusing mix of emotions. She loved being with her mother in this intimate way. However, in these moments, she also felt her mother's loneliness most strongly and this made her feel very sad.

Maggie remembered her parents drinking heavily and the verbal violence that always followed. She recalled their loud, damning attacks on each other which she sometimes arbitrated. Standing between two warring parents she learned to raise her voice, find solutions to end arguments and to physically defend herself when her father raised his hand.

Maggie said many of these fights were about her father's gambling habits. Over the years he squandered the family's savings and when Maggie was thirteen they had to sell their home and move in to a council flat. From then on, her father spiralled into alcoholic decline, sleeping late, missing appointments and brawling in the street. One by one the schools that employed him posted their 'sorry to inform you' letters which Maggie remembered him reading aloud at the kitchen table. Without a regular income and against her mother's will, he became dependent on social welfare. Maggie swore that when she grew up she would never marry, never be poor and never have children who would drain her energy and finances and then leave – as her siblings had done – without so much as a weekly phone call home.

Maggie spoke about her achievements with confidence and pride. She was the only one in the family to attend university and the only one to get out of Scotland and 'make it' in cut-throat, corporate London. According to Maggie, only the fittest survived. To be amongst the fittest, Maggie trained her body in the gym, cultivated her mind (she had recently been awarded a distinction for her MBA) and spent long hours expanding her online social and professional networks.

As Maggie talked I was struck by how flawless her current life seemed to be. Here was a beautiful, intelligent career woman living in style with, it would seem, abundant friends and a thriving social life. Yet it was also clear that an undercurrent of hostility and anger ran throughout her story. The need to battle, compete, overcome and win are strong indications that a person's habitual – although not exclusive – response to threat is *moving against*. I wondered whether, if this was so, it was a contributing factor in her workplace challenges.

I asked Maggie to tell me a little more about what she hoped to get from coaching. She said that she had been promoted to manage a 'difficult' group of mostly male, senior sales executives. She knew that to meet their high targets – which she was determined to do – the team needed to collaborate and share intelligence about customers. This would help with cross-selling and the exchange of best practice. However, the team members were focused on their individual targets and were competitive and hostile towards each other. Maggie felt that they had isolated themselves from crucial parts of the business and as a result were making unnecessary errors in product specifications and scope. It was not unusual for her sales team to sell products and services that could not be delivered to price, scale or schedule. Maggie wanted to help the team become more cohesive and to agree, and work to, a shared objective.

Maggie's coaching goals were well thought through and purposeful, yet as I listened I noticed the way her voice gradually lost energy as she talked about her team. It was as if she was telling me what she thought she *should* tell me and not what truly mattered to her. Often when we start speaking in the tone or language of 'should' we can be sure our inner critic is at play, judging, analysing and evaluating. Our inner critic voices many of our *threat brain* concerns and is born when we start to develop language to symbolise and mediate our experience.

Karen Horney referred to the 'tyranny of the should' and described a host of 'inner dictates' that propel us along a narrow path in life. The 'shoulds' are contained in the many demands and standards which our inner critic upholds. They are they often rigid, impossible to achieve and operate with a 'supreme disregard' for what we are actually able to feel or do at present. Their purpose is to ensure we conform to what society and others expect of us and therefore minimise the threat of rejection and abandonment.

You should compete and win this contract, our inner critic says, because somewhere in our experience we have learned that competing and winning secures us approval and belonging.

In this moment I thought Maggie's 'shoulds' were instructing her on how to conduct a 'proper' coaching session and how to be a 'good' leader. 'Succeeding' in coaching and leading may well have brought Maggie some rewards but I wondered whether these kinds of successes were what truly mattered to her.

Humble noticing

When I have a strong feeling or reaction to something a client says or does I usually talk about it with them to see if it has any shared meaning. I call this *'humble noticing'* and it is offered in the same spirit as Edgar Schein's 'humble inquiry':

> *...the art of drawing someone out, of asking questions to which you do not know the answer, of building a relationship based on curiosity and interest in the other person.*[91]

Humble inquiry is a skill we can learn and practice. It is the same with humble noticing. When we engage in humble noticing we learn to share what we feel, see, and hear, not as 'truth' or with the intention to define and determine a person or situation, but rather to create transparency and openness in the relationship and to encourage a humble inquiry that is rooted in the emotional intelligence of our bodies.

---

[91] (Schein, 2013)

As we have seen, the somatic unconscious is an important source of our knowing and it is unwise to ignore the significance of its intuitive, preverbal sensations. Frequent pauses to ponder feelings and meanings that are occurring *in the moment* offer opportunities for both coach and coachee to clarify and deepen understanding. Noticing in-the-moment sensations helps us to pay attention to experience which is often missed or ignored. Without acknowledgement or 'conscious attending' this information returns to its unconscious source and is hard to retrieve later. It is a bit like waking up from a vivid dream and then, because our mind quickly turns to the events of the day, the dream is lost. As the busy conscious mind carries us along in its flow, events and experiences stored more deeply in our memories sink and disappear.[92]

To honour my in-the-moment sensations, I shared with Maggie the energy I felt when she talked about her family and how I noticed that although her description of the coaching goals was clear and appropriate I didn't feel the same vigour and enthusiasm when she spoke of them. I said I'd like to know more about what brought vitality and meaning in her life and to explore whether that might be a starting place for our work together.

For the first time since entering the room Maggie looked uncertain and apprehensive. In the silence that followed I noticed her posture change. Initially upright and on the edge of her chair, she slowly slumped further into the cushions. Resting her head back she closed her eyes and started massaging the back of her neck with a manicured hand. When she spoke again she said, *"I feel so tired".*

I asked her to describe where in her body she felt the tiredness most. After some thought, she put her hand to her chest and described the tightness and pain she felt in that area. The word and image that came to my mind as she spoke was 'heartache' and again, I shared my noticing with her. To my surprise, her eyes welled with

---

[92] If you want to remember your dreams a simple tip is, on waking up, lie very still and don't talk. Stay in a half sleep state and replay what you remember. That allows the dream to be noted, processed and stored by our explicit memory system and is thus retained and available to consciousness.

tears and she began to silently weep. For a few minutes she sat, head down, shoulders rising and falling and her body shifting this way and that in what seemed like a contorted effort to control and prevent that which so strongly wanted to be released. She seemed angry with herself as she roughly wiped away the tears that she knew would leave messy, black streaks. When Maggie was able to speak again she began to tell me about the recent break up of 'yet another' short-term relationship and the increasing fear she felt about growing old, alone and childless.

Maggie had little faith in her ability to form reciprocal loving relationships. She had sought help for this yet had been unable to make significant shifts in her 'relating style'. A therapist, she said, had once diagnosed her with Narcissistic Personality Disorder. She knew that people at work called her a perfectionist and a slave driver. Maggie felt hated and criticised by the world and her response, it seemed, was to hate it back.

Again we can see the pattern of *move against* appearing as Maggie responds to challenges in her life. In this cluster of *threat brain* behaviours, we often develop an impenetrable body/mind armour that creates an aura of invincibility and toughness. Problems become invitations to conquer and control. When we *move against* we want to master a situation or other people and any sign of weakness in our self is perceived as a threat to this solution. Being vulnerable and thus open to reciprocal love and friendship is one such weakness and therefore avoided or rejected. When our solutions remain unconscious we act out these behaviours automatically even though their consequences often hurt rather than protect us.

Psycho-education – demystifying theory

Robert Leahy, a cognitive behavioural psychologist, describes the value of *collaborative* problem-solving and the importance of educating or 'socialising' the client in the intervention to be used.[93] This is sometimes called *psycho-education* and it can be useful when motivated not by the need to show my expertise as a coach, but by

---

[93] (Leahy, 2001)

my desire to *learn with* the client. For me, it means talking about and demystifying the theories, methods and approaches that inform the way I work *and* inviting the client to challenge, add to or reject them. One perspective I share and which I have described in this book, is how our *threat brain* habits can unconsciously influence and trap us in unhelpful feelings, thoughts and behaviours. This belief arises out of my personal and professional experience and research and informs my practice – so it is best out in the open!

When Maggie described her hostile feelings towards those who had failed her in relationships and her strategies for overcoming these feelings of rejection and hurt I once more sensed her tendency to respond to threat by *moving against*. I offered a description of *moving against* as a pattern of feelings and behaviours that can be aligned with the 'fight' response of the threatened brain and explained how this pattern differed from the flee or freeze response. I asked Maggie to remember a recent time when she felt anxiety or fear and to describe what her response was. She talked about her recent break-up and described how she had become extremely angry with her ex-partner. She had thrown a glass at him as he left her apartment and it narrowly missed his head.

Maggie remembered many instances of arguing, controlling and dominating others and could see how, at those times, she had felt under stress or anxious. She also recognised that sometimes she tried to hide her hostile emotions and as a result confused people, particularly work colleagues, by sending mixed messages. At work, Maggie was very polished and knew the right things to say and do[94] yet her body language and off-guard facial expressions often suggested the opposite and conveyed anger or disapproval. She reflected on whether this created distrust and confusion in her relationships and how the mismatch between what she felt and what she said might be experienced as dishonest and inauthentic.

All *threat brain* responses increase our stress levels and can benefit from soothing intervention. However, the 'fight' response is

---

[94] People whose solution is to master and conquer can also be very charming. They have learned that charm will get them what they want. This charm, whilst alluring, is often experienced by others as inauthentic and/or manipulative.

particularly stressful as it creates a motivation to aggress or dominate others which potentially puts us in *more* danger and triggers even higher levels of threat. A threatened brain trying to deal with another threatened brain is potentially explosive and usually highly unproductive. Thus, for those people whose survival strategy is primarily to *move against,* the soothing techniques of calm breathing, visualisation and time-out are particularly useful. When calm, the *safe brain* functions more effectively and enables us to notice and soften the tone of our self-talk from one of criticism to compassion and appreciation. Being kind to ourselves triggers a whole host of bodily reactions that includes being more able to perceive others as friendly or neutral rather than hostile. This is very useful when we are trying to negotiate difficult relationships. A calm voice, an appreciative perspective and a genuinely well-intentioned desire to work things through is the best starting point in a challenging conversation. Thus, self-compassion supports compassion towards others and reduces our urge to fight and argue – or conquer, master, solve, fix and win.

Warm awareness – insight without compassion hurts

Initially what mattered most to Maggie was the diagnosis she had been given by a previous therapist. Being told she had a Narcissistic Personality Disorder (NPD) had been both a relief and a shock. A relief because the explanation made sense and a shock because it seemed very negative and highly untreatable. She wondered whether the diagnosis had broader implications for how she related to others more generally, not just in intimate relationships.

Most of the literature she had read about NPD suggested poor prognosis. In other words, people rarely change. The same is true for those diagnosed as perfectionists and other disorders involving very defensive, rigid patterns of feeling, thought and behaviour. From our earlier discussion we know that our survival solutions, which become our *threat brain* habits, *are* tenacious and difficult to alter. Yet we are also learning that there *is* a way that can take us beyond survival. This is the way of *safe brain* where we begin by *warming up* our self-talk with kind, appreciative commentary.

When Maggie spoke or thought about herself as narcissistic she could hear her inner critic spring into action confirming the negative list of traits she had been diagnosed with and scolding her for being such a despicable, unlovable person. Our inner critic agrees with all this negativity as a way of scaring us into action. *"Work harder, be the best dressed, cleverest, strongest, most successful. That way they will never know the truth,"* it says.

The purpose of action, when driven by our inner critic, is to ensure that others never discover 'the truth' of how inadequate, incompetent and unworthy we feel deep down. If they do, we will be seen as weak and powerless and therefore more susceptible to abandonment or attack. These feelings of shame and self-doubt have probably been seeded in childhood and may reside in our deep memory. We may not be consciously aware of their influence. However, if we listen carefully to the way we talk to ourselves we will soon discover the individual characteristics of our shame-based feelings and the degree to which they impact our life. This is indicated by the tone of our self-talk and whether we are being motivated by an encouraging, kind voice or one which demands, threatens and commands.

In Maggie's case the NPD diagnosis provided 'evidence' of her unworthy character. To defend against the potential consequences of being 'found out' Maggie's inner critic told her to work harder, fight tougher and win more. These relentless demands exhausted Maggie and led to bouts of depression which, in turn, prompted Maggie's critical voice to scream louder. *These are weak emotions,* it told her, and weak emotions as we know are unacceptable to a person whose primary reaction to threat is to *move against.*

In this way, Maggie was caught in an unpleasant conflict between her need to love and be loved and her *threat-drive brain* strategy (arising from the belief that she was not loveable) to conquer and overcome. The more this conflict continued the more threatened Maggie felt and the more she resorted to the 'solutions' triggered by threat and resulting in toxic drive. Maggie was caught in a vicious loop. Yet her *moving against* solution was showing signs of wear, which is why she felt so tired and her tears were hard to contain.

To interrupt this internal war I offered a compassionate reframe of the diagnosis. Yes, you probably do behave in ways that conform to the narcissistic type, I said, and it is equally true that these behaviours have been *helpful* and *rewarding* to you for much of your life. When you were young, I reminded her, you managed the tensions at home by mediating arguments, taking a Saturday job to earn extra money, defending your mother from physical attack and focusing on your studies as part of your escape plan. All these strategies involved *mastering* a situation and *overcoming* difficulty.

Maggie felt fear and anxiety when her parents argued, when the rent man came to call or when her mother suffered a nervous breakdown. When this happened, she coped by fixing, solving, working harder and cultivating her independence. As a child, Maggie had acted with courage, tenacity and bravery to get through her particular challenges and these solutions formed part of her skilled and successful character repertoire.

Later, when Maggie began to practise this kind of appreciative reframing, she wrote a letter of gratitude to her younger self. In it she thanked her child self for all the innovative and brave actions she had taken to survive these difficult times. At the end of the letter the adult Maggie explained to the child Maggie that now she can rest for a while and let the mature, grown-up self look after things. This would involve learning some new ways of coping with threat and anxiety which, Maggie assured her young self, she *was* doing. She stopped evaluating herself in terms of good and bad and instead started asking "*are these solutions, once so helpful, still useful to me?*"

Diagnosing Maggie as narcissistic or perfectionist and identifying her moving against pattern may increase her awareness and help her notice and manage these behaviours. However, learning from Maggie's experience, we see that awareness without *warmth* is likely to trigger our *threat brain* and entrench us further in our problem habits. We need compassion to stimulate our *safe brain* so we can reflect deeply on what we are learning and stay open to, and trusting of, observations and feedback from others.

Before Maggie was able to articulate appreciative self-talk and writing she spent some time learning about and practising the basics of self-compassion described in Chapter Six. Those of us who have a strong inner critic and who are lacking in self-compassion cannot, at first, hear the harsh and punitive tones we drown ourselves in. My role, while she was developing her compassionate core, was to listen out for her inner critic, and to counter it gently with reminders of her strength and fortitude.

When Maggie started to explore her unconscious processes compassionately she learned about the source and strength of her habits and reflected on whether these habits were worth holding on to. In particular, Maggie was able to make compassionate connections between her childhood experience and current life that helped her reconsider how she dealt with conflict, how she related to her body and how she might integrate creativity into her pragmatic and corporate ambitions.

These connections enabled her to nurture a part of herself whose growth had been stunted. Karen Horney called this our 'real self'. Others have referred to this self that we rediscover and accept as our 'true',[95] 'actualised',[96] 'inherent'[97] or 'individuated'[98] self. I call it our *possible* self to avoid the problem of whether any part of us is more or less 'real' or 'true' and to emphasise that what may be *possible* is not necessarily a) probable or b) desirable. In other words, we may never discover more than we already know and even if we do we may choose to ignore or turn away from those discoveries in order to conserve our habits (problematic or not) and stay within the boundaries of what is familiar and known. A compassionate approach encourages the attempt and the effort to become more fully conscious *and* is accepting of other choices and outcomes too.

Maggie's possible self, always with her but deeply hidden, had a different understanding of how to be with conflict, physicality and

---

[95] (Winnicott, 1973)
[96] (Rogers, 1967)
[97] (Hollis, 1993)
[98] (Jung, 1961)

creativity. Our work was to surface this knowing and allow it to openly and helpfully shape and influence her life.

Holding the tension – from fixing to enabling

Once Maggie had learned the basics of self-compassion and started to practise this at work she noticed two important changes. First, that she genuinely felt less critical of others and second that her team members, who once simply wanted to 'download' information and leave, were now more willing to engage in difficult, strategic conversations. This occasionally led to heated discussions and differences of opinion in the team which, to her surprise, turned out to be insightful and produced some new thinking.

However, Maggie felt tense in these meetings. She continued to see her role as group arbitrator and frequently intervened with 'helpful' suggestions that cut short the conversations and resulted in what she began to understand as *passive resistance*. In other words, team members appeared to achieve consensus but in reality were simply agreeing to keep the peace whilst acting out their individual strategies privately and in their own departments. Maggie could see that her underlying fear of conflict was preventing the team from engaging in healthy dialogues that needed more time and a greater tolerance of discomfort. The result of this was ongoing fragmentation in the team and recurring problems relating to collaboration and productivity.

Maggie quickly made the connection between the way she tried to survive conflict at home and the methods she used as a team leader. She had learned that to survive conflict she needed to intervene and resolve. This childhood habit had evolved into a belief that good leaders should deal with disagreements by getting a quick resolution and taking action to ensure teams stay productive and cohesive. This belief is helpful for teams who experience danger, emergency or chaos yet in her industry and department this was rarely, if ever, the case.

Maggie's bold, confident approach in a competitive male environment *had* helped her survive. However, it was equally true – and this took some time for Maggie to recognise – that many of her interventions were making *no difference*. Arguments and hostilities recurred and sometimes got worse and team productivity was always below target.

As Maggie became more self-compassionate she was able to accept that the conflict between her parents was not her fault. Nor was it her fault that her naïve interventions did not save her parents' marriage. Maggie recalled with great sadness an evening when, very late and very tearful, she had taken each of her parents' hands and joined them together. "*Now make up!*" she had ordered. Despite her efforts, her parents separated and eventually divorced. In the same way, Maggie started to observe how conflicts she thought she had resolved in her team continued. She noticed her team hiding truths from her in an effort to appease and appear consensual and saw hostilities resulting from blocked or unspoken differences causing disengagement and a 'why bother?' attitude. She started to practise 'holding the tension' when conflict arose and resisting jumping in and fixing disagreements.

In her first attempts at 'stepping back' some team members experienced her as aloof and disengaged. They were unused to this version of Maggie. To develop her skill she practised 'warming up' her style by: voicing compassionate observations (I notice we are struggling with this client request), by being curious and inquiring in a non-accusatory way (is this conversation useful to us?), by owning her contribution to the problems (I realise I jump in and try and solve the problem too quickly) and sometimes by ending meetings not with an action point but with a simple, non-judgemental acceptance of the dilemmas facing them (this is a complex problem and it is not surprising we are finding it hard to resolve).

Slowly Maggie learned to facilitate more genuine exchanges between people without becoming threatened and resorting to her old habits. When she felt the urge to control and prematurely resolve she would practise the deep breathing exercises and visualisations that helped her feel safe and calm. By understanding that conflict was not her *fault* she was able to resist the desire to 'make things better'.

Accepting the gifts – learning to forgive

Maggie was always immaculately dressed in the latest, expensive fashions. With the advantage of natural beauty and posture she cut a glamorous and somewhat intimidating figure. Again, it did not take long for Maggie to make a connection between her mother's obsession with outward appearance and her own. As a child, Maggie learned that to avoid criticism and rejection she had to manicure, perfect and maintain a flawless and *conventionally* acceptable image. She had to show the outside world that things were going well, even when they were not. Yet as Maggie grew older her mother's version of 'well dressed' started to conflict with that of her peers. Maggie described the shame she felt at having to wear hand-knitted cardigans and skirts that were never the right length yet she did not want to upset mother by talking about it. Soon the teasing at school began and the threat of being rejected by her friends became stronger than the threat of disappointing her mother. Maggie found herself a job, studied fashion magazines and with her own money started to re-invent her wardrobe. She remembered bundling her old clothes into a black bin bag and with growing boldness instructing her mother to take them to the charity shop. Her mother quietly complied and the Singer sewing machine fell silent.

Not only did Maggie create a new image, she also anticipated trends and was the first to wear clothes that later became popular. Her looks and figure ensured that this brought her the admiration and status she craved. However, this local fame did not make Maggie feel good about herself. Maggie described how she had always had a very poor body image, how she struggled at times with binge eating and fast dieting and how her strongest and most vicious self-criticisms were directed at her appearance.

How does it come to be that such a beautiful woman lives in hatred of her body and face and that no amount of praise and compliment makes a difference? The simple truth is that our inner critic, the one that berates, shames and bullies us, is not there to deliver an accurate appraisal of life or help us feel good about ourselves. It exists to keep us on our toes, to keep us running and hiding from or fighting that which we deeply fear and to make sure we conform to the rules and expectations that are most likely to secure our belonging. Our inner critic is only interested in ensuring we survive; it is not interested in the *quality* of our life. Those of us driven by our inner critic and stuck in the loops of our survival strategies rarely experience inner peace, acceptance or contentment. Neither do we feel the vital energy (healthy drive) that comes from our full and unique participation in the world.

To interrupt this loop we need to understand and soothe the fears that keep it spinning. Often these fears operate at an unconscious level. We don't know what *exactly* we are afraid of and our conscious mind may misinterpret our fears. Maggie's conscious fears were related to being poor, being rejected for lacking social standing and being let down by people (mostly men) who were or might turn out to be weak and inadequate. However, at a deeper level, different fears, operating through unconscious processes, were disruptively influencing Maggie. Using free fall writing, metta meditations and voice dialogues, Maggie was able to get closer to these fears and, in doing so, begin to alleviate them.

Using the free fall writing method described in Chapter Six, Maggie explored her deepest fears. Her stem phrases included; 'my deepest fear', 'fearless' and 'when I am afraid'. However, her discoveries surfaced in less direct ways and appeared throughout her writing, first as themes loosely connected but gradually, as her writing continued, showing strong and recurring messages. Her fear of being found out and rejected was, for example, not only connected to shame around her family's status and behaviour but also to its opposite – of being held, embraced and submerged within the family unit. In her writing she rediscovered a deep love that bound the family and a fear of being caught within it. To avoid entrapment she had created a terrible version of her family, one which gave her reason to leave and establish herself as an independent and capable woman. In the story that got her out of Scotland and poverty her parents had nothing to contribute or offer. This belief generated an energy to survive in a world where no one would or could help her.

Maggie feared that if she allowed herself to openly love – and accept love from – her parents she would experience a vulnerability too painful and sad to bear. It would weaken her. Maggie could see how the story she had been telling herself about a hostile and incompetent world was fuelling her 'toxic drive' and interfering in her ability to form enduring relationships.

Events and people from our past may influence, but do not 'cause', our habits. It is our own repetitions of thought and behaviour, carried in and acted out through our 'stories', that shape our preferences. Telling a new story changes the way we perceive and interact with our world. For Maggie and others caught in *threat brain* habits, the most significant 'theme' to write into our story is self-compassion. In doing so, we reactivate our *safe brain* capabilities, diminish our inner critic and integrate threat experiences into a wider narrative.

Remembering the three components of self-compassion (Chapter 5) we see Maggie lacking not only kind self-talk but also feelings of common humanity; in other words the willingness and ability to honour the struggles and to forgive the imperfections that all of us experience and share. Maggie developed a greater sense of common humanity by reflecting on the qualities and gifts her parents had given her.

The work we did during this part of her development drew on the ideas of Bert Hellinger, a family therapist who writes about the significance of forgiveness in the healing process. Hellinger saw time and again the suffering of those who could not forgive their parents and who were unable to accept the gifts, no matter how small, that their parents had given.

> But feel what happens in the soul, when you imagine children saying to their parents, 'what you gave me first of all wasn't the right thing and secondly, it wasn't enough. You still owe me.' What do children have from parents when they feel that way? Nothing. And what do the parents have from their children? Also nothing. Such children cannot separate from their parents. Their accusations and demands tie them to their parents so that, although they are

> *bound to their parents, the children have no parents. Then*
> *they feel empty, needy and weak.*[99]

The most significant gift that her parents had given Maggie, in different ways, was the gift of creativity. She had a natural talent for writing, composing and drawing. She knew that her father's love of music and her mother's fascination with art and design had silently shaped her developing self. Maggie began to notice how these creative talents appeared in her life. Her work journals were a colourful and beautifully written account of team life, her clothes and even the way she coiled and plaited her magnificent hair showed an eye for design and everywhere in her life – although she had not seen it – was music. In her salsa classes, in the classical music she played in her office, in the biography of Billy Holiday she kept in her bag. Even her silk-covered journal was embroidered with musical notes. Contrast this version of Maggie with the one who came into my office describing herself as a pragmatist wanting to increase sales targets by controlling team dynamics.

Metta – or loving kindness – meditation is a practice used to develop our compassionate feelings towards others. It can develop our capacity to embrace common humanity, the third core component of self-compassion. Through loving kindness meditation we can practise accepting and forgiving the flaws and imperfections in ourselves and others and begin to see that they *define* us as individuals. We have been sculpted into works of art by the knocks, cuts and breakings in our lives. I introduced Maggie to this practice and over many months, for just a few minutes a day, she meditated on the *qualities* she had inherited and the *appreciation* she felt towards her parents.[100]

Towards the end of our work together Maggie brought in a small, tissue-wrapped parcel. She placed it on the coffee table in my office and for a while we sat in silence. There was obviously a great significance attached to this object. It turned out to be a nightdress that her mother had sewn for her when she was seven years old. It

---

[99] (Hellinger, 1998)
[100] (Salzburg, 2005); A guided practice audio version of Loving Kindness meditation.

was an exquisite garment made from pale cream silk and hemmed in delicate lace and something you might find displayed in an exhibition of antique clothing. Maggie unfolded the nightdress and held it up for me to admire. The woman who had sewn this, her mother, was clearly extremely talented. Everything she made, Maggie told me, had been of this quality – even those 'old fashioned' clothes she had contemptuously stuffed into the black bin bag.

During that session I noticed Maggie looked different. I remarked on this and she smiled broadly. No make-up! As I looked more closely I could see that even without mascara and lipstick Maggie was captivating. She wanted to try a more relaxed look. This meant flat shoes instead of six-inch heels, clothes that flowed in layers (some of which she had started to make) instead of tailored suits and less make-up. Once I even saw her in glasses and was delighted by her casual, shame-free admission that her contact lenses were too painful to wear that day!

Maggie's softening in relation to appearance had an impact on her team. The discussion about 'dress-down Fridays' was revived. Previously Maggie had not been an advocate of casual dress at *any* time in the calendar, let alone every Friday! Customers were always visiting the premises, she argued, and her sales team should be prepared for this. After a lengthy and honest conversation with her team Maggie accepted feedback that sometimes customers found the dress code overbearing. Maggie discovered that several members of the team had been asked by their customers to visit premises in 'less formal' attire. That they had not felt able to tell her this up until now was a great learning for Maggie.

Whilst her suggestion to bring in dress-down Fridays was seen as somewhat clichéd the team agreed to trial it. They also agreed that they should pay more attention to the context in which they were working and dress in ways that would best accord with their customer. Later Maggie reported that dress-down Fridays were often followed by a drink after work with most team members dropping by. This was a significant step forward for a team that had previously avoided social gatherings and maintained a strong demarcation between private and work life. It was also not the kind of 'pragmatic' solution Maggie might have first considered when trying to develop stronger team bonds.

Voice dialogues

As well as free fall writing and metta meditation Maggie experimented with a method called *voice dialogue* which helped her to learn more about her defensive unconscious. She discovered this method in one of the books[101] I recommended to her and wanted my help to try it out.

In voice dialogue we speak with parts of our self that we do not like, or which we fear. That self is invited or called forth with a simple sentence such as, "*may I talk to that part of Maggie which wants to be all powerful?*" or "*may I talk to that part of Maggie which hates men?*". We then speak with the coach or therapist through that voice. This is difficult work requiring experienced facilitation. However, when used correctly it supports a direct meeting with the shadow self that can be very powerful.

Voice dialogues are safer to use once we have gained some insight into our habits and have cultivated a degree of self-compassion. That way we are able to tolerate and accept whatever else we may find in our defensive unconscious. It is the difference between being overwhelmed by what jumps at us when we open the cellar door and being able to meet it – albeit on its own terms for a while. If our dark side is encountered when we are very vulnerable and unsupported or without recognition of its affirmative potential, our defence system will go into overdrive and *threat brain* habits will intensify.

Maggie wanted to use voice dialogue to talk with that part of herself which distrusted people and rejected intimacy. This could be described as a *moving away threat brain* habit and, as I have said, can co-exist as secondary or tertiary response underneath the primary or dominant pattern – which in Maggie's case was *moving against*.

---

[101] (Stone & Winkelman, 1989)

In the dialogues Maggie's suspicious, independent self described many, real events in her life where people had let her down. This part of Maggie could not bring herself to depend on others. At the same time she heard, through speaking aloud as this self, her own self-fulfilling prophecies at work. In believing that others were not dependable she treated them as lesser beings and in doing so contributed to the relationship's demise.

In Part One we explored how early attachment relationships can influence the way we relate to others as adults and how difficult it can be to interrupt these habits. Maggie did not begin a new relationship during the time we worked together. What did change though was the way she experienced her solitude. Her fear of being alone diminished as a different part of her – her possible self – began to emerge. This self became visible as Maggie began to experiment with her creative energy and to experience the 'self-forgetting' that happens in moments of total absorption and flow.

Creativity and Self-Forgetting

The final development in Maggie's coaching story and the one that is most ongoing, was her search to discover and nurture the creative energy within her. As we have seen, Maggie was already engaging in creative activities although these were not consciously acknowledged or given priority in her life. In her mind she had separated 'pragmatism' and 'creativity' and her *threat brain* habits promoted the former as a better way to survive in the world. Once Maggie learned to soothe her *threat brain* she was able to consider and experience how pragmatism and creativity could co-exist.

To begin with she made an intention to be more fully present in her dance classes and to reflect on how dancing contributed to her expressive life. After a few weeks Maggie told me that she was going to give up the salsa classes. She had joined, she said, not because she loved dancing but because she wanted to meet men and this was no longer a primary motivation in her life.

She was very interested in how art might enable self-expression and discovery and she experimented with several forms including clay sculpting and wood carving. By signing up to a few short courses and fully immersing herself in each experience she soon discovered a distinct and powerful love of oil painting. The smells, textures and techniques transported her, she said, into another world.

No art is produced when a person is in thrall to the inner critic. In the moment in which great work emerges, the critic and the observing, analytic self are silent or 'forgotten',[102] enabling a person to draw from the well of their unconscious knowing which holds unique insight, expression and truth. This was Maggie's experience. Her paintings, which she photographed for me to see, were mostly desolate mountain and lakeside landscapes that reminded me of her Scottish and even Italian ancestry. When I pointed this out Maggie was delighted. It gave her the idea to travel for a while to these places that she had visited or heard about as a child. Her father had often spoken of the northern Italian lakes and the walks he enjoyed as a boy. I know that Maggie later visited the place he was born and stayed for some time developing her art. I also suspect that the photo she sent me, some while ago now, of a dark skinned, smiling Italian in the foreground of the magnificent Garda mountains, might have been her partner. I'd like to think so any way.

Maggie still works in the telecoms industry although for a different company and in a more senior role. The articles and news stories that she circulates on LinkedIn are mostly about the value of creativity in innovation and how self-compassion nurtures open dialogue and grows resilience.

---

[102] See Lewis Hyde's *The Gift* which argues for the importance of creativity in our increasingly money-driven society.

Chapter Eight: Carl – Moving Away

Carl was referred to me for coaching by Anne, an HR business partner supporting an operational division of a global energy company. The Vice President of that division had approached her to discuss a talented employee – Carl – whose 'personality issues' were getting in the way of his career development. The VP wanted to promote Carl to a senior management role but felt that he lacked 'people skills' and was often withdrawn and perceived as moody. This was a shame, he said, because Carl's industry expertise could be put to good use in developing others.

Carl was a tall, thin man, in his late forties. His pale features gave him a slightly ghostly appearance and behind his delicate, frameless glasses I noticed silver grey eyes that looked inward, deflecting the world. Every time I met him he would be wearing a version of the same dark blue suit, a starched white shirt and a pale blue unpatterned tie. His white cuffs were visible half an inch below his jacket sleeve and I could see he wore polished silver bird cuff links.

Carl had a PhD in nuclear physics and more than twenty years' experience in the energy industry. His role was to advise on large-scale new-build projects. His work took him across the globe and his insight and expertise were in high demand. Mostly his work was to review evidence and recommendations and to produce viability reports. Now the VP wanted Carl to take a 'people role' and head up a team of consultants providing a complex range of services to a new client in China. The role required excellent interpersonal skills to manage the diverse professional groups involved in the project and mediate the many intercultural differences. The VP had given Carl six months to show he was capable of taking on the role. In the interim Carl had been assigned to lead a team of eight on a smaller project in the UK. To encourage and support him, the VP was prepared to offer weekly coaching and any other training Carl felt he needed.

Reframing reluctance

Over the years I have worked with many clients who do not want to take part in a 'personal growth' process. Of these, I can remember a few – and they number no more than four or five across a long career – with whom I have experienced a mutual dislike, mistrust and a strong intuition that the relationship would not evolve and enable either of us to fully enter into the work. As it happened none of these clients returned for a second session, partly due, I suspect, to my own lack of enthusiasm for the work. It is difficult to say much more about the unconscious processes that may have been operating between us to create this brief and mutual disinclination, although I have some personal insights about my own aversion and projections relating to a certain type of resilient scorn.

Thankfully these encounters are very rare. Usually I am curious about and able to work with the 'bad vibes' from angry, suspicious, bored, cynical, embarrassed and hostile clients. I have learned to cultivate my own resilience through reframing 'reluctance' not as a slight against me personally but as a *threat brain* reaction that appears in all three of our survival solutions. Reluctance from this perspective can be understood as *the fear of losing one's familiar and trusted method of coping*. This fear is understandably triggered in a coaching or therapeutic context where our habits are revealed and questioned. Whilst this is to be expected it is nevertheless a frightening prospect when, to begin with, no alternative way of living has yet been discovered.

How is reluctance expressed? In *moving against* the client may be angry and impatient about wasting time in a process that is highly unlikely (they believe) to result in anything new or productive. In *moving away* the client works hard to maintain emotional distance which involves withholding information about themselves that makes the work almost impossible. In *moving towards* a person may fear letting the coach down and thus becomes falsely appreciative, over-compliant and suddenly, problem-free.

In all three expressions of reluctance the client is protecting their known way of managing threat by raising the bar so high that the likelihood of change (experienced as fear of the unknown) becomes impossible. The 'high bar' in *moving against* requires, for example, change to be dramatic and quick – the problem must be overcome swiftly. In *moving away,* change must happen magically without the client's involvement – the problem is dissolved through an intellectual, emotionally detached discourse. In *moving towards,* change is dependent on the degree to which the coach can show unfaltering love – the problem is absorbed in the powerful union between coach and client. Of course, change rarely happens like this, yet for the reluctant client unless it does, the whole process is called into question.

A compassionate approach does not require a person to be willing, 'ready', enthusiastic, realistic or committed. Instead the work begins with the assumption that a person is stuck partly or wholly *because* they are caught in a *threat brain* loop. Thus all the emotions and thoughts that define *threat brain* experience need to be recognised and tolerated and then understood in terms of the patterns they reveal. In some ways, most of us are 'reluctant clients' when it comes to letting go of our habits.

Usually people express a *threat brain motif* that represents one of the three solutions. However, as we have already seen in Maggie's story, whilst individual experience is patterned it is also *kaleidoscopic* in that, depending on context, it sometimes mixes and radiates the colours of all three solutions. To begin with, though, it is useful to identify the dominant habits and work with those.

Approaching slowing – interrupting the desire to flee

Carl's *threat brain* habit was to *move away* from people. He cultivated a detached, aloof persona and ensured emotional distance from others. This meant he avoided or prevented encounters that might generate feelings of *any* kind whether they

173

be love, hate, excitement or fear. In the coaching relationship, those of us who *move away* present particular challenges – not least because coaching is felt as the ultimate intrusion on the privacy we so assiduously protect. Attempts to surface autobiographical details trigger a *threat brain* response that often results in us disengaging and dropping out of the process.

In our first few sessions, Carl's *moving away* tendency was very apparent in his short, vague answers, his long silences, his tendency to stare out of the window and check his watch, his unwillingness to share any autobiographical details and his clear statement that he didn't feel a need to change anything about himself. He told me that he was obliged to attend these sessions in order to secure a pending promotion. He then sat back and fixed his steely eyes upon me. This is a very typical starting point for those who *move away* and the more I learn about *threat brain* patterns the less I feel affronted or daunted by such disengagement. When *safe brain* is active we are able to express our opposition or differences in a respectful and open way. In its absence we often resort to the indirect, defensive and manipulative strategies of *threat brain* and often we are not even conscious we are doing so.

Assuming Carl was to some degree feeling threatened, and therefore not wanting to aggravate this further, I decided not to ask him to talk about his childhood. This would invite a level of intimacy, I thought, that would, for him, be far too uncomfortable. It is usually only when I sense a strong *move away* tendency that I hold back on inquiry of this kind. Instead, I invited him to share with me any personal and contextual information that might help us work on his 'promotion problem'. By situating the problem externally and thus more impersonally and by inviting him to choose his topic, I hoped to establish a safe enough space for him to participate. Mostly Carl talked about the company and its plans to attract new business in China. He also told me a few things about himself which strengthened my initial impressions.

Carl was proud of being self-sufficient. He described himself as resourceful, prudent and independent. In reality this meant Carl had few friends, no partner or children and, he said, he liked it this way. His father was no longer alive and his mother, whom he rarely visited or spoke to, lived a few hundred miles away in the southwest of England. Unsurprisingly, Carl's guard went up when I asked him (given he had raised the subject) to say more about his family life. He said he didn't remember much about it but in his estimation it was probably fairly normal and uneventful.

We know that the purpose of a compassionate inquiry is to stimulate *safe brain* as much possible. When the *safe brain* is functioning a person will be much more willing and capable of deep thought, imagination, reflection and the consideration of alternatives, plans and possibilities. The starting point for this, as we saw in Maggie's story, is to acknowledge the positive function of a *threat brain* habit. With Carl, I expressed curiosity about the subjective or personal *value* of his particular way of relating to himself and others and mentioned the spiritual and philosophical traditions that espoused independence, solitude and celibacy (his values) as the *highest* forms of human development. My intention was to emphasise the possibility that his behaviours were *useful* and had helped him succeed in life. Carl engaged enthusiastically in this intellectual discussion which deflected attention away from his personal story and suggested that we might solve the problem of his promotion through reason and discourse alone.

Moving away is the 'flee' component of the threat response and Carl seemed in flight throughout our first meeting. By not exacerbating this response, Carl and I were able to establish the basis of a relationship which enabled him to commit to the coaching process. In other words, Carl did not run away and willingly chose to come back for further sessions. This counted as our first small but important success.

Writing our way into feeling

Carl, like others who *move away*, prided himself on his observational skills. He was an onlooker in life and resisted participating in what he called the 'mediocre dramas' of the majority. Nevertheless, he maintained an acute interest – at a distance – in these dramas. He liked to sit in cafés and watch people over the rim of a book or, sitting quietly in team meetings, he would listen carefully and mentally make notes about his colleagues. Carl told me that this quality of observation helped him understand and anticipate situations very effectively. He was usually the first to spot an emerging trend or to remember the details of an event or conversation that others had forgotten. This gave him an advantage, he said, and it was one reason why he should be given the chance to lead the China project.

I asked Carl if he ever shared these observations with others. He didn't. I asked him if he ever wrote them down. Again, he didn't. I suggested that by writing about what he saw he might develop even greater understanding of the way others behaved and perhaps feel more compelled to share his perspective, thus achieving some of the improvements his VP was hoping for. Carl was curious about how writing could help him develop further insight or the interpersonal skills he had been told he lacked. I said that putting things down on paper can help us to clarify and 'see' our thoughts and intentions differently, particularly when we read back over what we have written and take the time to notice new or previously hidden connections between events, thoughts, feelings and actions. I also mentioned some techniques that might help him analyse the content of his written observations, particularly if they included verbatim accounts.[103] This would give him some new skills for understanding and improving the quality of team conversations.

I framed the purpose of writing to appeal to his preference for rational, methodological and logical thought – sometimes referred to as 'left brain' processing. This can be contrasted with those who demonstrate 'right brain' preferences like feeling, intuiting and thinking in images as opposed to words. At this stage I did not share with him another good reason for writing which Natalie Goldberg describes with naked (right brain) honesty:

---

[103] Verbatim accounts record the words that are actually said. They provide a rich description of an encounter. Usually a verbatim account is taken from an audio recording or is written as people are speaking. Verbatim accounts produced from memory are still useful but usually less accurate.

I write out of hurt and how to make hurt okay; how to make myself strong and come home, and it may be the only real home I have.[104]

To promote writing as a healing process would, I thought, have triggered Carl's defensive behaviours. Carl did not regard himself as wounded, nor did it occur to him that his life could be experienced any differently. He expected little and so his incentives to change were few. Furthermore, like others whose *threat brain* habit is to *move away*, he seemed to be on the look-out for 'intruders', in other words, anyone who threatened to come close to, interfere with or disturb the version of independence that was vital to him.

Threat brain solutions are limited in scope and have a compulsive and indiscriminate quality. In *moving away* we become hypersensitive to *anything* resembling suggestion or influence and we interpret this as an attempt to coerce or control. Protecting our uniqueness becomes an end in itself rather than a means, for example, to a more expansive form of self-expression and creativity. The question we most often ask about others is, 'will this person interfere with me?' Whereas when we *move against* we ask, 'will this person be better than me or useful to me?' and when we *move towards*, 'will he like me?' The fear of losing one's independence is at root a fear of experiencing the emotions that accompany both dependent and interdependent relationships. It was certainly so with Carl – and we will explore the origins of this shortly.

My suggestion that Carl write down his observations felt like a relatively safe task as it did not require any self-reflection or direct contact with others. My intention was to later invite him to share his notes with me so that together we could explore how his observations might translate into new leadership actions and practices. My hope was that if he shared his writing with me it would encourage 'vulnerability with purpose'[105] and in doing so develop trust in our relationship.

---

[104] (Goldberg, 2005)
[105] (Brown, 2012)

Carl agreed to buy a journal and during our first month of coaching (he came every week) he filled many pages with neat, comprehensive notes about his experiences at work. It was through regular journaling that Carl noticed two important themes that sparked some curiosity in him. First he identified recurring discrepancies between how he saw himself and how others saw him and second, he noticed that he was very attuned to and wrote mostly about *problems* at work.

He was willing to share these observations with me because, I suspect, he was satisfied that they passed as factual statements rather than emotional disclosures. However, as the weeks passed it became clear that recounting observations as facts and rigorously defending his own beliefs without deeper inquiry and reflection was limiting the potential of our work together.

Stuckness as opportunity

Carl's first journal entry contained details about the recent 360° feedback he had received from peers, the team he managed and the VP. In this report some people described him as disengaged, insensitive, rude, grudging and unapproachable. Carl was baffled by, and slightly contemptuous of, this feedback and dismissed much of it with his own counter analysis. Disengaged became 'quiet', insensitive became 'honest', rude became 'direct' and unapproachable became 'being busy doing real work'. Yes, he wanted the promotion but he did not see a corresponding need to change anything about himself. The problem, he thought, was that other people lacked insight and misunderstood him. As Carl talked he expressed significant inconsistencies between his interest in the promotion and his attitude towards achieving it. He said he had begun the coaching process to increase his chances of success, yet for the first few months Carl vigorously rejected any suggestion that he might need to develop.

We have seen that *moving away* involves defending the status quo and resisting change both as a means of attaining 'peace at any price' and a reaction to what is felt as external coercion. What then did Carl imagine we would do in our sessions?

As time went on it became clear that Carl enjoyed the opportunity to be in a relationship that made no reciprocal demands on him. Coaching for Carl was a one-way arrangement where he could philosophise to his heart's content without risk of generating friendship, intimacy or expectation. Or, conversely, rejection, criticism or judgement.

In some ways I had achieved what I had set out to. Carl felt safe enough to come to the sessions, talk with some openness, share his journal notes and contemplate (but always reject) trying out new behaviours. However, it also occurred to me that we were now flat-lining. In other words, there was no challenge, discomfort or *life* in the work. There was no momentum. We were simply turning over and reinforcing the status quo.

A compassionate approach is not indulgent, over-protective or naive. When we feel compassion we turn towards problems (within us or in others) with non-judgemental acceptance and at the same time with a will to take action in order to understand, challenge and may be resolve. Compassion is ultimately an active and courageous response to difficulty and suffering. Furthermore, we have seen how compassion stimulates our *safe brain* to produces emotions that motivate us to think carefully and act wisely. Actions that arise from this state are purposeful, value-driven and wholehearted. We are better placed to make plans, engage in activities and seek out resources that are healthy and contribute to our well-being. [106]

This was not happening for Carl. In between our sessions he returned to his *threat brain* loop and his *moving away* solutions. In some ways his journaling practice had made him *more* aloof and isolated. I wondered whether my growing feeling of being stuck in this coaching process might be mirroring Carl's own experience. I also contemplated how Carl might start to experience more healthy drive at work. How, for example, might he become more possibility- rather than problem-focused and open rather than

---

[106] Remember that, when *drive brain* is stimulated by *threat,* the actions that follow are likely to have a manic, addictive, overly competitive and exhausting quality.

defended? What might motivate him to willingly experiment in his relationships with others? What might change the dynamic between Carl and his colleagues so that there was at least some congruity in their experience of each other?

Having reflected on these questions at length I decided to share an observation that, given his *moving away* habits, had been puzzling me. At the same time I noticed my hesitation. *Moving away* solutions rely on keeping conflict out of awareness and the slightest hint of disturbance brought about by my provocation could trigger his 'flee' response. I did not want Carl to disengage given the small progress we had made, yet I knew my ongoing caution would eventually reinforce his habits.

In her book, *Our Inner Conflicts*, Karen Horney describes *moving away* as a resigned and apathetic adaptation to threat which often involves giving up on ambition and desire. I have observed this tendency in many of my coachees who deal with threats by disengaging and avoiding. Yet Carl was pursuing a promotion which would raise his profile and frequently involve him in challenging relationships and conflicts. Why? I was curious to learn more about his motivations. My hunch was that he probably felt ambivalent about the promotion and that by surfacing this conflict our work might find new direction.

So, I asked him how he truly felt about the prospect of obtaining this senior leadership position. What thoughts did he have about the extra work, the new relationships and high profile challenges it would bring?

Carl did not seem at all disturbed by these questions, in fact he seemed relieved and he queried why it taken me so long to ask! No, he didn't *want* the promotion. He did however feel that he was the right person for the job and, he added with scorn, there was no one he could think of with equivalent knowledge, skills set and vision. Additionally, he did not want to draw attention to himself by challenging the VP's strategy.

Underneath Carl's habit of *moving away* and avoiding emotion or conflict we can see secondary patterns relating to *moving towards* (complying and appeasing) and also *moving against* (arrogant, competitive). This underlying dynamic created a feeling of being 'torn' between options.

Of the three 'solutions' *moving away* is the most conflicted because it lacks clearly defined goals and values. Those who *move against* want to master, conquer and control. Those who *move towards* want to love, appease and belong. This wanting – even when unhealthy – gives *direction*. However, those who *move away* don't *want* anything. Their solution is to reject, detach and be free *from* – which is very different to wanting to be free *to*. This defensive 'lack of wanting' can manifest as procrastination, uncertainty and as with Carl, a profound feeling of being divided. Karen Horney suggested that those who 'choose' the *moving away* solution are more likely to have experimented with, and not fully relinquished, the other solutions. As a result, *moving away* contains within it the experience of, and residual cravings for, both closeness and aggressive domination. These contradictory values 'harass' and 'paralyse' their carrier.[107] We saw an example of this conflict earlier when Carl described both his disdain for people's mediocre dramas and, at the same time, his acute interest (observationally) in what they were doing.

I took Carl's provocation about why it had taken so long for me to ask these questions as an opportunity to talk about emotion and motivation using the *Trimotive Brain* approach and, in particular, the *threat brain* habits of *moving against, towards* and *away*. I said I sensed a *moving away* tendency in him and that I had been reluctant to aggravate this by asking personal or provoking questions too soon.

Carl was interested in neuroscience and liked the *Trimotive Brain* metaphor. He understood how Horney's three survival solutions could represent the complex, human version of fight, flee and freeze and he quickly identified with and became curious to learn more about *moving away*. This marked a turning point in our work together. Carl volunteered – in the name of furthering scientific inquiry, he said – some autobiographical details to help us

---

[107] (Horney, 1950)

explore how experiences in his personal history might have given rise to his *moving away* habits.

Carl had never spoken about his childhood. In many ways he had distanced and disassociated himself from this part of his life. However, fragmented recollections of the past lingered in his unconscious and strong, implicit memories continued to influence his beliefs and expectations.

Integrating unconscious memories into an open and conscious life narrative can be very powerful. We saw in Part Two how our unconscious processes are constantly 'messaging' us in a language of their own. When we can translate these messages through conscious processing they usually become less disturbing and more useful to us. Thanks to the evolution of consciousness we can do this with the help of our *explicit* memory system, described in Part One, which enables us to make sense, process and 're-store' old memories with the benefit of adult wisdom and perspective. Restored, integrated memories are less likely to interfere in or disrupt our lives.[108] Making sense of what has happened to us enables us to re-tag threat memories as coherent, meaningful and context-dependent and makes them less likely to trigger generalised, 'warning signals' that we misinterpret and misapply. By recognising that many of our *threat brain* habits are sustained by old memories we can learn to filter them and respond to new experience with more accuracy and skill.

Carl's story led him towards a greater understanding of his introverted, detached character and how change might paradoxically involve becoming *more* of himself not less. As with Maggie and Ronnie, Carl's story shows how patterns of adaptation to our particular environment and experiences emerge and how the interaction of nature (our biological inheritance) and nurture (our primary relationships) gives rise to very distinct habits of understanding and responding.

---

[108] Flashbacks, psychosomatic illness, phobias and insomnia are examples of how implicit memories appear in, and disrupt, our lives.

Vulnerability with purpose – Carl shares his story

Carl's father was a dominant, forceful character who believed his son should be taught the 'lessons of life' at an early age. Carl was told that hard work and discipline were the ingredients of a successful and worthy existence. At the age of five he was introduced to a strict regime which involved rising at dawn and helping out on his father's farm before walking the three country miles to school. After school he would complete his homework and then undertake a growing list of chores before falling exhausted into bed. Sometimes his mother would help with the tasks and on those evenings the two of them had secretive 'spare time'. This made Carl anxious. His father's approval meant a lot to him even though it was given sparingly and without warmth.

Carl's father ran a moderately successful business and approached his work in a highly competitive and exaggerated way as if, Carl said, he were running a multinational corporate. He was entrepreneurial and risk-taking and Carl remembered numerous ventures to diversify from milk farming. These included running a bed and breakfast, making artisan ice-cream and cheese and breeding rare pigs for the gourmet food industry. In many ways Carl's father exhibited *moving against* characteristics which, Carl noticed, became heightened when his father was under stress. His father had a bold charisma which Carl respected and probably, as a boy, tried to emulate.

Carl's mother, on the other hand, exhibited many of the behaviours of someone who was stuck in *moving towards*. Carl described her as placating, eager to please and constantly trying to anticipate and meet the needs of both her husband and son. Carl did not remember her taking time for herself or having any personal hobbies or interests. Carl believed his mother was a loving woman yet he was puzzled by how little 'warm' love he felt for her. It was a guilty love, he said. He felt he *had* to be grateful for the many things she did for him and he felt unable able to express dissent or difference. It was hard to be angry with her. Yet now he could see that he did feel anger – both then and now.

Carl talked about his mother's anxious determination to maintain harmony in the house. Every evening she would remind Carl not to upset his tired father. To keep the peace she lied about small things – what Carl had eaten that day, how long he had spent on his homework, what time he had gone to bed. These lies, to please and appease his father, created a fugitive bond between mother and son. Yet Carl did not like the conspiracy and subterfuge – it made him feel disloyal to a man he admired and feared.

Carl's most challenging childhood experience was the day he decided to tell the truth. When his mother lied about the hour spent on homework, Carl contradicted her and told his father that he had helped bake a cake and watched TV. On hearing Carl's version, his father became angry and struck his mother who fell, knocking her head on the stone mantel. Carl remembered the blood running down her cheek and his feelings of disgust and horror as he watched his apologetic mother struggle to her feet. Carl went to his room and sat in the dark with his hands pressed to his ears. Nothing more was said about the event and his life carried on as before.

Carl's parents were caught in loops of their own which combined to create an erratic and contradictory emotional environment. Carl was an only child and because of his strict routine had little time for friends. He kept his confusion and mixed emotions to himself. Often the best option for a child caught between the polarities of *moving against* and *moving towards* is to *move away*. To cope with his father's unpredictable moods (which made him anxious) and his mother's suffocating love (which triggered strong feelings of guilt), Carl sought distance from emotionality. Detachment took him away from the conflict, resignation ensured that the conflict did not return. In other words, by retracting any wish, desire or need that required others for its fulfilment, Carl ensured inner independence and freedom from the pain of relationship. Thus he learned to adapt and survive by repressing or locking-in all emotions. When we are caught in a *moving away* loop this locking-in often causes a visibly tense, rigid posture and a voice lacking in cadence and strength. This was certainly the case with Carl.

Carl went on to describe his successful university career. It was, he said, driven more by a wish to avoid the 'real world' of work than by personal ambition. He felt no particular pride in his PhD and afterwards chose his current job because it was a relatively solitary one compared to postgraduate teaching. Not much had happened since then, he said. His life was a predictable routine of work, the occasional cycling holiday and evenings in with a book.

Playing and experimenting – discovering introversion as a strength

Carl recounted his story as a series of facts devoid of feeling. Even when he spoke of anger his voice was toneless and flat. I asked him what it was like to reveal aspects of himself and he said it was surprisingly easy and, in some ways, useful. In talking about his family history he could see more clearly how his character had been influenced and developed. Externalising his thoughts by writing or telling a story about them, he reflected, made him see things differently. He had already begun to notice this effect through keeping a journal.

Carl was particularly interested in how his inner critic might represent the voice of *threat brain* and that it could be a restraining force in his life. Up until then he had only considered this voice as a helpful, driving force. Yet, when he listened carefully he could hear his father's tone and values in everything it said. That worried him.

To help Carl get to know his inner critic I suggested he make a list of all the things he believed he *should* think, feel or do. The list confirmed how his 'shoulds' supported the pattern of *moving away* already described. Carl's inner critic was very disparaging of others and didn't like 'feelings'. His inner critic told him he should trust only his intellect and stay free from emotional entanglements. Carl felt he should be independent, self-sufficient, unmoved by emotion, able to care for himself even when ill, unobligated to others, non-conformist and able to solve problems through reason and logic. When prompted to explore the unintended consequences or 'side effects' of these 'shoulds' he listed *a preoccupation with death and ill health, impatience and a reluctance to make future plans.*

His preoccupation with death and ill health came from his fear of being dependent on others. If he became sick, he said, he would have to seek help and this made him very anxious. Carl paid into expensive insurance policies to ensure he would receive the best private health care should he need it and he was very – if not overly – careful about his diet, weight and fitness. He hated, for example, being around people who were coughing or sneezing and as a result he refused to use public transport or to go to places where there might be a crowd, a queue or close interaction. His aversion to people made him intolerant and impatient of their mistakes, weaknesses and 'banal' interests. Carl expected little from life and had a tendency to see the future as fixed and unalterable. As a result, he didn't see the point in making long-term plans.

It was through our inquiry into the side effects of his *moving away* strategy (reinforced by his inner critic) that we eventually returned to the feedback provided in his 360^0 appraisal.

Picking up on Carl's own admission of impatience I invited him to read the reports out loud and *slowly*, taking in each word and resisting his urge to skip, jump to conclusions and dismiss. I also asked him to read the reports *as if* people's comments were true. Reading aloud enabled Carl to get feedback on and adjust his tone which, to begin with, was sarcastic and dismissive. When he started to read as if people had insight and compassion the words sounded and felt very different.

We had some fun with this exercise. I played 'director' and Carl the leading character. *"Make it sound as if you believe in it!"* I urged him somewhat theatrically and he, enjoying the process, rose to the occasion. During this play-acting Carl's usually soft, monotonous voice became animated and alive. In these moments he was not in a defensive *threat brain* state. Instead, he was able to experience, through playful and safe experiment, healthy drive that supported and accelerated his learning.

Later we contemplated the hypothetical impact of these 'truths' on the performance and productivity of the team. I encouraged Carl to imagine what it would be like to be the insensitive, moody, unapproachable person others described. What would be the behaviours and thoughts of such a person? What would be the consequences? This conversation – again, playful because it was imaginary – revealed the many opportunities for misunderstanding arising out of discrepancies between Carl's description of himself (quiet, honest, hard-working) and that given by colleagues.

Robert Bly in *A Little Book on the Human Shadow,* describes the value of play when we are trying to retrieve and work with aspects of our self that have been hidden away. However, playing rarely happens when we are in threat. That Carl was able to engage in our theatrical investigations indicated that both *safe* and healthy *drive brain* were active. This enabled him to imagine – and eventually accept – the multiple selves within him. All these selves were 'real' and their presence did not indicate insanity or ill health. They were simply less dominant, accepted or known to him.

Playing with truth is a gentle way of coming to know the whole self and acting 'as if' allows a person to temporarily enter into an alternative reality whilst still holding on to their stabilising habits.

Yet the simple act of telling a different version of the same story can bring a real-time shift in perspective and the possibility that other ways of experiencing are possible.

After these conversations Carl agreed to try an experiment which involved acting 'as if' he enjoyed the company of others. This felt safe and possible for Carl because it did not represent or require a commitment to change and, as he enjoyed playing these parts, he was willing to give it a go.

Carl's 'as if' experiment was to have lunch in the communal areas at work and initiate a different kind of 'social' conversation by sharing a few aspects of his private life. He prepared a few topics such as recent films he had seen, his cycling tour of Ireland and his interest in cricket. The aim of the experiment was to test the proposition that moments of sociability would enhance his experience at work without affecting his need for privacy and independence.

At first Carl found these 'socials' excruciating, maybe because he feared that opening himself to others in this way risked either rejection or intimacy. At the same time he noticed that the daily exchange of 'trivia' was not as boring or demanding as he had anticipated. After only a week of experimenting a colleague invited him out to dinner and, to continue the experiment, Carl accepted. It was, he said, a surprisingly pleasant evening.

Carl began to notice that his behaviour was frequently motivated by *anticipated* rather than actual threats. For example, his fear of ending up trapped in an emotionally difficult relationship led him to avoid social encounters. He was keen to explore what thoughts, feelings and behaviours he might experience if he acted as if people were *not* going to make demands or suffocate his individual needs. Thus Carl continued to develop his new friendships at work and became increasingly skilled at negotiating time in and time away from people. He was able to recognise and honour his needs without disparaging and disengaging from others.

As Carl's inquiry deepened he became interested in whether his preference for solitude was an enduring and stable characteristic appearing in many of his 'selves' and not just the self that responded to threat. His new friendships, he said, felt safe and stimulating, nevertheless he still wanted to keep these social engagements to a minimum. He didn't feel threatened by them, he just didn't want too much contact.

Carl's questions prompted me to share research that suggests there may be a biological predisposition towards introversion. I recommended he read Susan Cain's book, *Quiet*, which explores the possibility that that some babies are born with a sensitive nervous system that is more alert and responsive to novelty and potential threat in the environment. These infants are more likely to cope by withdrawing compared to those whose nervous systems are less reactive. This tendency – an aspect of our particular biological heritage – towards introversion only becomes unhealthy and rigid when it is regularly motivated by threat.

Carl started to see how a potentially healthy response could turn into a stuck, unhelpful habit. There is nothing inherently wrong, he realised, with wanting a quieter, less stimulating environment. Yet when that became his *only* response to life it diminished him.

By cultivating a mindful approach to his experience Carl was able to notice his defensive emotions as they arose and reflect on whether they were appropriate to his particular and current circumstances. Often they were not. The people in his life could not harm or control him as he had been harmed and controlled as a child and so his introversion and *moving away* habits were no longer required as a shield against threats that were no longer significant in his life.

Using kind and reassuring self-talk, Carl reframed his wish for privacy and solitude as a legitimate and productive way to re-energise and find inner peace. This softened the voice of his inner critic and made him less critical and suspicious of others. He no longer had to cast other people as problems in order to give himself a reason to live his solitary life.

Carl did not want marriage, children or significant contact with others. When he learned to compassionately accept this as an adult choice and preference he was able to reduce the guilt and shame that had originally been associated with being alone.

Thus, although Carl's *moving away* habits, motivated by threat, had become rigid and inflexible he began to see how the same habits, motivated by *safe brain* or healthy drive could result in a very different experience. To cultivate his *safe brain* and *drive brain* motivations Carl needed to soothe and manage his *threat brain*. For Carl this meant learning to accept and perhaps even like parts of himself that had been rejected or forgotten.

Owning our problems

Carl observed problems in the world but not in himself. This is not unusual. Often we don't hear or notice our own feelings and thoughts because we are too busy hearing and noticing them in others. This is especially true when it comes to feelings and thoughts that are painful, unpleasant or unwanted. Externalising these qualities and feelings helps to reduce inner conflict by turning them into someone else's problem. Whilst this can bring temporary relief, the longer-term consequences are that we fail to alleviate those feelings in ourselves and by seeing problems 'out there' we make our world unnecessarily difficult. For example, many of us will recognise the habit of projecting onto a partner or child our own bad mood. Through this misuse of our energy we infect others with our angry feelings and provoke arguments and hostility.

Our defensive unconscious processes, as described in Part Two, are responsible for managing what is difficult and disliked in us as its job is to protect us from experiences which cause us pain. However, the *long-term* distortion of reality is generally not good for us and does not in the end confer evolutionary advantage. There may be a few members of our society who *do* distort and bend reality to good effect without compromising the growth of their consciousness and capability. Perhaps artistic, scientific and inventive genius requires the defensive unconscious to cast its long shadow. The poet, Rilke, for example, needed his darkness and worried that if his demons departed, so too would his angels.

However, the majority of us do not thrive in these polarities and do not enjoy or want to live so close to the edge of what is known and given. For most of us it is useful to become more conscious of the forces that influence and direct our life and to manage those that are destructive. By taking back our projections, in other words owning our problems and personalities, we become more consciously aware of who we are and what we need. This in turn enables us to cultivate our possible self (or selves) and live in greater harmony with our internal 'family'.[109] The ego, that part of our self which is social, adapted to our particular environment, known to us and seen by others, does not represent the totality of our inner life. It is *'only one member of a commune'*.[110]

Ken Wilber, in *Meeting the Shadow*,[111] suggests that projection is very easy to spot. If a person or thing in the environment *informs* us, he says, we probably aren't projecting. However, if it *affects* us, if it generates surges of strong feeling in us, the chances are we are experiencing our own projections. Remember, we can project *all* the unwanted or unacceptable aspects of our self. In other words, we don't just throw out the embarrassing, ugly and shameful we

---

[109] For an overview and discussion on the ordinary and everyday experience of 'sub-personalities' see (Rowan, 1990)

[110] (Hillman, 1975)

[111] (Zweig & Abrams, 1991)

also, if we have not found a way to express them safely, throw out the heroic, creative, beautiful and spiritual. These latter projections can be seen, for example in our infatuations. We see our lover as faultless, heroic and saintly. They are, we say, 'our better half'. And this is partly true. We have projected onto the loved one those qualities and yearnings in ourselves that we have been unable to integrate as part of our own psyche and possibility.

By taking back our projections and owning them as parts of ourselves we will get to know the dark side of our nature *and* discover the precious qualities of our possible self that are awaiting expression.

Taking back our projections – reversal exercises

Carl got to know his unwanted, banished self by using writing exercises that surfaced and reversed his projections and helped him take responsibility for what he was doing to himself and for what he wanted from life.

He started by writing a list of the characteristics, habits and mannerisms he hated or strongly disliked in others. He considered traits or situations that *affected* him and created a strong surge of 'discordant'[112] emotion. This part of the exercise develops conscious responsibility for the feelings and thoughts we may wish we did not have. Free fall writing can have the same effect if, for example, we use a stem phrase starting with *I hate...* or *It disgusts me when....*

Carl wrote: "*talks loudly, overly concerned with appearance, hyper-critical, lazy, sentimental, overweight, ill-informed*".

I then asked him to write a paragraph for each item but reversing the characteristics he disliked in others and applying them to himself. So, *I hate people who talk loudly* becomes *when I talk loudly* and *I really dislike people who are overly concerned with appearance* becomes *when I am overly concerned with appearance*. The stem phrases helped Carl to explore how these disliked characteristics might live within him.

---

[112] Discordant/harmonious are used instead of negative/positive as they better represent the complexity of our experience. Negative and positive represent polarities that limit the way we understand emotions and their function.

The second exercise was intended to address Carl's reluctance to talk about personal desire, needs and goals. Remember an aspect of the *moving away* solution is to deny such things because they are likely to require others for their fulfilment. Discovering what we need or want beyond mere survival is one way we can start to understand what our possible, as yet unrealised, self is yearning for or to be.

For this exercise I asked Carl to write a list of five things he absolutely *did not* want to happen or experience in his life. This was easy for him. He wrote: "*I don't want to have children, I don't want to lose my job, I don't want to visit my mother, I don't want to be married, I don't want to be unhealthy*". I then asked him to do a simple reversal of those sentences and again write a paragraph for each. So, the first paragraph would start, "*I want to have children…*"

These reversal exercises are not to intended to create another set of 'shoulds' that one must act on. They are intended to stimulate an exploration of those parts of ourself which are in opposition to or different from the dominant and conscious self.

Carl was somewhat cynical of these exercises but each week, as his journal pages filled, he would return enthused and with new insights. In the reversal of disliked traits he discovered that repellent loud voices were most vocal in *him* and, that appearances mattered:

> **"When I speak loudly,** *I don't make sounds that others can hear but my head is full of cacophony, like rattling metal. My head hurts. So many loud voices all talking over each other. They've always been with me, like background music, so familiar I stopped hearing. But they are loud. My head is full of loudness."*

And

> **"I am concerned about my appearance.** *Overly concerned, perhaps. I don't want to stand out from the crowd so I wear the same regular suits every day. I want to blend in but I also don't want to be like them. I don't want to be ordinary. I spend a lot of time thinking about how I look. What would happen if I wore black? A bright scarf? A t-shirt!"*

When reflecting on the reversal of desires exercise he noticed that he had no strong feelings relating to the paragraph starting '*I want to have children*'. However, when he wrote, '*I want to see my mother…*'. He experienced a strong emotional reaction. At first he felt acidic anxiety in his stomach. As he continued to write, that sensation passed and was replaced by a softer feeling which he described as sadness. I asked him how he knew it was sadness and he said it was a feeling he recognised from the past. He recalled the moment when he discovered that one of the newborn farm kittens had been crushed when the herd were brought in for milking. His father had thrown the mangled body in the gutter to be swilled out at the end of the day. First he remembered the anxiety (*threat brain* response) and then the tender, open emotion that made him feel tearful and in need of comfort (*safe brain* motivating us to seek care and comfort). In those days, he said, he was quite a 'cry baby' but he didn't like to show his tears knowing that his father would disapprove and his mother would make too much of it. Thus although Carl started out with an active *safe brain* regulating his threat response, over time he learned that *safe brain* motivations could not be fulfilled. He would not get the comfort he sought, so it was better not to seek it and instead to find alternative emotional resolution. His anxiety was soothed by withdrawing and his need for love and comfort was thrown into the cellar of his psyche.

Carl's writing revealed a longing to be close to his mother again. It exposed a self that yearned to care and be cared for, a self that for many years had been kept at bay through defensive unconscious processes that warned him to stay away from other people.

In these two writing exercises Carl learned that he projected onto others or denied his shameful, or what he described as "useless", feelings. As he started to own these feelings he began to notice that the emotional conflicts he had tried to prevent were and had always been alive within him. He saw that underneath his independent and detached persona there existed the exact opposite qualities.

This troubled him. He did not understand how it was possible to think and 'be' one thing yet feel or want its opposite. He didn't understand why, if he so wanted to see his mother, he didn't just get on a train and visit. I asked Carl whether he would be willing to try a different method of inquiry that might offer deeper understanding of this conflict within him.

Carl had begun his 'shadow work' and its goal – to integrate our multiple selves into a harmonious, yet differentiated whole – cannot be achieved without patience, courage and forgiveness. You only have to imagine what it might take to heal a serious, long-term rift in your family to understand the challenges ahead. Carl Jung described the work as involving "long and difficult negotiations" and Connie Zweig and Jeremiah Abrams in their excellent compilation of shadow research and writing say:

> ...shadow work forces us again and again to take another point of view, to respond to life with our undeveloped traits and our instinctual sides and to live what Jung called the tension of the opposites – holding both good and evil, right and wrong, light and dark, in our own hearts... our beauty is deepened as our beastliness is honoured.[113]

Shadow work can also be understood as a way in which to regulate our *threat brain* by facing and coming to terms with our fears and it lies at the heart of all integrative work. When our motivation systems are working well together our experiences are less likely to be fragmented, rigid and limiting. Shadow work cannot be undertaken without self-compassion for when our different selves finally meet each other there is much to tolerate, forgive and accept.

Coming Home – returning to unfinished business

I suggested Carl deepen his inquiry using 'chair work' – a psycho-therapeutic intervention with origins in the Gestalt techniques pioneered by Frederick Perls.[114] The emphasis in Gestalt therapy is on taking personal responsibility and learning to experience life as it is happening *now* – not as it happened in the past. This means

---

[113] (Zweig & Abrams, 1991)
[114] (Perls, et al., 1986)

acknowledging and forgiving what has happened so that we become free to move on and create new experiences in our life.

There are different ways to carry out chair work but a popular method is 'two-chair work' involving a dialogue relating to a piece of 'unfinished business' in our life. Unfinished business describes a situation in which our vitality or growth is blocked by an ongoing connection to events or relationships that occurred in the past. These are often situations of trauma and loss.

The method involves placing two chairs facing each other. You sit in one chair and have a dialogue with the person (represented by the empty chair) with whom your unfinished business relates. In this case it was Carl's mother. Sometimes you move back and forth between the two chairs, speaking first from your perspective and then from the perspective of the other. The purpose of the dialogue is to bring into consciousness hidden thoughts and feelings about the person and the relationship in order to attempt resolution or release from the conflict.

Carl was curious to try it out so we set up two chairs facing each other with Carl sitting in one. I sat some distance away but guided him through the process. I began by asking Carl to tell his mother what he valued about her and their relationship and to speak as if she were actually sitting in front of him. This was to encourage a *safe brain* state of appreciation and pleasant memory which was not difficult for Carl as his mother had been a caring and kind person and he had already expressed gratitude towards her in some of his writing exercises. I then invited Carl to share any problems he had about her and the relationship. This was difficult for him. He fell silent and after a few minutes looked over at me and shook his head. *'I can't think of any.'*

I remembered that Carl had been very responsive to the 'as if' experiments so I offered an 'as if' visualisation that I hoped would enable him to connect with the anger and resentment he had previously alluded to when talking about his mother.

I said, "*Close your eyes and imagine you are dying. You are the age you are, lying in a hospital bed and the only person by your side right now is your mother. Bring your mother's face into mind and for a moment feel what it might feel like to know that you only have a few hours to live. You know that there is so much unsaid between you. You know there are many, many thoughts and feelings you have never expressed. Some good some bad. You have so little time left now, yet your mother is here in front of you. What is it you need to say now so that you can pass peacefully? Now open your eyes. See your mother sitting there. What is it you need to say to her?"*[115]

Again there was silence but this time his body, so often frozen and tense, folded forwards into a ball and from somewhere deep within him a cry, soft at first, filled the room. I have heard people make all kinds of noises in this work but Carl's sob was one that will stay with me. I made no movement towards him and I remained quiet. Often when people cry we feel compelled to comfort them with soothing touch or kind words. This can be helpful, however, it can also interrupt the experience of being fully with your emotion and learning to survive this experience *without* the help of your *threat brain* habits which mostly tries to distort, avoid or deny what is happening. Recent research explores the conditions in which crying acts as a self-soothing process that regulates mood and reduces stress by activating our parasympathetic nervous system. Results are varied, but studies suggest that a positive and accepting response from others, the possibility of problem resolution or clarity and an appropriate social context (e.g. in coaching, with friends, privately) support a self-soothing outcome.[116]

Carl found the two-chair work difficult. The only thing he was able to say – and he directed this to me and not to the empty chair – was, *"They didn't listen to me. They never listened."* Despite his difficulties, the experience brought him closer to his early, frustrated needs and the realisation that he had repressed and hidden them for most of his life. Carl went on to write about his experience privately and, he said, with much more raw emotion that he ever thought possible. He also noticed that when he gave full expression to his feelings and thoughts the 'noise' inside his head diminished.

---

[115] (Brandon, 1978)
[116] (Gračanin, et al., 2014)

The brilliant family therapist Bert Hellinger, once said that resolutions arise from a person's original feelings of love for the parents, not their anger and despair. Love, he said, is the first impetus and it is the root of all entanglement, suffering and psychic illness. In re-discovering love, the problems dissolve. Hellinger sought to discover the kind, forgiving, empathic elements in even the darkest stories. This is what we do when we cultivate our self-compassion. One way to do this is to reflect on the wider context into which we have been born:

> Our family is just one wrinkle of a collective event, important for you to know, perhaps, but not to be confused or treated as a cause.[117]

In Part Two we saw that by developing feelings of *common humanity* we start to see ourselves as part of a complex and mysterious web of relationships. Our selves were not born and shaped merely by our parents' will or desire, they also emerged as a result of ancestral experiences, peer group influence and biological and cultural forces.

Having disassociated himself from the past, Carl now became very curious about his extended family and the circumstances in which his grandfather had decided to move from London to a farm in the West Country. Carl's grandfather died before Carl was born so he only 'knew' him through his father's stories. On his deathbed his father said two things: "*I don't want to be buried. Make sure they cremate me,*" and "*my father was a good man. He was very strict. Now I know why.*"

Carl had not inquired further and a few days later his father was dead. The event, recalled recently in his journal, helped Carl to appreciate the complexity of his family relationships and how much he had forgotten as his energy became directed into managing unconscious conflicts.

As Carl's *threat brain* habits diminished he began to have more memories of peace, friendship and trust at home which enabled him to develop a less guilty, warm love for his parents and also, more

---

[117] (Hillman & Ventura, 1993)

significantly, for himself. As we continued to reframe and seek multiple perspective for events in his life, he was able to see how he had played a part in the *health* and *cohesion* of the family by being a quiet, obedient child. Although his *moving away* habits had become entrenched and problematic he was able to find a great deal of self-compassion for the resourceful and caring child these habits had taught him to be.

The two-chair work was the first of many imaginary conversations Carl had with his mother and then his father. Mostly these were private and contained within his journal but he wrote a few as dialogues which he wanted to read aloud, just as he had done when we played our 'as if' games.

A few months after our sessions ended Carl got on a train to visit his mother. He emailed me afterwards and this is some of what he wrote:

> *It was hard returning to a place that was a source of so much unhappiness for me. I've seen Mum in London. She visits once or twice a year but the last time I saw her in Devon was fifteen years ago. Dad was alive then. My mum still lives in the farmhouse but the land has been rented out. My bedroom is the same. She hasn't changed anything. Mum made one of her special cakes and we spent lots of time sitting at the kitchen table just talking about nothing much. No two-chair work or anything! What was strange was being in the house as a middle-aged man. I would have been eight when my dad was my age now. I felt like I was looking at things through his eyes. That was hard. Farming is not an easy life and I could see signs of hardship and poverty all around. You don't see this as a child. I had this odd feeling of love for them both. I suppose they did their best. I was surprised that Mum has kept Dad's ashes. They are in a silver jewellery box on the mantelpiece. They probably loved each other in their own way. That realisation has freed me somewhat from my own guilt and I feel I have let go of some of the heaviness that lives in me. I feel lighter.*

Carl had learned that his inner critic was the voice of his *threat brain* and that he possessed other voices or personalities which represented healthy drives and *safe brain* insights offering equally valid truths. By developing kind self-talk and by learning to accept the existence of contradictory thoughts and feelings Carl started to notice what he had in common with others and to bring a compassionate understanding to his relationships. Carl's email suggested that he was learning to forgive and to rewrite his narrative to include an appreciative perspective on what had happened and was happening in his life. Practising kindness, appreciation and tolerance towards himself and others enabled him to break free from his inner critic and enjoy many more moments of peace and equanimity.

Mid-way through our work together Carl received news that he would be promoted. Anne, his HR partner, had received excellent feedback from the UK project team regarding Carl's leadership. When Carl accepted the promotion he was given a further six months of coaching support, so overall our work carried on for over a year.

In that time I witnessed Carl unfurl and extend his wry, perceptive, kind and very caring being into the world. I also saw him embrace the possible self that he had for so long denied. This self led Carl along a different path. When we parted company, Carl was in the process of applying for a teaching position at a UK university. He wanted to develop his interest in the influence of nuclear reactions on stellar explosions and he had great fun in telling me that this could be described as 'dark matter research'. He intended, however, to complete his one-year secondment in China first.

Chapter Nine: Ronnie – Moving Towards

Ronnie was the Director of Communications and Marketing for a global Financial Services company. He was also a member of the Executive Board for whom I provided team coaching and leadership development. Ronnie had been very impressed with some of the methods I introduced within the executive team to improve the quality of their conversations and strategic thinking. He asked me if I would work with his Communications team to the same end.

Ronnie and I first met to discuss this piece of work at the end of an away-day I had facilitated for the executive team. Peter, the CEO, was a keen advocate of personal development and regularly scheduled off-site sessions for his team to reflect, learn and engage in challenging strategic conversations. Not only did Peter challenge and inquire with skill he also took personal risks that expressed his ability to be vulnerable and compassionate. As a result his team, which included Ronnie, were more cohesive than many I have worked with in the finance sector. They were clear about shared objectives, trusting enough to disclose their feelings and generally, with the exception of Ronnie, able to engage in productive conflict. Peter was fully supportive of team development across the organisation and he encouraged Ronnie's decision to begin a similar process with his own eight direct reports.

Part of the gang

Ronnie's story is not, however, about his team. It is about how he rediscovered deeply buried dreams and desires that helped him to stop being an ineffectual people-pleaser and to start making decisions and taking action guided by his own values and principles.

As a member of the executive team, Ronnie was, I thought, a leaf blowing across a gusty and exposed corporate terrain. I rarely had a sense of what he really thought or what he truly wanted to achieve. He offered his support and enthusiasm to most projects and generally went along with whatever the majority view was at the time. During the two years I had been working with the team I had never seen Ronnie disagree with, challenge or refuse anyone. In particular Peter.

Ronnie was in awe of his boss. In many ways this was understandable. Peter, the darling of the shareholders, had climbed the stairs from shop floor to boardroom in just fifteen years. He had started as a counter clerk having left school at sixteen and through hard work, charisma and sheer nerve had been noticed, promoted and rewarded consistently. Now at the age of 32, he was the youngest on the board, yet one of the company's most experienced. Ronnie wanted to emulate him but, more than that, he wanted Peter's unconditional regard and approval. To a lesser but still very high degree, Ronnie also wanted the approval of his peers, his direct reports, the customers, his PA, the office cleaner, the canteen staff and anyone else who might provide him with a sense of self-esteem, worth and belonging.

In our first meeting, Ronnie was on edge. He was keen to begin the development work with his team but asked me not to mention anything about it to his peer group. Peter, he said, was very supportive but the other directors might disapprove given the recent austerity measures that had been introduced across the company. I assured Ronnie I had no intention to discuss his requirements with the executives but I said it was unlikely they would not get to hear something about it. However, Ronnie insisted I work "*with discretion*" and encouraged me to find ways to ensure his team maintained confidentiality too.

When I asked Ronnie what outcomes he sought from the team development process he instructed me to "*ask them*" what they thought. Mostly he seemed curious to find out whether the team liked him and whether they felt he was doing a good job.

Ronnie's pattern of adaptation, the origins of which we will discover later, was to cope with threat by being self-sacrificing, excessively grateful, generous, sensitive and considerate. His time, resources and attention were directed in the pursuit of acceptance, approval and appreciation. His goal, it would seem, was to secure *love* and *belonging* in order to manage threat.

We know a *threat brain* habit is at work by the intensity of our reactions when the *opposite* of what is sought occurs – in Ronnie's case, rejection, disapproval or abandonment. If such experiences feel *devastating* or *catastrophic* we are likely to be caught in a *threat brain* loop, fearing something terrible will happen to us as a result. *Threat brain* loops are self-reinforcing, so when Ronnie was challenged or criticised in meetings he became *more* self-effacing, apologetic and eager to please.

In contrast to the *moving against* pattern of adaptation, *moving towards* is accompanied by an overt feeling and admission of failure. Ronnie had been made redundant by his former employer (a law firm) and before that he had been fired from an advertising company for failing to ensure the successful launch of a new toothpaste brand. When I first met Ronnie he came across as excessively modest, somewhat subdued and nervous about his position on the board. He showed no ambition and seemed overly concerned with managing the basic requirements of his current role. For Ronnie this meant doing whatever he could to please his colleagues and boss. If *they* were happy with his work, he said, then surely he must be succeeding? Ronnie found it hard to acknowledge his seniority and resisted the idea that he might command a powerful position in a growing business. For Ronnie his role was to *serve*. He rarely gave himself credit for any accomplishments he achieved.

Moving towards represents the 'freeze' part of the threat response. Not because it is 'inactive' – no solutions are – but because it involves a shrinking and silencing of the self. Personal needs, desires and ambitions are frozen or diminished because they divert energy away from focusing on what others want. Recent research has identified a physical reaction to threat that fits this pattern of adaptation very well. Shelley Taylor, for example, in *The*

Tending Instinct, shows how 'tending and befriending' others stimulates the hormone oxytocin and can create a feeling of safety in the face of threat. As part of a broader repertoire of soothing practices this is helpful. It is when this becomes the *only* solution to threat that we see unhelpful patterns developing.

The 'freeze' response enabled Ronnie to disappear himself, which is a survival tactic. Being noticed could, for example, carry the terrible risk of being humiliated, attacked or rejected. When our tendency is to *move away* we brush off achievements as 'mere luck' or recognise them with little emotion. Ronnie would say in a flat tone, *"People say I'm very supportive"* or *"Apparently the proposal I submitted was very good".*

Robin Norwood in her bestselling book, *Women Who Love Too Much,* describes a pattern of thought and behaviour called 'loving too much'. This pattern has similarities with the *moving towards* solution, yet it is a pattern Norwood almost exclusively attributes to women. Norwood argues that,

> *Due to an interplay of biology and culture men usually try to protect themselves and avoid pain through pursuits which are more external that internal, more impersonal than personal. Their tendency is to become obsessed with work, sports, hobbies while, due to the cultural and biological forces working on her the woman's tendency is to become obsessed with a relationship – perhaps with just such a damaged and distant man.*[118]

Norwood seems to suggest that men mostly *'move against'* and women mostly *'move towards'* and it is easy to see why when we consider the heavily promoted differences between men and women's relating styles and needs. However, whilst sociocultural forces play a role in shaping our *threat brain* habits, the three patterns of adaptation to threat are not *dependent* on gender but on the *success of the original solution* in resolving or coping with threat.

If a man has developed a *moving towards* response to threat he will react in the same way as a woman to frustration and challenge.

---

[118] (Norwood, 2004)

Very often, I observe men just like Ronnie *collapse* in the face of criticism or even mild disapproval from their boss or colleagues. They will immediately defer to the suggestions or demands of others to cope with their anxiety and diminish feelings of threat. Their goal is to be liked even if that requires inconsistency of opinion or an overnight switch in loyalties. These men are driven not by ambition, though they often believe this is their motivation, but by the need to secure and hold on to love.

In *moving towards* our inner critic insists that being helpful, generous, considerate, understanding and self-sacrificing is the path towards safety and survival and it admonishes us if we start to want something for ourself. Other people – if we treat them well – will protect us. This is a very different set of beliefs from those whose response to threat is to fight or compete with others (*moving against*) or to withdraw (*moving away*).

Moving towards also involves more general beliefs about achievement, self-expression and how to be effective in life. Modesty and self-sacrifice become core values. Pride is experienced as arrogant and self-assertion as selfish. Those who tend to *move towards* rarely want to be heroes, teachers, leaders or saviours. Situations that appear to demand this of them will send their threat response into overdrive.

Working with people whose solution is *moving towards* is challenging because they find it hard to focus on their *own* issues. Introspection and self-improvement is seen as selfish. Ronnie, for example, was always ready to listen to the other executives download their issues and requests but when it was his turn would frequently use up time asking questions and empathising with the previous speaker. His desire that I seek his *team's* opinions about the development agenda and his inability to articulate what *he* wanted from the process is typical of this pattern.

At the end of our first meeting, having noted Ronnie's requests and gained further insight into his *moving towards* tendency, I suggested that before meeting the team it might be helpful if Ronnie and I had a coaching session. I framed the coaching as a way to understand the relationship he had with each member of his team.

This insight would, I said, give me some context from which to structure my meetings with them.

Whilst I *was* interested in these relationships I was, at this stage, more interested in working with Ronnie's surface tension and anxiety, which I knew (through my work with the board) was affecting his credibility as a leader. Without addressing his threat-based behaviours and supporting him to develop integrity of purpose and clarity of mind it was unlikely the team intervention he sought would have much impact. The team, after all, needed a leader who could, in the eventual absence of the facilitator, make tough decisions, mentor and guide with compassion and, most importantly, enable the team to air their differences and engage in healthy conflict. Ronnie queried the need for coaching but, unable to say no, agreed to meet me for one session.

Being the Victim – the value of martyrdom

Ronnie and I met in his office on the fifteenth floor of a glass-clad building with views of Canary Wharf and the city sky line. I arrived on time and was shown into an empty office by his apologetic PA. Ronnie, she said, was running late. However, he had insisted that I make myself at home and order whatever refreshments I wanted.

Ronnie was often late to meetings. It was a consequence of his inability to enforce time boundaries or effectively wrap up a conversation. When he arrived he was, as always, flustered and contrite. I waited for him to settle and noticed, as he flopped down into his leather swivel chair, a thin coating of sweat darkening the rim of his shirt collar. Ronnie, for a man of 45, was unfit, overweight and full of nervous energy. He was unable to commit his attention to one activity or follow a train of thought for any significant period of time. During our short meeting he answered his mobile twice, left the room to remind his PA to prepare some reports for the morning, and when he was sitting down seemed unable to keep his eyes off the comings and goings through the glass office walls.

But, Ronnie, as always, appeared very glad to see me. He was full of warm, curious questions about my recent holiday, my children and the book I was writing. Having observed his *moving towards* patterns I was careful not to get pulled into this digression for long. After a few minutes I reminded him in a friendly way that we were here to talk about him. He looked momentarily startled and then suddenly began recounting in a bitter and angry tone the events of the meeting he had just left.

Apparently Ronnie had been 'grilled' by an unhappy Chairman who was highly critical of the latest television advertising campaign Ronnie's team had created. Ronnie felt manipulated, used, dismissed and belittled. He had, he said, worked hard to get the campaign out on time and to brief, yet one small error had led to the entire campaign being withdrawn. This was Ronnie in maximum threat mode having just been criticised and reprimanded by the top boss. Yet here he was ranting about the injustice done to him. How does this fit with a *moving towards* response that seeks to placate and please?

The answer can be illuminated using Stephen Karpman's concept of the 'drama triangle' of rescuer, persecutor and victim.[119] When *moving towards* is used as a response to threat it primarily involves a person coping by pleasing, helping, attending to and nurturing others. In Karpman's drama that's the 'rescuing' part. Once we have done all this good for others we get resentful and angry (the persecutor role) because the hoped-for solution – unconditional love and acceptance – is not forthcoming. Often this anger is repressed and hidden (hence the term passive aggression) but at other times it appears in behaviours such as sulking, moodiness or back stabbing. When we 'act out' in this way we notice others are even less likely to give us the appreciation and approval we demand and so we collapse into spiral of self-pity, hurt, sorrow and shame (victim). Melody Beattie, describing this pattern in her book, *Co-dependent No More*, writes:

> *This is the predictable and unavoidable result of a rescue. Feelings of helplessness, hurt, sorrow, shame and self-pity abound. We have been used – again. We have gone unappreciated – again. We try so hard to help people, be*

[119] In (Steiner, 1972)

good to them. We moan, 'Why? Why does this always
happen to me?' Another person has trampled on us, socked
it to us. We wonder, shall we forever be victims? Probably,
if we don't stop rescuing and caretaking.

Just as narcissism shares patterns with the *moving against* solution, so too does the 'disorder' of co-dependency share much with *moving towards*. What Beattie describes is the loop that defines this survival solution. Ronnie's strategy to rescue poor performing members of the team by taking on more work himself and by appeasing peers and stakeholders with over optimistic campaign reports did not bring him approval or appreciation. So his fear of being rejected increased, expressed itself briefly in an outburst of anger where he 'persecuted' by damning his colleagues and then, sank in to the more familiar misery and suffering of the victim.

Ronnie's unhappiness was very evident. It was not just the Chairman who failed to appreciate him, but Peter too. This was hard for Ronnie to digest. After all the hours of overtime, the late nights catching up with emails and his constant availability when Peter needed a friendly ear, he could not understand why Peter had not defended him in the meeting. He was bitter about this and told me a 'few things' about Peter which were less than complimentary. This switch in loyalties and 'u-turn' in his feelings about Peter was indicative of the *threat brain* motivation behind many of his significant relationships.

I asked Ronnie how he had responded to criticism from the board – although I had a fairly good idea having observed him in similar situations over the years. He confirmed my guess. Ronnie had accepted the admonishment, apologised profusely and promised a tough review with his team. I suspected the team review would never happen, that Ronnie would put in additional hours to realign the project and that his *move towards* loop would continue to repeat in much the same way it always had.

As I listened to Ronnie I noticed how increasingly unwell he was beginning to look. Every now and then he would loosen the knot in his tie and, in between pacing the room, take gulps of coffee from a cold cup. It's toxic here, he repeated. *Toxic.* I invited him to sit down and suggested he stop talking for a bit and practise some deep breathing. Ronnie knew about mindfulness practice from the work we had done in the executive team development. After a while he regained his composure and his angry mood deflated. *"This sort of thing triggers my depression,"* he said. *"and I've been depressed for years."* I had not known this about Ronnie, yet it made sense. The anger he was unable to express had probably turned inward.

Suffering – or being victim - is a key component of the *moving towards* solution and the perception that others are abusing or attacking us can provide a rationale for our protective, submissive response. We surrender in order to survive. At the same time it was clear to me that Ronnie's obsequious, sycophantic behaviour annoyed the Board and perhaps encouraged their hostile behaviours. Ronnie was blind to this. In his 'abuse narrative' he played the martyr role. Ronnie could not feel pride in his achievements but he could feel pride in his ability to tolerate suffering and 'forgive' those who brought such suffering upon him. This magnanimous, saintly person was the version of Ronnie that his inner critic promoted.[120] Suffering was his way of denying his rage and repressing deeply buried feelings of hatred and resentment.

When Ronnie admitted to having been depressed *"for years"* I asked him whether he had gained any insights into this depression. What followed was a sad and lonely story that held within it the origins of his current difficulty.

The Invisible Boy – Ronnie's story

When Ronnie was four his older brother was killed in a road traffic accident. His brother was six. They had been close companions and Ronnie felt his absence strongly. Overnight, home life as he had known it changed. Ronnie's mother blamed her husband for the loss. He had been driving the car that pulled out of a junction into the path of an oncoming van. The passenger side of the vehicle was

---

[120] In Ronnie's case, his Inner Critic scolded him when he showed any signs of fighting back. "We are safer submitting", it said. Thus, whenever Ronnie did experience his anger, he would later feel debilitating guilt.

crushed and Mark, Ronnie's brother, was killed instantly. Ronnie remembered his mother's fury and grief and his father's withdrawn and silent despair. His parents, lost in their own dark misery, did not have time or feeling left for Ronnie. From the day his brother disappeared, so too did he.

Soon after the funeral Ronnie was sent to live with his aunt for a while. He didn't remember much about this time except that his aunt, an older spinster, had little idea of how to relate to or care for a small boy. At nights the cold, spare room would cast shadows that terrified him. He would lie awake imagining that the creaking and shudderings of this old house were malevolent, ghostly voices.

Ronnie felt incomprehensibly to blame for his brother's death. Somehow he 'knew' that he had been sent to his aunt's house as a punishment and that he would only be allowed back once he had become 'good'. Some time after his fifth birthday Ronnie returned home and from that day forward was the well behaved, quiet boy he felt his parents expected and wanted.

A few years later, during a visit to his aunt, Ronnie found a local newspaper cutting from the year he had been sent away. The article reported that his father had been convicted for drunk driving and had received a suspended prison sentence for manslaughter. Ronnie felt a sudden surge of rage and hatred towards his father and then a crippling feeling of fear. He climbed back into the bed that had been the place of so many sleepless nights and wept. As the sun went down and the shadow of the tall lime tree fell across his bed he thought he heard his brother's voice. It startled him and he sat up in bed straining to hear. He thought the voice said '*Be still.*' Ronnie understood this as a message to do or say nothing. After tea with his aunt, during which she observed closely but said nothing, he returned home and carried on as before.

Ronnie lived with his parents until he was 25. He had tried to leave on several occasions but eventually returned to nurse his bedridden mother who had developed early dementia and become incapable of managing her basic needs. When Ronnie was 24 his mother committed suicide. He came home one day to find her in a drugged death sleep having overdosed on pain killers. He remained at home with his father who was demanding and bitter and made many claims on Ronnie's time and goodwill. Within a year he died from a heart attack on a night that Ronnie was out with his fiancée.

Ronnie married a woman whom he described as 'far superior' to him. She was a successful accountant, a semi-professional show jumper and a vocal member of their parish community. They had two children and Ronnie was fully involved in family life, whenever, that is, he could scrape time away from the office. I asked Ronnie what personal interests and hobbies he had and, unsurprisingly, he told me he did not have time for such things.

Ronnie had many dreams and aspirations though. He imagined learning to fly a light aircraft and backpacking through South America. He said he might begin a PhD or perhaps buy some land to build an eco-house. Of course, all these plans would need to fit in with his family and right now the timing was not good. Ronnie spent most evenings driving his children to and from clubs whilst his wife worked late, spent time at the stables or attended parish meetings. He was grateful and indebted, he said, to his wife for supporting him though his career mishaps.

I asked Ronnie whether his depression was related to these 'mishaps' but he repeated that he had 'always' been depressed. As a teenager he suffered 'some sort of breakdown' which resulted in a short admission to hospital. He was prescribed anti-depressants which he had been taking ever since. Ronnie told me that he had not had any formal counselling or therapy since his teenage years but that the few sessions he had back then sparked an interest in psychology, which he wanted to study at university. However, his father told him to do something he was good at, so he did economics. Nevertheless, he maintained his interest in psychology and over the years became familiar with the various schools and methods.

I asked him which psychological theories helped him understand his own circumstances and, to my surprise, he talked about his interest in *Active Imagination* and the work of Carl Jung. Ronnie, using Jung's methods, often entered into dialogue with the characters that appeared freely and vividly in his mind. It brought comfort he said and sometimes left him perplexed.

I must admit I was glad to hear this. It suggested to me that Ronnie was already familiar with some of the unconscious forces that have such influence in our lives. I asked him whether he wanted to talk about his use of this method as part of his development. Maybe, I said, those scenes that leave you perplexed are the very ones that will illuminate your way forward in this organisation. I also wondered privately whether the energy of his imaginal life was intensified by strong memories of his dead family and how their diminishing presence might release Ronnie to discover his unique and possible self. We will return to Ronnie's discoveries using active imagination shortly. Before that I wanted to draw Ronnie's attention to the *external* world and to explore the potential consequences of his strong *moving towards* habits.

Despite his theoretical insight and knowledge, Ronnie did not seem aware of how his behaviour appeared to, and affected, others. When he offered self-reflective statements they bore no resemblance to the Ronnie I saw in meetings and conversations. Ronnie spoke of himself as a 'broker', a skilled relationship manager who understood and was very responsive to the needs and requests of stakeholders. He did not talk about or recognise the problems of this 'supportive' approach which, given the requirements of his senior leadership role, lacked authority and direction.

At the end of this meeting, which I tried but failed to end on time,[121] I shared my observations about Ronnie's *moving away* habits. Using the flipchart that he kept in his office I drew Karpman's drama triangle and showed him, using the example of the meeting he had just come from, how it might play out for him. Ronnie listened quietly and with interest. When I finished we sat for a few moments and I watched him stare out of the window

---

[121] Ronnie was very skilled at keeping conversations going; it was part of his need to feel connected and bonded. He found endings difficult. I was pulled in to that strong undercurrent and in later sessions referred back to this experience as an example of the impact of *moving towards*.

mentally processing what he had heard. Finally he turned his worried gaze on me and said, 'Wow. That's me, isn't it?'

I suggested that, before we began the team development, Ronnie might have a few more one-to-one coaching sessions to work on his *moving towards* habits. "*It would help the team*", I said, "*if you came to the work with a greater sense of personal autonomy and strength*".

Ronnie agreed and, despite his anxious request to meet twice a week, we negotiated a fortnightly meeting. In the intervening weeks, I suggested a 'homework' task which was to notice and record moments in the day when he felt strong emotions. I asked him to make a few notes on the context, the people who were there, what was said and how he felt and reacted. It was my hope that he would get closer to the flip side of his compliance by noticing how frequent his aggressive feelings appeared.

Active imagination – surfacing and working with conflict

Our *threat brain* emotions are often triggered by *inner conflict* and our response is designed to minimise that conflict quickly. As we have seen, our solutions are not always appropriate or skilled, particularly when they involve distorting or denying our experience.

In *moving against* the inner conflict is between the overt urge to dominate and control and the covert desire to love and belong. In *moving towards* it is the opposite. Overtly we want to be liked, approved of, protected, guided and appreciated and we behave in ways that achieve these goals. However, underneath our compliance and 'good' behaviour are strong aggressive tendencies. In contrast to the apparent need to please and serve we also experience a lack of interest in others, a desire to manipulate, punish or exploit and feelings of defiance and anger. That we have opposing drives is not abnormal, it is a sign that our motivational system, with its range of emotional responses, is alive and well. It is only when our drives become imbalanced through repression (of the unwanted) and amplification (of the desired) that we start to experience the turmoil, confusion and unease that fuels our problem thoughts and behaviours.

As a child, Ronnie feared that if he was demanding, aggressive or 'bad' he risked losing his parents' love and care. As children, we think about morality and justice simplistically and so Ronnie may also have believed – consciously or unconsciously – that his brother died *because* he was bad. Thus he rejected 'bad' impulses and locked them in his cellar. He refused to hear the noise they made even when, as in his angry outburst, they escaped and appeared right in front of him.

The diary Ronnie brought back two weeks later was full of accounts of angry emotions that he felt but kept to himself. He was surprised by this and, he said, ashamed at the extent to which he harboured grudges and criticism about his colleagues. He was, he said, now trying much harder to be a decent person and felt these thoughts to be unacceptable and unfounded. This is an example of how his inner critic controlled him and directed him back to his familiar *moving towards* habits.

This was a good moment to talk about *threat brain* and how we can easily get trapped in self-reinforcing loops of reactive behaviour. Often, I said, the *threat brain* is responding to unconscious or 'implicit' memories rather than 'here and now' experience and one way of interrupting these loops is to become more conscious of the memories that motivate them.

Ronnie had already made a connection between his brother's death and his decision to be a 'good' child. It did not take him long to see that this same tendency played out in his adult relationships. Upsetting people meant risking abandonment and losses as grievous and painful as the first. This pervasive and core belief was seared into his implicit memory and left little room for other truths to thrive. Ronnie became very animated by talk of the unconscious and asked if he could share with me the contents of a recurring active imagination scene that he had been working with for some years.

Active imagination is a method of exploring the unconscious by having a dialogue with different parts of yourself that appear, just like in your dreams, as images, only in active imagination you are fully awake and interacting with these images. These images are *symbols* representing less familiar or known parts of ourself and in active imagination our conscious, 'ego' self has a conversation with them. If this sounds a bit like talking to yourself – it is. Only here the talk takes place with the full focus of your attention. This means preparing for and taking time to be with your imagination without interruptions or distractions. You need to find a quiet, private space and enough time to enter into and return from the experience. It also means recording what happens. The simplest way to do this is to give each image a name and then, using their initials, track the dialogue as if you were writing a play. As in free fall writing, you write with the flow and don't stop to correct, analyse or edit. Some people record their active imagination in drawings or music but if you are not familiar with these forms of expression, writing is probably the easiest.

It is not my intention to go into the full details of this method – for that I recommend Robert Johnson's book, *Inner Work*. My purpose here is to distil Ronnie's *learning* and how he eventually applied that learning in his day to day experience.

Ronnie had a summer house at the bottom of his garden which he had converted into his office. His wife and children rarely interrupted him there as it had a reputation for harbouring an unusual number of spiders. Ronnie liked to perpetuate and embellish this rumour as it enabled him to maintain his privacy without having to refuse their entry.

For some years, since attending a weekend course on Jungian psychology, he had been going there to experiment with active imagination. Each time he called forth images from his unconscious he would see and enter into what he described as his 'Narnia' – a snow-drenched, wooded landscape where figures of his family stood frozen between the trees. Ronnie appeared as a faun with furred goat legs and a muscly human body. The only other living creature in this drama was a bad-tempered witch, who had a cauldron that bubbled and boiled all day and all night over an open fire outside her door. This, she said, kept away the spirit child who was made of ice and had cursed the forest. She had never seen this spirit but she heard it speaking through the trees which, although frosted on their lower branches, had verdant canopies that swayed in the wind and appeared to be reaching towards a clear blue sky.

Ronnie had already made a number of interpretations and connections that cast the images and characters as actual people from his life. He believed that if he could fully come to terms with his brother's death there would be a thaw in his own heart and a resolution to the emptiness he so often felt. He spoke to the spirit child as if it was his brother who was part of this frozen landscape and also separate from it. He wasn't sure, however, who the witch was. Their conversations were mostly about Ronnie's family. The witch watched Ronnie's life though a cracked mirror that hung from the branch of a dead willow tree. She spat out her scathing opinions about his wife and children and scolded him for being a weak and ineffective parent.

Johnson, when describing this method, warns against casting the images as actual people who we know. This tempts us to literalise our imagination by, for example, trying to continue conversations with people in real life that we began in active imagination. Johnson calls this 'acting out'. If we *imagine* that we are wielding a sword against our father that does not mean we should actually drive over to his house to provoke a violent argument.

Active imagination is not about other people, it is about you and your unconscious, interior life. If an image of someone you know does come forth, it is better to stop and change their appearance and you can do this as part of the dialogue. Johnson suggests saying something like, *"Look, I don't know why but you look exactly like the guy at the office that I'm mad at, since I know that you are an energy system inside me, please change your appearance. I don't want to confuse what is inside me with a person who is outside me."*

I reminded Ronnie to cast his images as parts of himself and to understand the spirit child, frozen family and witch as his own energy. In our conversations about his active imagination he began to see the witch as his anger and the spirit child as his possible self.

Our conversations about his scenarios were rather like two people discussing a film they have seen. We both had different experiences, questions, interpretations and interests and in sharing these we came to a fuller understanding of what motivated and also what blocked Ronnie. We do not need to be Jungian experts to work with our imagination and to play with the stories that pour forth. We do however, need to have emotional resilience in order to tolerate the twists and turns of plot and character and the insights that emerge about ourselves. Self-compassion is an essential requirement because it is likely that our unconscious will deliver up some unpleasant and unwanted 'truths'.

Ronnie learned about the underbelly of his compliant self by writing about his witch, whom he came to understand as representing the denied and hidden aspects of himself. For Ronnie to meet and integrate his witch he had to explore the unresolved grief around his brother's death and safely rediscover the anger and 'bad' emotions that he had supressed since then.

Seeking resolution – disentangling from the family

Many years ago, I practised as a family therapist and was introduced to the work of the German therapist[122] Bert Hellinger, whose ideas I have already referred to. Hellinger only asks about the *events* in a family – not the thoughts and feelings attached to those events. He then encourages his client to state, in one sentence, the problem for which they are seeking resolution or understanding. With this information Hellinger guides his client through the process of setting up a *constellation*, using workshop participants to represent the people and relationships involved in the problem – or 'entanglement' – described. From this representation of his client's family dynamic, Hellinger is able to see what is missing, unresolved and in need of reparation. Resolution comes, he says,

> When each person is in the right place; when each is being true to what is important to that person; when each is attending to his or her own life and not interfering with the others. Then everyone has dignity and self-esteem and feels good.

We become entangled when we unconsciously take over the fates of members of our family and start to live these out as if they were our own. In my work the most frequently discussed entanglement is

---

[122] Hellinger describes himself as "a caretaker of the soul".

that of family break-up and divorce. The strategies we use to keep our parents together and to cope with the intense feeling of loss and loneliness that ensues when we inevitably fail, striate our being and powerfully motivate our subsequent relationships. We explored the significance of early attachment and separation in Part One.

A less frequent, yet powerful, experience is that of a death in the family. Too often deaths are not fully acknowledged and the deceased are not openly grieved, spoken about or honoured. This can cause problems and emotional 'blockages' for surviving family members.

Hellinger, who worked as a missionary in South Africa, describes rituals that help families live in harmony with death. The Zulu people, for example, bury their dead and, after a year, welcome them back into the house. Family members take a branch, which they imagine the deceased member is sitting on, and drag it back into the house. The branch is left in a corner of the hut that is reserved for the ancestors. Apparently this is the corner where the beer is kept! Many such rituals honour and acknowledge the dead as a presence in life. According to Hellinger, when this is the case the dead 'find their place'. They are peaceful and experienced as a powerful energy.

Before my father was interred I saved a portion of his ashes and, in a ritual of my own, mixed them with some brightly coloured gem stones and placed them in a small crystal box. My father liked to buy us jewellery and watches and I know he would have appreciated this gesture. More so, he would have been delighted to have a place in my office amongst the books and photos of our family. My father has found his place above my desk in a box that catches the light like a fine cut diamond. Although we had a difficult relationship my memories of him are peaceful now and I feel immense gratitude.

In a family constellation the dead are brought back into the picture so that they can be reintegrated. This is made possible when we see and appreciate the *whole* dynamic or pattern that has been in motion since the death and then the way in which that pattern could shift to create greater peace and harmony.

I suggested that Ronnie attend a Constellations workshop to see whether he could move closer to resolution of his own.[123] The value

---

[123] For more information see www.thecsc.net

of placing people to represent you and your family system is that the representatives usually go on to 'tell' a different version of your story by describing how *they* feel in the positions you have placed them. The facilitator, after hearing from each representative, asks them to move to where they feel more comfortable or 'right'. Usually this creates the representation of a healthier system. The facilitator observing this process can also move representatives and, in the *re-constellating* of the system, insight and resolution occurs.

Resolution means we experience our story or problem differently. The difference usually involves less guilt, more compassion, forgiveness, relief and a feeling of freedom to live our own lives.

Ronnie attended two workshops. In the first he observed the process and in the second he volunteered to share his problem. He gave a few details of his circumstances – mentioning the death of his brother but not his mother's later suicide and then set up the constellation to show what it was like living in his family after the death. He chose representatives for himself, his mother, father and brother and placed them in relationship to each other.

Ronnie reflected at length on this experience and told me how powerful the re-constellation had been. Listening to the representatives describe their feelings and watching their movements, he realised that for many years he had been afraid that his mother wanted to 'leave' the family to be with her dead child. 'Leaving' can be experienced as emotional absence or an actual departure through death, divorce or hospitalisation. Throughout his childhood and early adult life Ronnie had unconsciously known how much his mother wanted to leave and, in the constellations workshop, he learned that the desire to join a dead loved one is not an uncommon experience. He also learned that when it is the parent feeling this way it is not unusual for a remaining child to develop illnesses and 'problems' in order to prevent their departure. If I am ill, says the child, you will have to stay to take care of me.

The constellation gave Ronnie a different perspective on his depression. He now understood it as an attempt to keep his mother from leaving. He also realised that his strategies had to be extreme to match the force of her desire to leave – which was expressed, in the end, through her suicide. When the representatives re-constellated the family they created a scenario in which Ronnie's parents were with the dead brother (Mark), but this time the three of them were turned to face Ronnie and had moved close to him. The representatives had not known that in the end this is exactly what happened. Both Ronnie's parents died within a short time of each other and Ronnie was left on his own.

When Ronnie described his constellations I drew them and I was very moved to see that when the representatives re-constellated they clustered the family tightly together and each member was facing in (see figure 9, drawing 2). Although they did not know that Ronnie's parents had died, the constellation hints at this outcome and suggests it as a peaceful resolution. Of course, our stories, including those told in constellations, are open to interpretation, editing and change. This method, which can sometimes feel uncanny or preternatural, can be understood in more simple terms – it gives visual voice to new possibilities for re-authoring our lives.

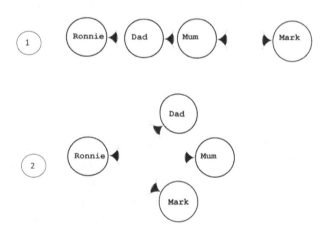

Figure 9: Ronnie's family constellation

The constellations helped Ronnie tell a different version of his story which was more compassionate and forgiving – of himself and his family. It helped him let go of the guilt he had carried and to understand, particularly in relation to his mother, the powerful forces that turned her towards her dead son. He imagined the death of his own children and found great empathy for her in this analogy. He began to experience fewer mood swings and felt confident to gradually lower his dose of anti-depressants. It also gave him the courage to address some of the problems in his marriage which were part of his *moving towards* pattern. He asked his wife to attend one of the workshops with him in which he set up a constellation based on the problem statement, "*I am unable to assert myself in my marriage*". Having set up the representatives in relation to one another in a way that reflected his inner image of his marriage and family, Ronnie and his wife watched the facilitator inquire and provoke the system into a new 'order' that both illuminated and unlocked the problem.

Changes in our private life often affect us at work and vice versa. As Ronnie became more assertive and confident in his home life so too did he feel able to address the problems in his team and at work.

We began the team development a year after Ronnie's first request. It had taken him that time to work on his issues and make progress personally. By then Ronnie was keen to explore how constellations could be used in his team to surface and relieve some of the problems that had been growing as a result of redundancies, falling share price and the sudden departure of Peter, the golden CEO.

When I started to meet Ronnie's team to find out what they wanted from team development most of them said they wanted Ronnie to be more 'present' in team meetings, to offer clarity on strategy and more opportunities for team discussion. Ronnie's restless habit and his tendency to talk a lot and provide disconnected pieces of information was affecting the learning and productivity in his team. In addition the volatile business climate was creating uncertainty and fear throughout the organisation. In Ronnie's team this was felt as covert suspicion and conflict between certain members.

Before addressing the group dynamic – which we will end this chapter with – I wanted to draw Ronnie's attention to this feedback and relate it to the work we had begun around noticing emotion states and their impact on threat, safe and drive motivations.

Playful Inquiry – a safe way towards disruptive thinking

Clarity and presence were the two themes I focused on and I began by asking Ronnie to give me an overview of the People Strategy which had just been signed off by the Executive Team. I asked him to imagine he was briefing his team. Again, we had some fun with this as I took the role of various team members to challenge, inquire and provoke Ronnie as he delivered the brief.

What surfaced in this short session is that Ronnie's brief was anything but brief. He talked, without pause for breath, providing a large quantity of information which veered further and further away from the executive summary. Ronnie spent time drawing flow charts and diagrams on his white board that were intended to clarify processes, objectives and relationships but in the end were a confusing array of arrows, circles, ticks and crosses. Even though I had been present when the People Strategy was signed off I could not make sense of Ronnie's presentation. I noticed in myself a mixture of frustration, impatience, anxiety and disengagement. This, I thought, could be what it feels like to be in Ronnie's team.

Ronnie was caught in a loop which is probably familiar to most of us. He was drowning in 'information overload' – the recipient (as we all are) of vast quantities of facts, figures, opinions and advice which only made him feel *more* ignorant. This overload leads to feelings of inadequacy and incompetence. Many of us try to hide these feelings by pretending that we *do* know and that we have the 'answers'. Yet the vast expanse of the unknown which is illuminated by all this 'information' can return us to childhood feelings of fear in the face of the unfamiliar and unpredictable. Our *threat brain* begins to pulse, anxiety grows and our ability to feel, think and act clearly and accurately is disturbed. Unless, of course, we can interrupt the loop, regulate these feelings and reframe our uncertainties as opportunities for learning and growth.

Joichi Ito, Director of MIT Media Lab, suggests that to do this we must become *neotenous* (neoteny describes the retention of childlike attributes in adulthood) and rediscover the characteristics within us that once – no matter how briefly – made learning a joyful, wondrous, exciting activity and the unknown simply a wide open space for adventure. In short, we must learn to play again.

Ronnie practised playing with questions. Instead of sweating on the answers he could present to impress or placate his team, he contemplated how he could invite a playful inquiry that might stimulate collective learning and shared understanding of strategy.

I am using 'playful' to describe the open and genuinely curious tone in which a question is asked. We ask because we truly want to know and because we trust and value the interdependencies in our relationships. In other words, we are not frightened to say *"I don't know, can you help me understand?"* Or *"What do you think?"* There is a spacious quality to playful inquiry – we give ourselves time to 'not know' and time to discover that which, within or around us, is seeking to be known. Our questions turn the keys in doors to our cellars and secret gardens.

Padgett Powell in *The Interrogative Mood*, writes an entire novel from questions and provides an entertaining example of the infinite possibilities for inquiry, if only we were prepared to play and were tolerant of play. He writes:

> *If someone approached you saying 'lead me to the music,' how would you respond? Is there a name to complete this progression: Rasputin, Robespierre, Robbe-Grillet, Robert Goulet and...? If you could spend some time with a young Judy Garland or a young Lucille Ball, whom would you pick? If you had house painters drinking on the job, would you provide them booze? Is there anything or anyone that you'd say you are 'enamoured of'? If you could disappear from your native country and live comfortably in another, what country would you choose?*[124]

To exercise your curiosity muscles you could, like Padgett Powell, write a few pages of questions in free fall fashion. This is what Ronnie did and soon discovered that below the surface of his ever-present anxiety was his very playful 'spirit child' waiting to be invited into his conscious life. In conversations with his spirit child

---

[124] (Powell, 2010)

Ronnie talked about how he could acknowledge and work with the growing tensions in his team. What was the question that might release healthy energy into the group?

We worked on powerful questions that might support team development and explored Peter's parting words to the executive team – that they needed to be *creatively disruptive* to meet the challenges arising out of the turbulent and unpredictable economy.

The *creative disruption* Peter referred to was an invitation not just to disturb but also to *transform* the business in a way that he, in the end, could not do. Peter had become locked in a conflict with the new chairman who had placed major constraints on him. Peter had believed in development and wanted his organisation to feel, think and act freely. Ronnie, who mourned his departure, wanted to honour his legacy and this was a strong motivation to let go of his *moving towards* habits – which he described as 'vague and invisible' – and to challenge the unhealthy patterns of thinking and behaving that were adversely affecting team creativity and performance.

In the constellations workshops Ronnie had successfully addressed some of these patterns and he wondered whether a similar exercise could work in his team. He also thought it would be a good way to make his presence felt by suggesting – and leading – a different approach to team development: one which, he hoped, would provide a new kind of clarity. The core question Ronnie framed to begin his team development was: *How can we improve the quality of relationships in this team so that we have more conversations that create shared meaning and purpose?*

Team Constellations – opportunities for clarity and presence

A year after our meeting in his glass office, Ronnie and I facilitated the first of six team gatherings intended to address his core question. We met regularly for half a day over nine months. In the second session Ronnie invited the group to take part in a constellations exercise to explore relationships in the team. Prior to this the team had done some work to agree the purpose and parameters of the development and to develop openness and trust.

It was a small group of six direct reports. Two individuals had left during the difficult, preceding year of redundancies and restructuring. The remaining members were unsettled and wary of change. Understandably, their *threat brain* was on high alert. In our meetings they expressed relief at being able to talk for the first time about their fears and experience, yet when given the time and space to do so it was hard for them to share their concerns. The conversations were cautious and defensive. I also sensed that several members were unsure whether to trust Ronnie. He had, after all, been part of the staff 'elimination' process.

When Ronnie asked me to facilitate a constellation I wondered how useful or appropriate it would be given the levels of threat and conflict in the team. In these situations, to avoid provoking further problems, the constellations are often set up in an artificially harmonious way and representatives are vague and non-committal. Gunthard Weber, an experienced constellations facilitator, warns that the method should not be used as a 'parlour game':

> *Experience shows that a constellation makes a strong statement when the person setting it up has a burning, important issue and is willing to put something at stake to risk finding a solution.*[125]

Weber advises that constellations be used only to solve immediate and specific individual problems. I did not feel the team would benefit from the full method, so I suggested the constellation could be used *lightly*, in adapted form. This is a simple, yet powerful exercise which involves each member taking a turn to place the others and lastly themselves in a configuration that represents how they experience the team relationships, feelings and behaviours. Placing involves using distance from each other, body postures and even facial expression to convey the relationships.

When framing this exercise I emphasise that *every* representation is valid and no constellation holds more 'truth' than another. I encourage the team to take part with respect and interest in each person's team story. Once a constellation is set up, I invite

---

[125] (Weber, 2000)

the team, one at a time, to talk about what it feels like to be in the position where they have been placed. Afterwards, when everyone has had a turn (and a break) I invite the members to take time alone to reflect on what has happened and then to draw on a flipchart their version of an 'ideal' configuration. In other words, what would the constellation look like if the team were working and relating to each other optimally?

Our workshop ended with the team talking about each of these drawings to get a sense of the hope and potential for development within the group. These flipcharts became a very useful reference point throughout the work and we brought them out at the end of the nine months when the team re-constellated to see how close they were to their 'ideal' states.

This chapter is not, however, about Ronnie's team but about his own learning and growth and, in particular, his efforts to manage his *threat brain* habit of *moving towards*. If Ronnie had approached the exercise in *threat brain* he would have created the artificial harmony that is so detrimental to this discovery process. Ronnie's tendency to appease, smooth over conflict and 'rescue' people would have closed down difficult expression and conversation.

He, as leader of the team, needed to set the tone for the work and, in doing so, create 'permission' for others to follow. In this case Ronnie needed to show that he would not appease or rescue and that he was prepared to risk disapproval and tolerate disagreement in order to create an open, honest space for dialogue. Ronnie needed to show that it was possible to speak your truth, survive the tension and grow from it.

To frame the purpose and intent of the constellations exercise Ronnie shared his own experience of using the method to understand events and relationships in his life that, he felt, were holding him back from realising his full potential. He invited me to talk about 'possible' selves and what happens when we live through our *threat brain* responses. However, mostly *he* led as well as participated in the process and in each constellation spoke his perspective from the heart, which meant giving both challenging and vulnerable feedback. He expressed his feeling of being an outcast, a pleaser and in one difficult moment, his ongoing impatience and estrangement from a colleague. The way he spoke and took part was exemplary. Here was the clarity and presence – I witnessed both gravitas and humour in his actions – that some of the team needed in order to feel confident. The constellations enabled Ronnie to *show* his team that he was capable of leading with purpose, direction and strength and that it was possible to embrace and work with the differences in the team in a healthy and considerate manner.

During our year together Ronnie learned to centre himself and speak not from a position of threat but guided and soothed by his *safe brain* voice which, as we have learned, is mindful, kind and conscious of our common humanity. Ronnie had developed a compassionate voice which enabled him to speak his truth with respect and care. He worried much less about being rejected or criticised and had come to appreciate that he did not need uniform approval to survive and thrive in his life. In fact, by pruning people from his life he started to experience *himself* fully – what he wanted and needed and what he believed and thought. He began to spend longer in his summer house, planning a trip to South America, which he intended to take on his own. Like active imagination and playful inquiry, this also nurtured his imaginal mind by giving space for long-forgotten dreams of exploration and adventure and it inspired him to discover how traditional Amazonian villages and ways of life could inform his own interest in eco-living.

Ronnie's team went on to launch a successful new product that contributed to a share price rise and enabled the company to survive the reverberations of the 2008 global crash. But in 2012 the organisation underwent further structural changes and as part of this process, Ronnie accepted voluntary redundancy. He decided, with his wife's support, to re-train and begin a new career in social work. He also bought a flat-pack eco-home which, when I last spoke to him, he was building in the footprint of the old summer house.

Epilogue: Moving On

Freud once said that he cured the miseries of the neurotic only to open him up to the normal misery of life. What he was getting at, but did not fully conceptualise, was that no matter how capable we are of soothing our threatened brain or how practised we are at re-finding our centre, the fact remains that we cannot transcend the limits of our human condition. The result is that the fear of death – expressed in the kinds of 'survival solutions' we have learned about – remains a primary motivating force. Freud did not openly acknowledge the significance of this fear. Late in his life though, he proposed that aggression was the expression of a 'death drive' and existed as a separate, "original and autonomous disposition". This was a big addition to his system of thought because it pointed at motivations which were not part of the libidinal, pleasure-seeking system (part of *drive brain*) which he had been preoccupied with for most of his career.

We could re-cast this 'autonomous disposition' as the *moving against* part of our *threat brain* which then helps us understand what Freud meant when he said that the aggressive impulse represents "the greatest obstacle to civilisation". Perhaps Freud's pessimism came from the observation that too many ordinary people (he called them "trash") were caught in what I have called *threat-drive brain* loops. I have suggested that this version of 'normal misery' – or 'toxic drive' – is motivated not just by aggression but also by avoidance and compliance and organisations, as well as civilisations, will be injured by these 'obstacles' if we remain unconscious of them.

Freud knew that awareness by itself is no cure for normal misery and he did not go beyond this realisation. Some since Freud *have*, though. In this book I have proposed that warm awareness is the antidote to many of our problems and it may be the antidote to the fundamental problem of existence – our mortality. Why? Because warm awareness is forgiving. It knows that there are some things we need to keep at bay, some things that we had better not be too cognisant of lest they de-rail us for good. For each of us, those 'somethings' are personal and particular and remain in the dark matter that appears in dreams, in inexplicable moments of anxiety, in the habits we cannot relinquish. Warm awareness will soothe us when the bad dreams come, when we relapse into our old habits and when fear sweeps over our life, like a winter storm. Warm awareness leads us into new territories and also tells us when it is time to return. There is, after all, only so much each of us can take – or let go of.

At the same time, warm awareness will gently pull us to our feet when we inevitably stumble or fall. It will revitalise us and re-direct our energy towards the nurturing of what Ernest Becker beautifully described as our own 'creative myth' which is a story about our self that accounts for and releases our potential. It is a *safe brain* story and different from the one we tell our self when we are in threat. In this book I have suggested cultivating self-compassion, exploring our unconscious beliefs and motives, and re-imagining our life: these are all ways in which we can make our own creative myth.

In making our creative myth we learn to accept the inevitability of our eventual 'nonbeing' without becoming engulfed or embittered by the problem of meaninglessness that death confronts us with. We make our meaning – or author our lives – in the full knowledge that our story is both arbitrary and essential. We have seen how our beliefs make our reality and affect our actions and we have learned that these personal 'truths' are pliable – making it possible to construct our narrative in a way that serves us and others well. Our biological inheritance and our lived experience give us the raw material to do this and, as I have tried to show, once we have developed a degree of cognitive maturity, we can learn how to edit and revise our stories if we wish. As we make and practise our revisions we could follow Becker's advice and "leave tragedy behind".

There are many things about life that are poignant and painful, yet to make life generally tragic or dangerous is to live in the narrow confines of *threat brain*. Given that we are only here for such a short time, and given that our *Trimotive Brain* offers richer possibilities for living, that seems wasteful.

Living courageously, creatively and from our centre starts with soothing our threatened brain, with turning towards the aggressive impulse that Freud so feared and seeing it for what it is. The shadow looming large on the wall is not in the end a wild and ferocious beast but a small part of ourselves that has something important to say. Sometimes that part of us will speak some useful truths and sometimes it won't. With warm awareness we listen openly, take what is helpful and leave behind what is not. We are all, as the opening quote from Carl Jung suggests, in need of the alms of our own kindness and it is that quality in particular which enables us to endure the uncertainties of creation and our own vulnerable place within it.

Warm awareness has, for me, a golden hue. It is a summer afternoon walking hand in hand through tall cornfields that surround my grandmother's farm and, somewhere else, waiting at the window to see my father turn in to the drive. It is a cake with my name piped in icing, my brother sticking up for me at school and mittens my mother lovingly strung through my winter coat. I forget these things when I'm in threat; when I remember, I make meaning, my myth, differently and life feels more possible.

In the end, the best we can do is to make meanings and myths that help us live with greater equanimity and grace in the face of disappointment, difficulty and suffering. This is how it would be to live beyond threat.

Thank you...

Ruth Moody for compassionately reading the first drafts and offering your non-wounding, early perspective. Tom Jones for your direct feedback and long lived ambition for this work. Rovarn Wickremasinghe for our esoteric conversations and your unconditional praise. Jim Cookson for scribbling thoughtful and appreciative words over the manuscript. Liz Straker for your boundless optimism and encouragement. Matt Jacobs for taking on even more reading and giving your non-corporate observations. My mother, Aru, for quiet faith and unfaltering help with the daily juggle. And, Andrew Carey, a patient, sagacious and subtly swashbuckling editor.

Bibliography

Baldwin, C., 1996. *Calling the Circle.* Gateway Books.

Becker, E., 1973. *The Denial of Death.* The Free Press.

Begley, S., 2009. *The Plastic Mind.* Constable.

Bly, R., 1988. *A Little Book on the Human Shadow.* HarperCollins.

Bowlby, J., (1969) 1997. *Attachment and Loss.* Pimlico.

Brandon, N., 1978. *The Disowned Self.* Bantam Books.

Breines, J. & Chen, S., 2012. 'Self-Compassion Increases Self-Improvement Motivation', *Personality and Social Psychology Bulletin,* Vol. 38, pp.1133-1143.

Brown, B., 2012. *Daring Greatly: How the Courage to be Vulnerable Transforms the Way We Live, Love, Parent and Lead.* Penguin.

Cacioppo, J. T. & Patrick, W., 2008. *Loneliness: Human Nature and the Need for Social Connection.* Norton.

Cain, S., 2012. *Quiet: The Power of Introverts in a World That Can't Stop Talking.* Penguin.

Capra, F., 2002. *The Hidden Connections.* HarperCollins.

Carr, N., 2011. *The Shallows: How the Internet is Changing the Way We Think, Read and Remember.* Atlantic Books.

Collins, S., 2016. *Neuroscience for Learning and Development.* Kogan Page.

Corkin, S., 2014. *Permanent Present Tense: The Man with No Memory and What He Taught the World.* Penguin.

Csikszentmihalyi, M., 1992. *Flow: The Classic Work on How to Achieve Happiness.* Rider.

Curran, A., 2008. *The Little Book of Big Stuff About the Brain.* Crown House.

Damasio, A., 2012. *Self Comes to Mind: Constructing the Conscious Brain.* Vintage.

Depue, R.S. and Morrone-Strupinsky, J.V., (2005): 'A neurobehavioral model of affiliative bonding' *Behavioural and Brain Science*, 28, 313-395

Eagleman, D., 2015. *The Brain: The Story of You.* Canongate Books.

Eisold, K., 2009. *What You Don't Know You Don't Know.* Other Press.

Eliot, T.S., 1936. *Collected Poems 1909-1962.* Faber and Faber.

Foer, F., 2017, *World Without Mind: The Existential Threat of Big Tech,* Jonathan Cape.

Frankl, V., 2004. *Man's Search for Meaning.* Rider.

Freud, S., (1930) 2004. *Civilisation and Its Discontents.* Great Ideas ed. Penguin.

Fromm, E., 2010. *The Heart of Man.* American Mental Health Fnd. Books.

Gilbert, P., 2009. 'Introducing Compassion-Focused Therapy' in *Advances in Psychiatric Treatment,* Vol. 15, pp.199-208

_____ 2010. *The Compassionate Mind.* Constable.

_____ 2012. 'Compassion Focused Therapy' in *Cognitive Behavioural Therapies.* Sage.

_____ 2014. 'The Origins and Nature of Compassion Focused Therapy' in *British Journal of Clinical Psychology,* Vol. 53, pp.6-41

Gilbert, P., et al., 2011. 'Fears of Compassion: Development of Three Self-Report Measures'. *Psychology and Psychotherapy: Theory, Research and Practice,* Vol. 13, pp.239-255.

Glouberman, D. D., 2003. *The Joy of Burnout.* Hodder & Stoughton.

Goldberg, N., 2005. *Writing Down the Bones: Freeing the Writer Within.* Shambala.

Gračanin, A., Bylsma, L. & Vingerhoets, J. J., 2014. 'Is Crying a Self-Soothing Behavior'. *Frontiers in Psychology,* 28 May, Vol. 5, pp.1-15.

Greenfield, S., 2014. *Mind Change.* Rider.

Harlow, J. M., 1869. 'Recovery from the Passage of an Iron Bar through the Head'. *Publications of the Massachusetts Medical Society,* 2(3), pp.327-347.

Harrison, P. J., 2004. 'The Hippocampus in Schizophrenia: A Review of the Neuropathological Evidence and its Pathophysiological Implications'. *Psychopharmacology,* 174(1), pp.151-162.

Harris, S., 2012. *Free Will.* Free Press.

Hellinger, B., 1998. *Love's Hidden Symmetry: What Makes Love Work in Relationships.* Zeig, Tucker and Co.

Helliwell, J., Layard, R. & Sachs, J., 2017. *World Happiness Report 2017,* Sustainable Development Solutions Network.

Hillman, J., 1975. *Revisioning Psychology.* Harper Row.

Hillman, J. & Ventura, M., 1993. *We've Had a Hundred Years of Psychotherapy and the World is Getting Worse.* Harper.

Hollis, J., 1993. *The Middle Passage: From misery to meaning in middle life.* Inner City Books.

Horney, K., 1945. *Our Inner Conflicts: A Constructive Theory of Neuroses.* W.W.Norton.

_____ 1950. *Neurosis and Human Growth: The Struggle Toward Self-Realization.* W.W.Norton.

Hyde, L., 2012. *The Gift: How the Creative Spirit Transforms the World.* Canongate.

James, W., 1890. *The Principles of Psychology, Vol. One.* Holt.

Jamieson, J., Nock, M. & Mendes, W., 2012. 'Mind Over Matter: Reappraising Arousal Improves Cardiovascular and Cognitive Response to Stress'. *Journal of Experimental Psychology,* 141(3), pp. 417 -422.

Johnson, R.A., 1986. *Inner Work: Using Dreams and Active Imagination for Personal Growth.* HarperOne.

_____ 1991. *Owning Your Own Shadow: Understanding the Dark Side of the Psyche.* HarperCollins.

Jung, C.G., 1961. *Memories, Dreams, Reflections.*Random House.

_____ 1968. *The Archetypes and the Collective Unconscious.* Routledge.

_____ (1933) 2001. *Modern Man in Search of a Soul.* Routledge Classics.

Kabat-Zinn, J., 2001. *Full Catastophe Living: How to Cope with Stress, Pain and Illness Using Mindfulness Meditation.* Piatkus.

Kolts, R., 2012. *The Compassionate Mind Approach to Managing Your Anger.* Robinson.

Konnikova, M., 2014. 'What's Lost as Handwriting Fades'. *New York Times,* 2nd June.

Laing, R.D., 1959. *The Divided Self.* Tavistock Publications.

Lakoff, G. & Johnson, M., 1999. *Philosophy in the Flesh.* Basic Books.

Leahy, R. L., 2001. *Overcoming Resistance in Cognitive Therapy.* Guilford Press.

LeDoux, J., 1998. *The Emotional Brain.* Phoenix.

_____ *Anxiety: Using the brain to understand and treat fear and anxiety.* Penguin.

Lifton, R. J., 1993. *The Protean Self: Human Resilience in an Age of Fragmentation.* Basic Books.

Longe, O. et al., 2010. 'Having a Word with Yourself: Neural Correlates of Self-Criticism and Self-Reassurance'. *NeuroImage,* Vol. 49, pp. 1849-1856.

Maitland, S., 2008. *A Book of Silence: A Journey in Search of the Pleasure and Powers of Silence.* Granta.

Mangen, A. & Velay, J.-L., 2010. 'Digitizing Literacy: Reflections on the Haptics of Writing'. In: M. H. Zadeh, ed. *Advances in Haptics.* Intech.

Miller, A., 1987. *The Drama of Being a Child.* Virago.

Moore, T., 2001. *Original Self: Living with Paradox and Originality.* Perennial.

Morgan, G., 1997. *Images of Organisations.* Sage.

Munro, G. & Munro, C., 2014. "'Soft' versus 'Hard' Psychological Science: Biased Evaluations of Scientific Evidence that Threatens or Supports a Strongly Held Political Identity'. *Basic and Applied Social Psychology,* 36(6), pp.533-543.

Neff, K., 2011. *Self-Compassion.* Hodder and Stoughton.

Newberg, A. & Waldman, M., 2012. *Words Can Change Your Brain.* Hudson Street Press.

Norretranders, T., 1998. *The User Illusion.* Penguin.

Norwood, R., 2004. *Women Who Love Too Much.* Arrow.

O'Connor, R., 2015. *Rewire: Change your Brain to Break Bad Habits, Overcome Addictions and Conquer Self-Destructive Behavior.* Plume.

Perls, F., Hefferline, R. & Goodman, P., 1986. *Gestalt Therapy.* Souvenir Press.

Perry, B., 2002. 'Childhood Experience and the Expression of Genetic Potential'. *Brain and Mind,* Vol. 3 pp.79-100.

Polyani, M., 1962. *Personal Knowledge: Towards a Post-Critical Philosophy.* University of Chicago Press.

Powell, P., 2010. *The Interrogative Mood: A novel?* Profile Books.

Reich, W., 1972. *Character Analsysis.* 3rd ed. Farrar, Straus and Giroux.

Rilke, R. M., (1923) 1985. *The Sonnets to Orpheus.* Simon & Schuster.

Rogers, C., 1967. *On Becoming a Person: A Therapist's View of Psychotherapy.* Constable.

Rowan, J., 1990. *Subpersonalities: The People Inside Us.* Routledge.

Salzburg, S., 2005. Loving Kindness Meditation Audio CD. Sounds True.

Sapolsky, R., 2004. *Why Zebras Don't Get Ulcers.* St Martin's Press.

Sartre, J-P., 1946. *Existentialism and Humanism.* Methuen.

Schein, E., 2013. *Humble Inquiry: The Gentle Art of Asking Instead of Telling.* Berrett-Koehler.

Senge, P. et al., 2008. *The Necessary Revolution: How Individuals and Organisations are Working Together.* Nicholas Brealey.

Shaw, J., 2016. *The Memory Illusion: Remembering, Forgetting and the Science of False Memory.* Random House.

Siegel, D., 2010. *Mindsight: Transform your Brain with the New Science of Kindness.* Oneworld.

Sroufe, L., et al. 2009. *The Development of the Person: The Minnesota Study of Risk and Adaptation from Birth to Adulthood.* The Guilford Press.

Steiner, C., 1972. *Scripts People Live.* Grove.

Stone, D., Patton, B. & Heen, S., 1999. *Difficult Conversations: How to Discuss What Matters Most.* Portfolio Penguin.

Stone, H. & Winkelman, S., 1989. *Embracing Our Selves.* New World Library.

Swabb, D., 2014. *We Are Our Brains: From the Womb to Alzheimer's.* Penguin.

Szasz, T. S., 1974. *The Myth of Mental Illness: Foundations of a Theory of Personal Conduct.* Harper Collins.

The Arbinger Institute, 2006. *Leadership and Self Deception.* Penguin.

Weber, G., 2000. 'Organisational Constellations: Basics and Special Situations'. In: C. A. S. Verlag, ed. *Praxis der Organisationsaufstellungen.*

Wenger, E., McDermott, R. & Snyder, W., 2002. *Cultivating Communities of Practice.* Harvard Business School Press.

Wickremasinghe, N., 2021. *Being with Others.* Triarchy Press.

Wilson, T., 2002. *Strangers to Ourselves.* Harvard University Press.

_____ 2011. *Redirect: The surprising new science of psychological change.* Little Brown.

Winnicott, D., 1973. *The Child, the Family and the Outside World.* Pelican.

Winterson, J., 2012. *Why Be Happy When You Can Be Normal?* Vintage.

Zander, R. S. & Zander, B., 2000. *The Art of Possibility: Transforming Professional and Personal Life.* Harvard Business School Press.

Zweig, C. & Abrams, J., 1991. *Meeting the Shadow: The Hidden Power of the Dark Side of Nature.* Tarcher Penguin.

Index

Maggie, 162; and physical intelligence, 69; and the PNS, 33; for Ronnie, 209
Brexit, 119

C

caring, 28, 31-32, 198-199
centredness, 14-15, 18, 27-28, 85, 119, 145, 227, 229, 231
Chua, Amy, 59-60
collaboration, 116, 161
communities of practice, 116
compassion fatigue, 28
compassionate inquiry, 148-149, 175
constellations, 217-221, 225-226
core beliefs, 89, 128-133, 214
corporate psychopath, 58
corpus striatum, 62-66, 69, 133
cortisol, 28-29, 39, 66
creative disruption, 224
creativity: for Carl, 177; and kindness, 113; and machines, 118; for Maggie, 160-161, 166, 169-170; and self-forgetting, 169-170; and the unconscious, 78
crying, as self-soothing, 196
culture, 94, 97, 204; and meaning, 86; modern, 117, 118; in organisations, 75; scarcity, 38
curiosity: and *drive brain*, 37; naming emotions, 84; and free fall writing, 139, 223; and humble noticing, 153; 223; and warm awareness, 103-104
Csikszentmihalyi, Mihaly, 89-90

D

Damasio, Antonio, 81, 98-99
dark side, 92-94, 119, 133-134, 168, 191

death, 93, 185-186, 210-221, 229-230
depression, 10, 30, 100-101; bi-polar, 149; cause of disability, 143n87; and control, 60; for Miller, 58; for Ronnie, 209, 211, 219
depth coaching, 19, 77, 143-146, 150
divorce, 55, 102, 218-219; and threat, 29, 148
drama triangle, 207, 212
drive brain, 25-28, 31, 37-39, 86; and Carl, 179, 187, 189; and false self, 57-60; Horney and, 47; looping 39-40, 102-106, 113, 123-124, 141; and Maggie, 150, 158

E

emotions: and awareness, 99; and breathing, 140; for Carl, 173, 177, 184, 188; and children, 35; and core beliefs, 129; and *drive brain*, 37, 103; and feelings, 25-26; and habits, 45; for Maggie, 151, 156, 158; and memory, 61-63; Miller and, 60; and nervous system, 25; for Ronnie, 213-217; and *safe brain*, 19, 33; and somatic unconscious, 82-86; and *threat brain*, 18, 30, 39, 124
endorphins, 33, 125-127
entanglement, 197, 217
equanimity, 15, 199, 231
evolution, 23-24, 31-33, 37, 72, 97-99, 141-143
experimenting, 11-13, 15; for Carl, 180-181, 185-189, 195; for children, 51; 107, 124; for Maggie, 168-169; and play, 132, 141-142, 145-146, 185-189

F

Fight, flight, freeze, 28-32, 48-49, 54; and breathing, 126; for Carl, 181; for Maggie, 156-158; for Ronnie, 205; and the SNS, 84; and submitting, 143-144

flow, 89-90, 169

forgiveness, 11, 56, 120, 165, 194, 219

Frankl, Victor, 116

free fall writing, 137-141, 164, 191, 215

free will, 98, 124

freedom: to choose, 98-100, 103; to live, 219; from pain, 184

Freud, Sigmund: and aggression, 229, 231; and childhood, 45-46; on drives, 93-94; and the preconscious, 124; and repression, 70; and the unconscious, 64, 78-79

G

Gage, Phineas, 34-35

Germer, Christopher, 107, 120-122

gifted child, 58

Gilbert, Paul, 25, 100, 103-105, 107, 100

Goldberg, Natalie, 137, 176-177

grandiosity, 58

grief, 51-52, 121-122, 210, 217

H

habit, 13-15; addictive, 57; 'as if', 132; breaking, 108, 120; bundles, 75-79; destructive, 59; gambling, 151; *moving away*, 180-182, 189, 198, 212; new, 41; *moving towards*, 212-214, 224; perfectionist, 58; problem 19,

26, 31, 39, 43-45, 49-55, 100, 124; *threat brain*, 102-103, 144-149, 156-157, 165, 168-169, 173-177, 182, 196-197, 203-204, 226

Hellinger, Bert, 165-166, 197, 217-218

hippocampus, 62-68, 88

homeostasis, 80-81, 91

Horney, Karen, 30, 46-52, 153, 160, 180-181

humble noticing, 153-155

humour, 91-92

I

identity, 61-66, 130, 133, 143, 145

imagination, 31, 64, 94-95, 117-118, 175, 211-217, 227

inner conflict, 90-91, 180, 189, 213

inner critic, 47, 106-113, 131, 138-141; for Carl, 185-186, 189, 199; for Maggie, 152-153, 158-160, 163-165, 170; for Ronnie, 205, 209

integration (and dis-integration), 26, 40-41, 43, 47, 57, 67-69, 81

intelligence, 64, 68-72, 78, 81, 87, 148, 150-153

intimacy, 52-54, 129, 168, 174, 179, 187

J

Johnson, Robert, 97, 215-216

Jung C.G., 64, 94, 97, 194, 211, 215-216

K

kindness, 19, 33, 46, 132, 199; and metta, 166; and self-compassion, 108-113, 121

Kolts, Russell, 109-110

L

M

N

O

P

About the Author

Dr Nelisha Wickremasinghe is a psychologist, family therapist, author, educator and organisational change consultant. She has worked in the field of human development for 30 years.

Her work at the boundary of psychotherapeutic practice and management development has taken her across the globe to support organisations to develop their leaders and implement complex change. In addition to her role at Saïd Business School, Nelisha is the founding director and lead practitioner in The Dialogue Space, which provides therapeutic depth development for individuals, families and employees within organisations. She is also a regular contributor to *Psychology Today*.

Previously Nelisha developed and ran a successful organic food business and restaurant and, for ten years, was a clinical and management lead in the mental health and social care sector.

By the same Author

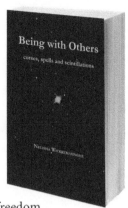

Being with Others

In *Being with Others*, Nelisha explores how it is impossible to build relationships based on openness, trust and respect when our brains and bodies are in threat. Following on from *Beyond Threat* she unravels why so many of us are often in threat, and how we can overcome these feelings to find freedom, authenticity and forgiveness in our relationships. In *Being with Others* we learn how:

- We are cursed by our ability to think and remember, and by the dictates of culture, family and our own conflicted characters.
- Unconsciously, we cast 'spells' – in the form of psychological defences – to try to rid ourselves of these curses.
- Our most trusted spell is the belief that magical 'Others' – partners, children, celebrities, gurus or gods – can heal, protect and save us.
- Perception practices help us to recognise our curses, cast off our spells and wake up to the scintillations of insight that take us beyond threat.

Being with Others is an invitation to reclaim our imagination, our intuition and our body from the grip of our threat brain emotions. It is a book for all of us who want to grow richer relationships with others and with our own selves.

www.triarchypress.net/bwo

About the Publisher

Triarchy Press is an independent publisher of new and alternative thinking about government, finance, organizations, society, movement, performance, walking and the creative life. Other Triarchy authors whose books seek to raise awareness of ways we can transform our organizational and daily life include:

Russell Ackoff	*Differences that Make a Difference*
	Systems Thinking for Curious Managers
Rosalind Armson	*Growing Wings on the Way*
Vince Barabba	*The Decision Loom*
Nora Bateson	*Small Arcs of Larger Circles*
Margaret Hannah	*Humanising Healthcare*
Margrit Kennedy	*People Money*
Graham Leicester	*Dancing at the Edge*
	Transformative Innovation
Bernard Lietaer	*Money and Sustainability*
Barry Oshry	*Context Context Context*
	The Organic Systems Framework
Sandra Reeve	*Body and Awareness*
John Seddon	*Systems Thinking in the Public Sector*
Bill Sharpe	*Three Horizons: The patterning of hope*
Phil Smith	*Covert*
	Mythogeography
William Tate	*The Search for Leadership*
Daniel Wahl	*Designing Regenerative Cultures*

For details of all these authors and titles, please visit:

www.triarchypress.net